THE COHERENCE THEORY OF TRUTH:

A CRITICAL EVALUATION

BY

HAIG KHATCHADOURIAN

M. A., PH. D.

Associate Professor of Philosophy
American University of Beirut

WIPF & STOCK · Eugene, Oregon

Wipf and Stock Publishers
199 W 8th Ave, Suite 3
Eugene, OR 97401

The Coherence Theory of Truth
A Critical Evaluation
By Khatchadourian, Haig A.
Copyright©1961 by Khatchadourian, Haig A.
ISBN 13: 978-1-60899-803-6
Publication date 7/9/2010
Previously published by Beirut American University, 1961

To my wife, Arpine

CONTENTS

Abbreviations Used For Titles Of Books Frequently Utilized
Preface vii
Introduction ix
Chapter I   The Coherence Theory Of Truth: An Exposition . 3
Chapter II   The Doctrine Of Internal Relations 20
Chapter III The Doctrine Of Internal Relations (Cont'd.) . . 42
Chapter IV Coherence As The Criterion Of Truth: A Critique . 100
Chapter V   Coherence As The Nature Of Truth: A Critique . 143
Chapter VI The Doctrine Of Degrees Of Truth And Falsity . 185
Index 228

Abbreviations Used For Titles Of Books Frequently Utilized

A. R.	*Appearance And Reality*, F. H. Bradley.
C. E.	*Collected Essays*, F. H. Bradley.
E. T. R.	*Essays On Truth And Reality*, F. H. Bradley.
I. C. S.	*Idealism: A Critical Survey*, A. C. Ewing.
L. S.	*Logical Studies*, H. H. Joachim.
N. T.	*The Nature Of Thought*, B. Blanshard.
P. L.	*The Principles Of Logic*, F. H. Bradley.

PREFACE

The present work, in a somewhat different form, was originally submitted in partial fulfillment of the requirements for the degree of Doctor of Philosophy at Duke University, Durham, North Carolina, U. S. A. Thanks and grateful acknowledgments go to the Graduate School of Arts and Sciences of Duke University, and to the Department of Philosophy as a whole. Special thanks go to the members of the Committee which supervised the writing of, and examined, the thesis: in particular, to my advisor, Dr. Glenn Negley, and to Dr. Charles A. Baylis, Director of Graduate Studies in Philosophy.

Last but not least, thanks and grateful acknowledgments go to the American University of Beirut, Lebanon, and in particular, to its Publications Committee, for the generous financial help which made the publication of this work possible.

American University
Beirut, Lebanon

29 March, 1961

Haig Khatchadourian

INTRODUCTION

The coherence theory of truth is historically associated, primarily, with the so-called Absolute Idealists of the nineteenth and twentieth centuries—with such names as Hegel in Germany, Bradley, Bosanquet and Joachim in England, and Blanshard in the United States. But, on the one hand, there are some Absolute Idealists who do not hold the theory, such as T. H. Green and McTaggart; and, on the other hand, there are non-idealists who hold it, for instance Samuel Alexander. Also, there are some Logical Positivists, like Neurath and Hempel, who hold what might be called a form of the coherence theory, though the theory they hold differs in important respects from the traditional coherence theory, that is, from the theory as held by the Absolute Idealists. Finally, there are thinkers who hold the theory as an account of the test of truth, but reject it as an account of the nature of truth. A. C. Ewing is a good example.

This being the case, we shall arbitrarily limit ourselves in this work mainly to the theory as expounded and defended in the writings of Bradley, Bosanquet and Blanshard.

In giving an exposition of it, and especially in criticizing it, we shall further limit ourselves to the theory as an account of the nature and the test of empirical or synthetic statements. We shall not concern ourselves with the theory as an account of truth and a test of mathematical, logical, and other types of analytic statements. It is true that the idealist advocates of coherence do not regard such statements as analytic. But this is contrary to what is generally held at present and to what the present author himself holds. At any rate, even with this exclusion, there is no danger of making the coherence theory too circumscribed and restricted, or of robbing it of its significance and essential tenets. It affords wealth enough and to spare to anyone who wants to explore and evaluate it.

For the exposition and especially for the criticism of the theory, we shall use as foundational the formulation and defence of the theory set forth in Blanshard's *The Nature Of Thought*.

There are several reasons for doing so. First, Blanshard gives a detailed, systematic and clear account of the theory (something which cannot be said of some of its other advocates) showing clearly its place in the idealist's general scheme: its logical relations to the Idealist's conception of thought in its various forms and stages, and to his conception of the nature of the universe—in short, its metaphysical presuppositions. Second,—and this is the main reason for our choice—Blanshard gives the most important arguments which have been raised against the theory, both as a conception of the nature of truth and as a conception of the test of truth (as well as against the conception of reality as an internally-related whole) from the time it was first formulated, and marshalls many if not all of the counter-arguments which the Absolute Idealists have been rallying to their side, beginning with Bradley and Bosanquet. Thus he offers the critical student of the theory a clear vista of the battlefield, so to speak, a vantage point from which it becomes possible to distinguish between the invalid and the valid criticism, the valid and the invalid defence. Finally, both in the exposition and in the defence of the theory, Blanshard, as a contemporary philosopher, has had the advantage of profitting from the arguments and from the errors of his predecessors, and therefore of presenting the theory in a more refined, sophisticated and better-fortified way, making use of developments in philosophy which have appeared since Bradley and Bosanquet lived and thought.

However, it should be stated that our aim in this essay is analytic and critical, not historical or expository. We are not ultimately concerned with disproving the views of any particular thinker as much as with attempting to show that the coherence theory, in its traditional form, is untenable both as an account of the nature of truth and as the test of truth. What truth there seems to us to be in the theory, we shall also, of course, attempt to bring out.

The present work consists of six chapters. The first chapter is a general but summary outline of the coherence theory of truth developed and presented in the context of the idealistic philosophy as a whole. No attempt is here made to be exhaustive, since the chapter as a whole is only designed as a general introduction to the theory; hence only those aspects and tenets of the idealistic epistemology and metaphysics (especially the latter) are outlined, which have a direct bearing upon the theory. Further, even in the case of the former, including the coherence theory itself, the discussion does not go beyond a mere sketch. The analysis of the view in its ramifications and implications, the important arguments of its advocates in support of it, and their defence against criticism, has been left to the succeeding chapters. Chapters four, five and six deal with three important aspects of the theory (coherence as the test of truth, coherence as the nature of truth, and the doctrine of degrees of truth, respectively). The second and third chapters deal with one of the basic metaphysical presuppositions of the coherence theory, namely, the doctrine of internal relations. In each of these chapters the particular aspect of the theory in hand (and in chapters two and three one of its main metaphysical presuppositions) is criticized. In the course of this the theory is analyzed as exhaustively as the limitations of time and space permit, and its general pattern and intricate details are brought out as sharply as possible into relief.

THE COHERENCE THEORY OF TRUTH:
A CRITICAL EVALUATION

CHAPTER I

THE COHERENCE THEORY OF TRUTH: AN EXPOSITION

In order to understand clearly the Coherence Theory of Truth as held by Bradley, Bosanquet and Blanshard, we have to understand the nature of the mental activity which aims at truth, and to discover how this activity operates in the process of arriving at it. This mental activity is thought, and it is to thought that we have to turn first.

Thought, according to the Absolute Idealist, is one in essence in all its forms—whether in reasoning or inference, explicit judgment, or perception. But though one, it varies in complexity and degree of explicitness.[1] The simplest form of thought is judgment, and the simplest form of judgment is judgment involved in perception, or judgments of perception.[2] Since also it is in perception that the mind first comes into contact with the external world, and truth involves a relation between thought or mind and reality, it is doubly important to turn to perception as the starting point in our analysis of thought and through that of truth itself.

We said that thought manifests itself in perception, explicit judgment, and reasoning or inference. But it is judgment or belief which is present in all these. As a matter of fact, it is present in all mental activities. "It [judgment or belief] is present, and indispensably present, in perception and reflection, in desire and will, in memory and expectation, even in imagination and doubt."[3] In other words, it is "... present wherever we have an object at all before the mind...."[4] Nay, judgment or belief "... is virtually

---

1 B. Blanshard, *The Nature of Thought*, New York, 1940. vol. I, p. 117. Hereafter cited as N. T.
2 *Ibid.*, p. 51.
3 *Ibid.*, p. 115.
4 F. H. Bradley, *The Principles of Logic*, [N. P.], 1928, second edition, revised, vol. I, p. 39. Hereafter cited as P. L.

identical with mind on its intellectual side."⁵ Or "The whole of consciousness, in as far as it is the consciousness of a single world that shares the reality of our waking self, may be regarded as a continuous judgment...."⁶

All perception is a complex of two elements: an element which is given to the mind from the outside in sensation, and another element which is added by the mind, i. e., judgment or belief or interpretation of that which is given. But perception should not be thought of as a mechanical sum of sensation and interpretation or judgment. We do not first have the given in its nakedness, and then belief or judgment is added to it: "... the two present themselves together; the ground [the given] comes clothed or invested with the belief."⁷ This means, first, that we cannot draw a sharp and fast line in actual perception (though we can still distinguish the two logically) between what is given and the judgment which rests on it, and second, that we cannot have a pure sensation, or a sensible datum stripped of all mental accretions. It is true that perception is a matter of degree, and varies from almost pure sensation⁸ to almost pure conception. But even when I merely perceive a certain patch of blue, say (if that is possible), some judgment is already present. Thus the pole of pure sensation can be approached as a limit, but can never be actually arrived at.⁹ Put in other words, what this means is that there is no such thing as perception which is wholly immediate, in the sense of being "... the direct awareness of an independent fact... a solid constituent of reality, presenting itself, entire and complete, to the passively accepting observer."¹⁰ To hold that sense perception is immediate is to hold that what we perceive is "... in no sense

---

5 N. T., vol. I, p. 115.

6 B. Bosanquet, *Logic*, 2 I. 84. Quoted from N. T., vol. I, p. 115.

7 N.T., vol. I, p. 118.

8 But pure sensation is not perception proper for the Idealist: "... If sensation is present alone, we are below the perceptual level...." (*ibid.*, p. 53) Cf. also H. H. Joachim, *Logical Studies*, Oxford, 1948, p. 83. Hereafter cited as L. S.

9 N. T., vol. I, p. 118; Bradley, *Essays On Truth And Reality*, Oxford, 1914, pp. 119-120. Hereafter cited as E. T. R. On the other hand, there is always, in perception, some element which is given, which is not thought. We should not go to the extreme—the advocate of coherence warns us—of resolving the given into thought.

10 L. S., p. 80.

bit-beside-bit or bit-after-bit; in no sense affected in their existence or character by what precedes, succeeds, or environs them; in no sense linked to one another by any third or middle, so that 'perceived' and 'perceiving' unite only through an intermediary to constitute the sense-perception."[11]

That sense-perception is not immediate in the foregoing sense is shown, according to Joachim, by the fact that what a percipient perceives is private to him, and differs from one person to another, due to differences in their sense-organs and their powers of attention.[12] Similar considerations, which are the stock-in-trade of the epistemological dualists, all show that what is perceived is not the public object or quality it is supposed to be. The "real" object or quality, such as the "real" flash of lightning which different observers are supposed to be perceiving—

Is that which all the observers postulate on the ground of the 'appearing flashes' or presentments.... It is the product of an inexplicit and confused thinking, a thinking immersed in and inseparable from sensation. It is the hybrid offspring of that blend of sense and thought which goes by the name of 'sense-perception'.[13]

Blanshard takes another line of approach in showing the non-immediacy of sense-perception. An analysis of the genesis of perception in the infant (so far as we know its nature) shows that the perception of any particular sensible quality, as a particular quality, e. g. of a colour blue as blue, requires its perception as an instance of a universal, i. e., as a quality which can be exemplified in other objects. And this can occur only if and when we perceive the quality in relation to, or as set off against, something else; in other words, only when we apprehend a quality as the embodiment of a universal.[14]

Similarly, for Bradley, the so-called "given" in perception, or "facts", are never merely given facts. "The merely given facts are... the imaginary creatures of false theory. They are manufactured by a mind which abstracts one aspect of the concrete known whole, and sets this abstracted aspect out by itself as a real thing."[15]

---

11 L. S., p. 80.
12 Ibid., p. 83.
13 Ibid.
14 N. T., vol. I, pp. 53, 61, 62.
15 E. T. R., p. 108.

We have been reiterating what seems to the Idealist to be the fact that perception involves judgment. The next question is: What is the nature of such perceptual judgment; or, in other words, what exactly is added by thought to the given in perception? According to Blanshard, this addition can be divided into three types of ideas: (1) The sense-qualities which are perceived are grasped as belonging to a whole, to a thing, although what is given in perception at any moment is only a part of this whole. Thus we only see one side of an orange, one side of a tea-kettle; and yet we attribute this side or part to a whole, the orange or the tea kettle, to something which is more than what is sensed at any one moment. (2) The categories, "... in both the Aristotelian[16] and the Kantian senses, are there in perception from the beginning...."[17] These include the thought of space and time, and also "... all manner of qualities and relations present in perception, but grasped only implicitly."[18] (3) What is sensed is not only grasped implicitly as part of sensible wholes and as related spatially, temporally and in other ways to other things or wholes, but is also grasped as within a setting or background provided by past experience. "... Focal experience is what it is because of a great fringe of retained experience, but the retained experience, when we come to look for it, is conspicuously not there."[19] In other words, this kind of perceptual idea "... is present only in the form of a disposition."[20]

To put the matter in general terms, judgment in perception involves the perception of what is given as a part of a greater whole, as related to other things; i. e., it involves synthesis. But it also involves selection.[21] And the nature of the particular selection and synthesis is partly determined by the percipient's interest

---

16 The universal forms of thinking, which "... determine the structure of any world we can think about...". (N. T., vol. I, p. 154)
17 *Ibid.*, p. 523.
18 *Ibid.*, p. 525.
19 *Ibid.*, p. 526.
20 *Ibid.*
21 Cf. Bosanquet, *Logic*, Oxford, 1888, vol. I, pp. 82-83.

and purposes. Thus perception is teleological. I say "partly determined" because our construction is always partly determined by the nature of the categories of thought.[22]

The view that all perception is teleological brings us to a point of central importance for the Absolute Idealist; it also points the way to the manner in which ideas or judgments of perception (or 'tied ideas', to use Blanshard's expression) pass into free ideas or explicit conception.

It is the essential mark of thought that it is teleological, that it is governed by an end, an ideal, which it strives to realize.[23] Thought is a striving, seeking thing, seeking to realize a peculiar end. This end or ideal, immanent in the very nature and process of thought (hence called the immanent end by Blanshard) is understanding, intelligibility; and the moving force of the process of thought is the desire for a peculiar satisfaction, the desire to understand, the desire to see things in relation, as parts of a coherent, systematic, intelligible whole.[24] In other words, thought is a process of self-development or self-realisation, and in that sense, therefore, every act of thought is an act of will.[25] Hence the refusal of the Idealist to draw a sharp distinction between intellect and will.

But the end of thinking is also knowledge of the nature of reality, i. e., of things as they are. This constitutes the transcendent end of thought or the activity of knowing. And thought achieves satisfaction and realizes itself as thought only in such knowledge. Thus in ideal or perfect knowledge the immanent and transcendent ends of thought coincide. However, such perfect coincidence is only an ideal and forever eludes our grasp; at any given moment, both in the case of the individual and of the human race, the coincidence of the two ends of thought is only partial, and hence the urge to

---

22 Which are also ontological categories according to the Absolute Idealist.

23 N. T., vol. I, pp. 458, 459, 464, 472, 473. E. g. "Everywhere and always... thought does have an end of its own.... The Pragmatists are clearly right that thought is an end-seeking activity...". (*Ibid.*, p. 472)

24 Cf. Joachim, "... To 'conceive' means for us to think out clearly and logically, to hold many elements together in a connexion necessitated by their several contents. And to be 'conceivable' means to be a 'significant whole', or a whole possessed of meaning for thought". (*The Nature Of Truth*. Oxford, 1906, p. 66)

25 N. T., vol. I, p. 526.

understand, and the satisfaction of knowledge, are incompletely realized. The mind apprehends reality in the degree in which it realizes its immanent end, the ideal set up by its own nature; and conversely, the immanent end of thought is realized in the degree in which it apprehends reality.

We have seen that in perception the mind is already at work in ordering and relating, and therefore systematizing, the given, that perception involves going beyond what is momentarily presented.[26] But this process is only realized very imperfectly at the level of perception, and only implicitly.[27] This process is further continued in explicit thought or conception, where thought is no longer tied down to the sensuously given. Thus judgment becomes explicit and reflective and fully conscious when it transcends the tied ideas of perception in free ideas and images (all three types of ideas being simpler types of ideas), and still more completely, in general ideas or concepts.[28]

For Bradley, given experience (which he sometimes calls "feeling") is non-relational. "... It is an unbroken fluid totality containing in one 'now' an undivided lapse, and is in itself foreign to any terms or relations as such."[29] But this immediate, felt content, which "... is all one blur with differences, that work and that are felt, but are not discriminated"[30] "... is developed in such a way that it goes beyond and conflicts with the form of feeling or mere immediacy."[31] And this going beyond is the explicit activity of thought: explicit judgment and inference which, like all judgment and inference, are relational in nature. The felt

---

26 Cf. Joachim's view that sense-perception involves the "consciousness of a world", "... a relatively enduring system of fact, within a reality spatially and temporally 'beyond' the particular perception". (L. S., p. 89)

27 Cf. Joachim's view that the object of perception is "... not distinctly conceived elements intelligibly related". (*Ibid.*, p. 84)

28 Although Blanshard uses the expression 'types of idea', he warns us that strictly speaking there are no types of ideas at all, "... but only stages in the development of a single function". (N. T., vol. I, p. 567)

29 E. T. R., p. 152.

30 *Ibid.*, p. 157, footnote 1.

31 *Ibid.*, p. 157.

content is not an explicitly unified, integrated whole, "... not distinctly conceived elements intelligibly related."[32]

Although thought is by its nature necessarily relational, its end is to transcend relations, to achieve a supra-relational unity, and therefore to cease to be thought. As Bradley puts it, its end is to commit suicide as thought.[33] But this ideal is never completely realized, although Bradley intimates that in aesthetic contemplation or intuition and in moral insight we come closest to achieving it. In terms of inference, this means that inference is defective. Inference is the ideal (in the sense of logical) self-development of an object;[34] but though in that sense it is necessary, it is also universal, going beyond its "this", "here", and "now."[35] But inference involves a puzzle. Inference means the advance of the object beyond its beginning. "But, on the other hand, if the object passes beyond what is itself, the inference is destroyed[36]". The solution lies in the fact that—

The object not only is itself, but is also contained as an element in a whole; and it *is* itself, we must add, only as being so contained. And the difference of the object from, and its essential identity with a whole beyond itself... is the key... to this puzzle of self-development. On the one side the special object advances to a result beyond the beginning, and yet its progress throughout is nothing beyond the intrinsic development of its proper being. For that which mediates and necessitates its advance is implied within its own self.[37]

Let us look at the matter from another angle. An idea has an objective reference, is the idea of an object. As the idea of an object it must in some sense be like or even identical with its object. And yet it must be different from it.[38] How can this be? The answer is that:

---

32 L. S., p. 84.
33 *Appearance And Reality*, London, 1925, second edition, eighth impression, pp. 181 ff. Hereafter cited as A. R.
34 P. L., vol. II, Terminal Essay I, p. 597, and *passim*.
35 *Ibid.*, p. 598.
36 *Ibid.*, p. 599.
37 *Ibid.*, p. 600. Italics in original.
38 N. T., vol. I, p. 473.

The idea is... both identical with its object and different from it. It is identical in the sense in which anything that truly develops is identical with what it becomes. It is different in the sense in which any purpose partially realized is different from the same purpose realized wholly.[39]

In other words, an idea is its object partially realized, a potential object:

If thought can be seen as a stage on the way to its transcendent end or object, as that end itself in the course of becoming actual, the paradox of knowledge is in principle solved. The idea can then be *both* the same as its object *and* different; the same because it *is* the object *in posse*; different because that object, which is its end, is as yet incompletely realized.[40]

This is in line with the nature of thought, which we saw is teleological, the progressive self-development and self-realization of an idea.

But how can an idea itself be a partially realized object? The idea is universal, while the object, on the face of it, is an individual thing. The chasm between the two seems insuperable.

Reflection, however, shows this not to be the case. To begin with, sensible qualities are not particulars, as they are ordinarily regarded, but universals, being capable, in principle or logically, of existing identically at different times and in different places, i. e., of repeating themselves.[41] Further, reflection also reveals that so-called individual things—tables, chairs, trees, mountains—are nothing but a complex of sensible qualities in certain spatial, temporal, causal and other relations. There is no such thing as a Cartesian or Lockean material substance underlying sensible qualities. This being so, it follows that "individuals" are really nothing but congeries of universals. Hence the apparent difference in kind between objects and ideas is seen to be illusory.

Now we have said that thought realizes itself in a system of judgments or universals, i. e., in a logically-coherent whole. Hence, if in realizing itself fully it becomes identical with its objects (if

---

39 *Ibid.*, p. 473.
40 *Ibid.*, p. 494. Italics in original. Also pp. 496, 550, and *passim*.
41 Cf. *Ibid.*, pp. 631 ff.

the immanent and transcendent ends of thought coincide),[42] it follows (a) that the object of thought in the fullest sense must itself be a systematical and coherent whole, a system of universals and not an aggregate of particulars, a network in which every part is related essentially and necessarily (i. e., internally) to every other part and to the whole; and (b) thought, in its full actualization, merges and passes over into Reality and thereby ceases to be thought. This means that thought as thought—

Cannot get the content into a harmonious system. And in the next place, even if it did so, that system would not *be* the subject. It would either be a maze of relations, a maze with a plan, of which forever we made the circuit; or otherwise it would wholly lose the relational form. Our impossible process, in the first place, would assuredly have truth distinguished from its reality. For it could avoid this only by coming to us bodily and all at once, and, further, by suppressing entirely any distinction between subject and predicate. But, if in this way thought became immediate, it would lose its own character. It would be a system of relations no longer, but would have become an individual experience. And the Other would certainly have been absorbed, but thought itself no less would have been swallowed up and resolved into an Other.[43]

Still, "There is nothing foreign that thought wants in desiring to be a whole...."[44]

Judgment and therefore inference implies a dichotomy between subject and predicate, fact and idea, the "that" and the "what", existence and content. But the grammatical, or even the logical, subject of a judgment is not the true subject. The logical subject is as universal as the logical predicate. The logical subject is not a self-contained whole, but involves relations to other things going beyond it. The true or metaphysical subject is "... not this or that finite person or thing, but the ultimate reality."[45] Thus in

---

[42] And it is the firm conviction of the Absolute Idealist that knowledge is possible and that we do have some knowledge, i. e., the immanent and transcendent ends of thought do coincide to some extent in actual knowledge (Cf. E.T.R., p. 16). However, the perfect coincidence of the two ends of thought is only an ideal never actually realized or realizable.

[43] A. R., p. 179. Italics in original.

[44] *Ibid.*, p. 181.

[45] P. L., vol. I, p. 181, and *passim*. Quoted from N. T., vol. I, p. 647.

inference, although the particular premise is some particular content, what is implied by it is the entire Reality. "The inference here may be called arbitrary, so far as the point where you happen to begin, and so far again as the result—where, short of the whole, you are pleased to stop—are taken to depend on your choice."[46] And Bosanquet—

> It follows from the nature of implication that every inference involves a judgment based on the whole of reality, though referring only to a partial system which need not even be actual. You cannot draw a conclusion *from* a mere and pure supposition, though you may draw one which explicitly refers to such a supposition and nothing more. Every assertion, when its explicit condition is discounted, asserts absolutely of reality as a whole.[47]

Hence every judgment and every inference is conditional and presupposes the whole system of reality.[48] Only the whole of reality can be the unconditioned subject of judgment and inference. But if the whole of reality is taken in this way, there will be nothing left outside it; the distinction between the "that" and the "what", fact and idea, is overcome. But if this happens, judgment and inference themselves cease to be and thought itself ceases to exist.

For Bradley, any particular "that" which is the object of perception or of thought is a fragment torn from the whole of reality, a particular which is seen apart from and shorn of its relations to the rest of reality. And in that sense it is only appearance. Hence any judgment about it, which does not take its relations to the whole within its content, is bound to be partial and fragmentary. To see it, on the other hand, as real and not as appearance, means to see it in relation to the whole, which really means to take the whole of Reality as the subject of judgment.

---

46 P. L., vol. II, *Terminal Essay* I, pp. 601-602.

47 B. Bosanquet, *Implication And Linear Inference*, London, 1920, pp. 4-5. Italics in original.

48 Cf. C. R. Morris, *Idealistic Logic*, London, 1933, p. 148. Idealistic logic "... insists that the characteristic mark of judgment is ... that it is essentially bound to other judgments—that when you make one judgment you are asserting a whole system of judgments"...

But what is the coincidence of thought with reality but truth, and therefore what is the system of thought, which is thus true, but the system of knowledge? Since the coincidence of thought and reality is realized in system, system constitues the nature of truth. But the coincidence of thought and reality, or of the immanent and transcendent ends of thought, is a matter of degree, and its complete realization is only an ideal which always eludes us. Hence truth (and knowledge) is a matter of degree, depending on the extent to which system is achieved. But in perfect system thought would become merged into and one with reality and would cease to exist as thought. Hence perfect truth can never be realized so long as thought is thought.

The coincidence of thought and reality in truth is not a case of "correspondence" or "copying", which could only be the case if thought and reality were externally and accidentally related. It is far from that. For since thought is its object partially realized, the two are essentially related. The essence of a thing is what it actually becomes; and to say that the two are related essentially is to say that the two are related internally, necessarily. But internality of relations and necessity are again matters of degree. The degree of internality corresponds to the degree of system achieved, and that in turn means the degree of necessity realized. (On the side of the system of thought or judgments, degrees of necessity, essentiality and internality involve degrees of entailment or implication. But more of this later).

It is important to keep in mind that coherence as the nature of truth logically presupposes that reality is an internally-related system. Without this, coherence would become nothing more than logical consistency and logical entailment, and the truth of any such "coherent" system becomes something which its coherence can in no way guarantee or determine. Further, if the relation between the ideal system of thought and the system of reality (here the totality of real things) were external and not internal, the relation between the system and reality which we call truth would no longer be coherence but rather a form of correspondence—the correspondence of the entire system of thought (and not of isolated, individual propositions) to the entire system of "fact."

We said that for the Absolute Idealist coherence is not mere logical self-consistency or the mere absence of self-contradiction. A logically-coherent system may still be false. In a fully coherent system every judgment[49] entails and is entailed by the rest of the system. "The truth is the whole."[50] We can think of the ideal system of truth as "... a single judgment, the judgment which sustains the ideal structure of the real word."[51] Thus no system is fully coherent in which there are postulates which lie outside the system, which entail it but are not entailed by any constituent judgment, or even by the entire body of judgments, within it. From this it follows that no actual system, even such a system as Euclidean geometry, is fully coherent, since its postulates are always unproved and independent of each other.[52] And Bradley: "Truth... must... fail to satisfy its own claim, and must remain imperfect, even as truth, so long as it falls short of the entire Reality."[53]

It is important to emphasize that truth consists in system which is both self-consistent and comprehensive, embracing all facts in the universe. Logical self-consistency by itself does not constitute truth; nor can comprehensiveness as such be taken as the nature of truth. Truth consists in a system of knowledge "... as wide and as consistent as may be... If we separate coherence [self-consistency] from... comprehensiveness, then... neither of these aspects of system will work by itself."[54] Consistency (or formal validity) is a necessary condition for coherence,[55] and therefore is

---

49 The view that in a perfectly coherent system a *single* proposition entails all other propositions in the system, jointly or singly, is, according to Blanshard, not essential for the definition of 'coherence'. But Blanshard follows Joachim in regarding it as characteristic of a perfectly coherent system. (N. T. vol. II, pp. 265-266, footnote 1).

50 B. Bosanquet, *Logic*, vol. 1, p. 3.

51 *Ibid.*, p. 6. Cf. also pp. 2-3.

52 N. T., vol. II, p. 265.

53 P. L., vol. II, *Terminal Essay* XI, p. 704, footnote 1; also E. T. R., p. 114.

54 E. T. R., pp. 202-203. Bradley, in the quoted passage, is speaking about the test rather than about the nature of truth. But the quotation also represents his conception of the system of knowledge which constitutes truth. See, for instance, A. R., 363.

55 Note that Bradley uses the word 'coherence' for what we ordinarily call "consistency." But we are using the term 'coherence' throughout the present work as Bosanquet, Joachim, and Blanshard use it, namely, for Bradley's "coherence" together with what he calls "comprehensiveness."

a negative condition for truth. But it is not a sufficient condition. No system can be true which is not valid. But a valid system may still be false.

Joachim defines truth as systematic coherence, and then defines systematic coherence (though only provisionally, and as a rough formulation) as "conceivability." But to "conceive" as used by him, means "... to think out clearly and logically, to hold many elements together in a connexion necessitated by their several contents."[56] And to be conceivable—

> Means to be a 'significant whole', or a whole possessed of meaning for thought. A 'significant whole' is such that all its constituent elements reciprocally involve one another, or reciprocally determine one another's being as contributory features in a single concrete meaning. The elements thus cohering constitute a whole which may be said to control the reciprocal adjustment of its elements, as an end controls its constituent means.[57]

Thus coherence does not mean the external relatedness of the constituent propositions, which would be the case if coherence were mere self-consistency. Every proposition in the whole is determined as to its nature by its relation to the whole, and ceases to be what it is if isolated from the system. "'Coherence' cannot be attached to propositions from the outside: it is not a property which they can acquire by colligation, whilst retaining unaltered the truth they possessed in isolation."[58] It follows that no proposition is true or even has any meaning in complete isolation from the whole. What meaning and what truth it has derives from the meaning and truth of the whole system.

From this it further follows that meaning and truth are a matter of degree. No actual system of knowledge, which by the fact that it is an actual system of knowledge is imperfect and falls short of the ideal system of knowledge, is completely coherent "... if only for the reason that it is growing in time."[59] Hence it is only true to a degree (or has relative truth) and not perfectly

---

56 H.H. Joachim, *The Nature of Truth*, p. 66.
57 *Ibid.*
58 *Ibid.*, pp. 72-73.
59 *Ibid.*, p. 114.

true (or lacks absolute truth). And the degree of truth (and of meaning) it possesses corresponds to the degree of its coherence. For since coherence constitutes truth (and meaning), degrees of coherence determine the degrees of truth. Also the meaning a proposition possesses is derived from the system of which it is a part —ultimately from the ideal system. Any actual system, and therefore every constituent proposition in it, is meaningful and true in the degree in which it approximates to the perfect system of knowledge or perfect coherence; and correspondingly, it lacks meaning (or is unintelligible) to the extent in which it falls short of the ideal system. Thus to every degree of truth there corresponds a degree of falsity, and any system, and any constituent proposition in that system, is both true and false in some degree. Only the ideal system is absolutely true and has no element of falsity whatever.

But if all actual systems and all actual propositions are true and false in some degree, there are not—and cannot be—any propositions or systems which are completely false. For a proposition which is entirely false is meaningless, and therefore is not a proposition at all. As Bradley puts it, "There will be no truth which is entirely true, just as there will be no error which is totally false."[60] And again, "... truth and error, measured by the Absolute, must each be subject always to degree."[61]

We have seen that partial knowledge consists in the partial, and complete knowledge in the complete, coincidence of the system of thought and reality. We have also seen that this entails that if any knowledge, let alone perfect knowledge and therefore perfect truth, is to be possible, reality itself must be a coherent system. This is another way of saying that if thought progressively realizes itself in becoming its object, the latter, when it is realized, must likewise be a coherent whole; since this self-realization consists in progressively greater and greater systematization and coherence. Thus we are brought to the view that reality must be a coherent system. We have already said something about the nature of a coherent

---

60 A. R., p. 362. Cf. also E.T.R., p. 232.
61 A. R., p. 362.

system of *thought* or of propositions. And as we expect, we find that, *mutatis mutandis,* the way in which we have characterized the former applies equally to the latter. To begin with, an essential feature of a coherent system of thought is that all of its parts are related essentially or logically and necessarily. Similarly, a coherent system of reality is a system in which everything is related in essence to everything else, i. e., is related "internally" and not "externally." What a thing is, is determined not merely by some of its qualities (called "essential" qualities), or by these plus some of its relations, but by *all* its qualities and *all* its relations to everything else in the universe. Conceived thus, reality is a tightly-knit and closed web or network where every strand and knot is what it is by virtue of the nature of every other strand and knot: which really means that it is determined by the nature of the web as a whole. Hence any modification, any change, however slight and insignificant, is inevitably felt in the entire network. Any and every change in any quality or relation in any part, results in corresponding changes in every other part and therefore in the whole. Hence any *knowledge* of any part of the system entails some knowledge of other parts of the system, and complete or perfect knowledge of any one part entails some knowledge of the whole of reality. Tennyson's now-famous poem "Flower In The Crannied Wall", though well-worn by quotation, illustrates this point admirably.

Again, in the same way as there are, in systems of thought, degrees of coherence or implication or necessity, there are degrees of reality itself and corresponding to each degree of it, a degree of internality of relations. Truth and reality are two sides of the same coin, so to speak, two ways of looking at reality. An idea is real in the degree in which it realizes the nature or character of the object or is identified with it; that is, in the degree in which it is systematic and coherent. But it is *true* in the degree in which it is systematic and coherent. Hence it is real in the degree in which it is true, and true in the degree in which it is real. This makes it easy to see why perfect truth merges or is identical with perfect reality, the Absolute. For the standard of both truth and reality is the Absolute, the entire system of Reality; therefore, reality and truth coincide in it. "Perfection of truth and of reality has in the end the same character. It consists in positive, self-subsisting individuality..."[62] To quote Bradley again:

> The truth and the fact, which, to be converted into the Absolute, would require less re-arrangement and addition, is more real and truer. And this is what we mean by degrees of reality and truth. To possess more the character of reality, and to contain within oneself a greater amount of the real, are two expressions for the same thing.[63]

Further, "To be more or less possible, and to be more or less true, and intrinsically necessary,—and, from the other side, to be less or more contingent— are, in the end, all the same."[64]

If truth is necessity, reality, internality of relations, falsity, contrariwise, is contingency, unreality, externality of relations. A proposition is false in the degree in which it is torn from the context of the whole of knowledge, the smaller the number of its apprehended relations; and an object is unreal or an Appearance (to use Bradley's expression) in the degree in which it is fragmentary, isolated, torn out of the context of the whole of Reality. But in the same way as no proposition can be completely false without being completely meaningless and so ceasing to be a proposition at all, nothing can be completely torn away from its relations to other things; hence nothing can be completely unreal. To be an Appearance, for Bradley, does not mean to be completely unreal; to be an Appearance is not to be nothing at all. Reality manifests itself in its Appearances; and to hold that Appearances are completely unreal is to hold that Reality does not manifest itself, or that it does not appear—which is certainly contrary to Bradley's thought.

If coherence constitutes the nature of truth, it follows that coherence is also the test of truth.[65] To show that a judgment is

---

62 *Ibid.*, p. 363. I. e., in being the entire system of Reality, which alone has perfect individuality; since it is a concrete universal, unrepeatable even in principle.
63 *Ibid.*, pp. 364-365.
64 *Ibid.*, p. 394.
65 This is not, however, the reasoning Blanshard, for instance, follows. As a matter of fact, he follows the converse method. He first tries to show that coherence is the test of truth, and uses this as an argument (though not the only one) to show that coherence must also constitute the nature of truth.

true is to show that it coheres with a system of judgments which is true—ultimately, with the ideal system of knowledge. Hence it is the coherence or lack of coherence of the judgment which tests its truth. However, since the ideal system of knowledge is, at any moment, beyond our reach, the test of truth consists in discovering the degree of coherence and lack of coherence of a given judgment with the actual system of knowledge which we at the time possess; and since such an actual system itself is true only to a degree, the coherence of a judgment with the actual system shows the judgment to possess a certain degree of truth—the degree of truth the system as a whole possesses. Lack of coherence with the system would indicate that the judgment has a degree of truth less than the degree of truth of the system, and therefore requires modification, in order to fit into the latter. Of course it is logically possible that a judgment which does not cohere with the present system of knowledge may have a *higher* degree of truth than that system, and that therefore the system itself has to be modified to make it possible for the judgment to fit into it. But this is less likely, other things being equal, the greater the inclusiveness (or "comprehensiveness") of the system.

This in brief and in a very sketchy form is the picture of truth which the Absolute Idealist draws for us, and with it, the wider framework of reality within which he places it. Our task in the remainder of this work lies in finding out the adequacy or inadequacy of this picture of truth (and space and time permitting, as much of the metaphysical framework as an examination of the problem of truth involves). The questions we shall raise are: Does coherence constitute the nature of truth? Does it constitute the test of truth? Are there degrees of truth? Are all relations internal? These are large questions. But they are as important as they are large, and to them we now turn.

CHAPTER II

THE DOCTRINE OF INTERNAL RELATIONS

The doctrine of internal relations is an integral part of Idealism, and closely connected with the coherence theory of truth.[1] Indeed, as we shall attempt to show in this chapter, it is logically presupposed by the coherence theory of truth, in some crucial sense or senses of 'internal relations.' If so, no criticism of the coherence theory can be adequate or complete without a discussion and criticism of this doctrine.

The term 'internal relations' has been and is used in different senses by the advocates of the doctrine of internal relations. A. C. Ewing's ten senses of this term are well known. But since our purpose here is only to analyse the doctrine of internal relations in so far as and in the sense or senses in which it is crucial to the coherence theory, we shall concern ourselves primarily with only a few of these senses. Still, it is necessary to mention here the various senses which Ewing distinguishes, since, as distinguished by him, they will be foundational in our discussion and criticism of the doctrine in hand.

The ten senses of the term which Ewing discovers are the following: An internal relation is a relation (1) which falls within the nature of the related terms,[2] or (2) which is essential to its terms,[3] or (3) which is itself identical with certain qualities,[4] or (4) which involves some kind of genuine unity between its terms,[5] or (5) which alters or modifies its terms[6] or (6) which is "grounded in the nature of the related terms,"[7] or (7) which 'makes a difference'

---

1 *Idealism: A Critical Survey*, London, 1933, chapter IV. Cited hereafter as I. C. S.
2 *Ibid.*, p. 119.
3 *Ibid.*, p. 121.
4 *Ibid.*, p. 122.
5 *Ibid.*, p. 124.
6 *Ibid.*, p. 126.
7 *Ibid.*

to its terms,[8] or which is (8) such that "... from a knowledge of one term and the relation in which it stands to the other term we can infer with logical necessity that the other term possesses a certain *determinate* or relatively determinate characteristic other than the characteristic of standing in the relation in question,"[9] or (9) which is such that one term of the relation could not exist unless the other term existed and was related to it by that relation; i. e., one term is dependent on its relation to the other term;[10] or, finally, (10) which is such that "... one term is not only dependent but logically dependent on its relation to the other and *vice versa*."[11]

What Ewing calls the third sense of 'internal relations' ((3) above) is really not a sense of this term at all, but rather a conception of relations as such, whether these are conceived of as external or as internal. As a matter of fact, in this conception of relations the question of whether or not all relations are internal does not arise; unless we think of the question as being whether or not some qualities—those to which relations are reduced—are "essential" to the entities of which they are qualities. Since this is not what we are chiefly concerned with in our discussion of the doctrine of internal relations, we shall ignore this "sense" of 'internal relations.'

In Chapter I it was stated that the Idealist advocates of the coherence theory with whose views we are concerned in this work (with the exception of Bradley) hold at the same time that reality is an all-inclusive coherent system of interdependent parts, taking this view of reality as the fundamental presupposition of the coherence theory. The question now before us is this : in what sense, if at all, is the doctrine that reality is an all-inclusive system *logically* presupposed by the coherence theory of truth. For though the advocates of the coherence theory do as a matter of fact regard the doctrine that reality is a coherent system as a logical presupposition of the coherence theory of truth, it may turn out

---

8   *Ibid.*, p. 130.
9   *Ibid.*, p. 135. Italics in original.
10 *Ibid.*, pp. 135–136.
11 *Ibid.*, p. 136.

that they are mistaken; i.e., it may be that the coherence theory of truth can logically rest on other metaphysical grounds. In that case, criticism of the coherence theory of reality would not necessarily disconfirm the coherence theory of truth, but would only show that the metaphysical ground on which it has as a matter of fact been based is untenable. It would leave open the possibility that the coherence theory may be true. On the other hand, if it can be shown that the coherence theory of truth logically presupposes some form of the coherence theory of reality, it cannot be true if the latter turns out to be false.

This question now resolves itself into another and prior question. For, as Blanshard rightly maintains,[12] the coherence theory of reality itself presupposes the validity of the doctrine of internal relations in some sense or senses of 'internal relations.' Reality can be an all-inclusive system only if *all* things in existence are related internally to *all* other things. If this is the case, our main question now becomes whether or not the coherence theory of truth logically presupposes the doctrine of internal relations, and if so, in what sense or senses of 'internal relation.' For if the coherence theory of truth logically presupposes the coherence theory of reality, in some form or other, and the latter theory in that particular form logically presupposes the doctrine of internal relations in some form or other, it logically follows that the coherence theory of truth logically presupposes that particular form or forms of the doctrine of internal relations which is presupposed by the particular form of the coherence theory of reality.

According to Blanshard, the crucial sense of 'internal relations' in which the Idealist holds that reality is an-inclusive internally-related system, is the following: "A relation is internal to a term when in its absence the term would be different...."[13] Elsewhere he says, "By an internal relation between two parts we mean a relation such that neither could be different without entailing a dif-

---

[12] Cf. "...The world could be accounted intelligible only if it were a system, all-inclusive and perfectly integrated, and... such integration would be achieved only if the parts were internally related." (N. T., vol. II, p. 475)

[13] *Ibid.*, p. 451. Cf. also p. 452.

ference in the other."[14] The first definition, as will be observed, is sense seven of Ewing's ten senses. Ewing concurs with Blanshard in holding that this sense "... is perhaps the most important sense in which relations are maintained to be internal. If the 'internal' view is true in this sense, it means that all reality is an interconnected system such that a difference in one part would always involve a difference in others."[15]

Before we go any further, we have to see what Ewing's so-called seventh sense of 'internal relations' involves or means, since a good deal of what follows in this and in chapter III depends on a clear understanding of it. According to Ewing's definition of this sense of 'internal relations,' a relation is internal or "makes a difference" to its terms if the latter would not or could not be the same if the relation were absent or different. And according to Blanshard's definition, "a relation is internal to a term when in its absence the term would be different." But these definitions are ambiguous, and allow at least two different interpretations. Only in one sense or interpretation would they be equivalent to saying that the relation makes a difference to its terms in the sense that it *determines* them. A difference in the terms A and B of a relation r would be involved if one or the other of the following conditions obtains: (i) if r, by its presence brings about (logically or causally) some change in A or B, or in general (partly) determines their nature: or (ii) if A and B wholly determine r or make it what it is, by virtue of their nature. For if A and B wholly determine r, r's absence would logically *presuppose* a difference in either A or B or both, i. e., either A or B (*qua* A or B) would be absent. R's absence would itself be a *consequence* of a logically prior change in A or B; hence r's absence *would* imply that A or B or both are different. In these cases the statement "Relations make a difference to their terms" or "Relations are internal in Ewing's seventh sense of 'internal relations' " is logically equivalent to—being the contrapositive of—the statement "Terms wholly determine the nature of their relations." But the last statement merely states that relations are internal in Ewing's *sixth* sense of

---

14 *Ibid.*, p. 475.
15 I. C. S., p. 133.

'internal relations.' Hence here there is really no new sense of internality of relations involved, besides the sixth sense.

As for sense (i) above of 'internal relations,' in which a relation, by its presence, brings about some change in one or both of its terms, this may mean either (a) that a relation logically generates relational characteristics in its terms, or (b) that it causes a change in its terms; or both. In the former sense, *all* relations are internal, if we assume the existence of relational characteristics. But this sense of internality is trivial. In the latter sense, on the other hand, *no* relations are or can be internal, as we shall later attempt to show.

It appears, therefore, that only in the case of those relations (if any) whose character is only partly determined by the nature of the terms, could we have a seventh sense of 'internality of relations' distinct from Ewing's sixth sense—if of course a difference in a relation so determined does imply a difference in at least one of its terms. But to anticipate once more, we shall attempt to show that this is not true.

Nonetheless, in the present and in succeeding chapters, we shall continue to speak of internality of relations in Ewing's seventh sense, in the manner defined by Ewing himself; namely, that a relation is internal in this sense if it is such that both of the terms could not have been what they are (in respects other than that of the relational characteristic of standing or not standing in that relation) without the relation holding between them.

Now on the coherence theory of reality or the view that the universe is an internally-related system, the universe is such that no part of it could be what it is without every other part of it, and the universe as a whole, being what it is. A difference in any part of the universe, therefore, would involve a difference, directly or indirectly, in every other part of it, in the universe as a whole. Suppose the universe to be composed of four terms A, B, C and D, as follows:

THE DOCTRINE OF INTERNAL RELATIONS

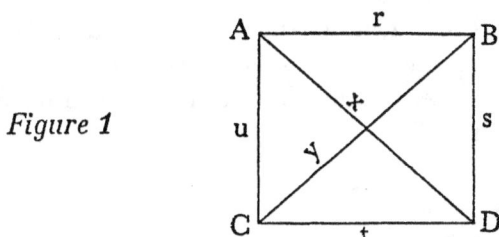

Figure 1

In such a system (if it is to be an internally related-system), the follwing *minimal* conditions are requisite:

(1) (a) That a difference in A (say) sould involve a difference in relations r, u, and x, and

   (b) That a difference in r, u and x should involve a difference in B, C and D;

or alternatively,

(2) (a) That a difference in A should involve a difference in B, C and D, and

   (b) That a difference in A should involve a difference in all the relations in the system, r, s, t, u, etc.

In both cases (1) and (2), a difference in every other term and in all relations in the system would obtain, directly or indirectly, as a result of a difference in any one term. But this system, as an epitome of the actual universe, is assumed to be dynamic and changing. Consequently (1) and (2) have to be modified to satisfy this condition, if the system is to be and to remain an internally-related system throughout its existence. That is, it should be the case either:

(A) (i) That any change in A, directly or indirectly, involves a change in r, u and x, and

   (ii) That any change in r, u and x, directly or indirectly, involves a change in B, C and D; or

(B) (i) That any change c in A, directly or indirectly, involves a change in B, C and D, and

   (ii) That the same change c in A, directly or indirectly, involves a change in r, s, t, u, x and y.

If These minimal conditions are not satisfied, a change in A would not involve a change in every other part of the system and therefore the system would no longer remain an internally-related system, even if it is so at its inception. This is most easily seen as follows: Suppose A at time T_0 to change to A_1 at time T_1. And suppose that, as a consequence, a change obtains at time T_1 in every other part of the system except B. We should then have the following situation at time T_1:

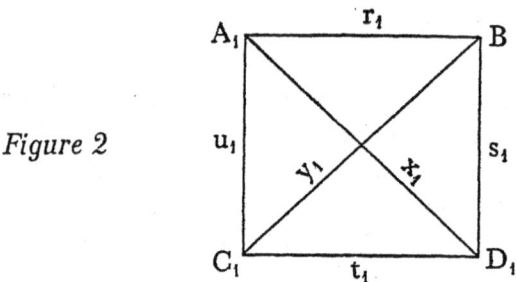

Figure 2

For the system a time T_1 to be internally-related, it has to satisfy conditions (1) and (2). That is, if A_1 were different, every other part of system should be different. But at time T_0, A_1 *is* different, being A. Hence at time T_0 every other part of the system, including B (at time T_1), should be different—i. e., should be not-B, not-C_1, not-D_1, and so on. Of these, C and D are not-C_1 and not-D_1 respectively; but B is of course *not* not-B. Hence A, B, C and D would not form an internally-related system, though A, C and D would still be internally-related.

Now (A) (i) would be true if relations are partly or wholly determined by the nature of their terms; that is, if all relations are internal in Ewing's sixth sense. (A) (ii) would be true if either (a) all relations generate relational characteristics in their terms, or (b) a change in any relation logically presupposes a change in *all* its terms, or (c) a change in any relation causes a change in all its terms. (B) (i), on the other hand, would be true if either (a) a change in any one term in the universe produces, directly or indirectly, a change in all other terms in it, or (b) relations form part of the nature of all their terms. Finally, (B) (ii) logically follows from (B) (i) and would be true if (B) (i) is true, or if a change in any one term in the universe would result, directly or indirectly, in a change in *all* the relations in it. Since the coherence theory of reality would be true if either condition (A) or condition (B) is true, it would be true under the above-specified conditions which make the latter true.

Our next question is to find out whether or not the coherence theory of *truth* (here the theory that coherence constitutes the *nature* of truth) logically presupposes the coherence theory of reality, and therefore the doctrine of internal relations.

(A) If perfect or ideal truth consists in an all-inclusive system of propositions in which every part[19] entails and is entailed by every other part, and if such a system is a system of true propositions (as the advocates of coherence hold), this system must reflect reality in the sense that it must be true of it.[20] This means that the

---

19 I. e., a single proposition (Joachim, Blanshard), or a set of propositions (other advocates of the theory).

20 The relation between truth and reality envisioned here is of course very different from correspondence as envisioned by any of the advocates of the so-called Correspondence Theory. But I think we should say something about this theory (or rather, theories) and about "correspondence," since we shall occasionally mention the former and shall make use of the notion of "correspondence" in criticizing the coherence theory. It is common knowledge that the Correspondence Theory has been and is held in different forms. Correspondence, the relation constituting truth, has been variously held as one of copying or photograph-like likeness (e. g. Locke), as a one-to-one correlation (e.g. Russell, *The Analysis of Mind*), or as a kind of "accordance" (Ewing). Also, it is variously held as a relation between propositions and facts, judgments and facts, acts of judging and facts, or beliefs and facts. And facts, which constitute one term of the relation, are themselves variously conceived. But in all the forms of the Correspondence Theory that I know of, with a single exception, correspondence is conceived as a dyadic relation. The one exception is Russell's theory (*Philosophical Essays*), later abandoned, which conceives it as a polyadic relation between the mind and objects related in one manner or another.

Among the recent holders of the Correspondence Theory we might mention here G. E. Moore, Russell, Stace, and Ewing. G. E. Moore (*Some Main Problems of Philosophy*) conceives truth (in one important sense of 'true') as an unanalysable relation between a belief and a fact, a relation which does not obtain in the case of falsity. Thus to say that a given belief is true is "... to say that there is in the Universe *a* fact to which it corresponds; and that to say that it is false is to say that there is *not* in the Universe any fact to which it corresponds." (*Ibid.*, p. 277. Italics in original) But here a fact is not an actual physical or psychic event, a physical object or set of objects. The belief "Moore has gone away," supposing it to be true, corresponds to the fact '*that* Moore has gone away,' and not to Moore's actual act of going away itself. Russell (*An Inquiry Into Meaning*

propositions constituting the system, and the logical relations between them, must express the nature of the constituent parts of reality and their connections with one another. It follows that the ideal system of truth logically presupposes the coherence theory of reality in that it requires that the nature of everything in the universe be determined by the nature of the universe as a whole; that

---

And Truth) defines the Correspondence Theory as the theory "... according to which the truth of basic propositions depends upon their relation to some occurrence, and the truth of other propositions depends upon their syntactical relations to basic propositions." (*Ibid.*, p. 289) This theory he accepts. We might add that he distinguishes two forms of the theory: the epistemological and the logical forms. In the former, the relation of correspondence is held to obtain between basic propositions and experience; in the latter, it is held to obtain between basic propositions and facts which may or may not be experiences. (For Stace's and Ewing's versions of the theory, the reader is referred to *The Theory of Knowledge And Existence*, pp. 419 ff. and to I. C. S., pp. 207-208.)

We must now say a word about our use of the term 'correspondence' (or, sometimes, 'agreement') when expressing or intimating our personal views, as against our use of the term in comparing and contrasting the coherence theory with the various Correspondence Theories. I do not personally hold that 'truth' *means* correspondence with facts, nor that correspondence constitutes *the* test of truth. However, it is my belief that in our ordinary uses of the terms 'true' and 'truth' when applied to propositions, beliefs, or statements, there is involved some particular kind of reference to existent things and or events, which is absent in the case of our ordinary uses of 'false' and 'falsity' as applied to propositions, beliefs, or statements. And it is merely this reference which I allude to by my use of 'correspondence' or 'agreement,' for lack of a better name. Moreover, I hold that this reference is involved in the case of *individual* propositions, beliefs, or statements, though only in particular concrete contexts and not in a contextual vacuum.

This is not the place to give a positive analysis of the meaning of 'true' and 'truth.' But in order to make the above vague notion of "reference" clearer, let me state one way in which this reference can be understood. If the notion of denoting is regarded as applicable to statements, then this reference will be nothing but denoting. A true statement will be one which denotes what it purports to denote, i. e., will have denotation. A false statement will be one which does not denote what it purports to denote, i. e., it will have zero denotation (C. I. Lewis). (It is not maintained that this analysis would necessarily be applicable to all kinds of empirical statements.)

Finally, denoting statements, except those which expressly purport to denote the entire universe, like "The universe is four-dimensional," would have to be taken as purporting to denote, and as denoting, a limited segment of the actual world—a limited complex of objects and or events—and not the entire actual world.

any difference in any part of reality imply a difference in every other part of it. So for the coherence theory of truth to be true, the coherence theory of reality must be true. And we saw a little earlier what minimal conditions should be satisfied to make the latter true.

(B) The coherence theory of truth, in addition to the above, logically presupposes the internality of relations between *propositions* in the sense that (a) a difference or change in any one proposition should directly or indirectly involve a difference or change in any one logical relation in the ideal system of propositions; and (b) any difference or change in any one logical relation between any two or more propositions should imply a difference or change in all propositions in the ideal system. For unless these two conditions are satisfied, we cannot have a system of propositions in which every part—every proposition and every logical relation in the system—entails and is entailed by every other part and therefore by the system as a whole.

There is one further point which we have to discuss before we pass to a criticism of the arguments presented by the advocates of the doctrine of internal relations in support of this doctrine, and to the positive arguments in support of the doctrine of external relations. This is the contention that the coherence theory of reality itself logically presupposes and rests upon the conception of reality as an underlying or transcendent unity where the distinction between terms and relations, and therefore terms and relations themselves, do not exist. Put in other words, this contention consists in the view that ultimate reality cannot be a system of terms in (internal) relations, and that, therefore, to take such a system for ultimate reality is to falsify the nature of the latter.

This contention is historically associated in Anglo-American Idealism chiefly with Bradley; but it is also held by Royce.[21] We shall call this theory, for covenience, the underlying-reality theory,

---

21 E. G. Spaulding, in his *The New Bationalism*, New York, 1918, in addition to Bradley and Royce, mentions Card, Calkins and Green as exponents of this position. G.F. Stout, though not an Absolute Idealist, also holds the position. Blanshard, however, does not seem to hold it. He seems to hold the coherence theory of reality.

borrowing the term from E.G. Spaulding.[22] As stated by Spaulding, this theory is "... expressed by $\underset{U}{a\,R\,b}$, meaning by this, that, if two terms are related, and whether they modify each other or not,[23] there is an *underlying* or *transcendent* reality, U, to mediate this relation, indeed to make it possible at all."[24]

Bradley's arguments for the view that a system of terms in relation is not ultimate and self-sufficient, but requires a supra-relational reality to make it possible, are based on his attempt to show that the notion of relation is self-contradictory, so that in order to relate its terms, another relation is necessary to link the first relation to its terms, and this in turn requires another relation to relate it to the whole complex; and so on *ad infinitum*. He concludes that if this vicious regress is to be overcome, there must be something which is neither a relation nor is relational, which makes it possible for a relation to relate its terms. But terms, or qualities, require relations to be qualities at all; and relations require qualities or terms. Hence relations and qualities cannot be ultimate, and are only Appearance. However, he holds that the view that all relations are internal is nearer to the truth, is less

---

22 *The New Rationalism*. Spaulding regards this theory as an aspect of the theory of internal relations, the other aspect of the theory, according to him, being what he calls the "modification theory" of relations (which is actually a form of the doctrine of internal relations as we have discussed it). But it is clear that the latter is not really an aspect of the doctrine of *internal relations* (see footnote 23) but rather a metaphysical conception of reality as a whole, which, however, is based on, and involves a particular conception of the nature of relations. It would be merely a theory of *relations* only if the underlying reality is regarded as some sort of relation. But this is precisely what the advocates of this theory do not hold. On the contrary, as will be clear when we discuss the theory, it cannot be considered as a relation without either destroying the theory, or, if it is to be preserved, without positing another reality, itself not a relation, underlying *that* relation.

23 I. e., as formulated by Spaulding, the theory is independent of the doctrine of internal relations (the "modification theory" of relations) and is compatible with the doctrine of external relations. But we are here concerned with theory in so far as it is alleged to be logically presupposed by the conception of reality as a system of *internally*-related terms.

24 *Ibid.*, p. 177.

false—or more precisely, has a higher degree of truth—than the view that relations are external.

This view that relations are ultimately self-contradictory has been criticized by a number of writers[25] as resting on the supposition that a relation is a distinct and separate entity, a third term, a thing or a quality. Thus, Pratt says, "The difficulty is an entirely artificial one and evaporates at once if we refuse to make the fatal mistake of starting with a "relation" which does not and cannot relate."[26] Again, in criticizing Bradley's view that (in Stout's words) "... in affirming relations we affirm what is false," Stout says that if, whenever we say that any two things are related, we always say what is false, "... it must always be true that any two things, A and B, are not related, and never true that they are related."[27] However, Bradley does hold that so far as the world of Appearance is concerned, things *are* related, and related internally; i. e., that the doctrine of internal relations is true so far as this world is concerned. He does not deny that sensible objects are related, but denies that ultimate reality is a relational complex.[28] Further, since he holds

---

25 For instance G. F. Stout, *Studies In Philosophy And Psychology*, London, 1930, chapter ix; Aliotta, *The Idealistic Reaction Against Science*, translated by Agnes McCaskill, London, 1914, pp. 108-109; J. B. Pratt, *Personal Realism*, New York, 1937, p. 32; C. D. Broad, *Examination of Mc Taggart's Philosophy*, Cambridge, 1933, vol. I, p. 85; A. C. Ewing, *Idealism: A Critical Survey*, Chapter IV, p. 147. Ewing mentions Hobhouse, *Theory of Knowledge*, chapter xii; Schiller, *Humanism*, essay xi; Cook Wilson, *Statement and Inference*, vol. II, p. 692 ff., as well as Stout, as writers who have made the same criticism.

26 J. B. Pratt, *Personal Realism*, p. 32.

27 G. F. Stout, *Studies In Philosophy And Psychology*, p. 186.

28 Cf. Bosanquet on Bradley: "We are told that Mr. Bradley pronounces relations impossible. But there is more likely to be error, the author [Carr] continues, in his very subtle argument, than in so patent a fact as the inter-relatedness of things in the world. And then mention is made of experiment and the empirical outlook in contrast with *a priori* errors, quite after the manner of John Mill.

Now the author seems to me not in any way to imagine how totally foreign all this suggestion appears, rightly or wrongly, to the problem at issue as others among us see it." (*Science And Philosophy*, London, 1927, p. 28)

Again: "Mr. Bradley has, one might say, exhausted his very considerable resources of language in pointing out the two-sidedness of the problem, and how, if you cannot do with relations, no more can you do without them." (*Ibid.*, p. 29)

And again: "In the first place diversity is present, according to Mr. Bradley

the doctrine that internality of relations is a matter of degree, the sharp dichotomy between "A and B being related" and "A and B not being related" does not arise. Only if we first show that the doctrine of degrees of internality of relations is untenable (something which Stout does not do in his criticism) can we validly argue against Bradley from this dichotomy.[29] Again, Stout argues that if a thing is self-contradictory, it cannot exist. He says: "If, for example, space and time were self-contradictory in their very essence, it seems ... that space and time could not exist at all. There would be no space and no time."[30]

This criticism, if valid, also applies to relations. If the notion or relations is self-contradictory, then relations could not exist, even as Appearance; for Appearance itself is not nothing, as Bradley himself holds. But this argument, again, would only be valid if self-contradictoriness cannot admit of degrees (and therefore also, if reality cannot admit of degrees). If self-contradictoriness is a matter of degree, these relations would exist in so far as they have a degree of self-consistency. For if a thing or notion is not completely self-contradictory, it is not perfectly *not* self-consistent; which means that it is self-consistent in some degree. But if that is the case, relations exist in so far as they *can* and *do* relate; for as we said, their self-contradictoriness arises for Bradley in their *inability* to relate. Consequently, in so far as and in the degree in which relations do relate, they will have a degree of reality. But the view that relations do relate in some degree, is precisely the view that relations are internal in some degree since for Bradley to say that a relation relates is tantamount to saying that it is internal, and to say that it is external is to say that it does not relate; i. e., is not a relation at all in the proper sense of

---

as I read him, both in primary feeling and in the Absolute. In the next place, his attitude to relational diversity is really, it seems to me, quite simple. He, of course, so far from rejecting all diversity, was one of the first who fought for and established the principle of identity in diversity in English philosophy. It was his great contention. His books are full ot it. What he in principle refuses to accept I understand to be bare conjunction that is, the bringing together of differents, without mediation by any analysis of their conditions satisfactory to thought. Very likely no such analysis is ultimately and completely satisfactory." (*The Distinction Between Mind And Its Objects*, Manchester, 1913, p. 59)

29 For this, see Chapter VI of the present work.
30 *Studies In Philosophy And Psychology*, p. 187.

"relation." And the doctrine that relations are internal in a degree and therefore are external in a degree means that they relate in a degree but fail to relate completely. This shows why, according to Bradley, there cannot be a completely external or a completely internal relation. In the former case such a relation would not exist, since to be completely external means not to be capable of relating at all: and something which is incapable of relating at all cannot be a relation. On the other hand, a completely internal relation would entail the complete identity of the related terms, and therefore, again, would preclude the possibility of a relation. In order to relate, a relation must relate (at least numerically) discrete entities; and such discreteness is incompatible with perfect relatedness. So long as they are discrete, a relation is possible; but then the relation does not relate them completely. But if a relation does relate perfectly, there will be no discreteness and therefore no relation. This is the consequence of what Bradley expresses by saying that qualities (terms) cannot exist without relations and relations cannot exist without qualities (terms).

The foregoing also makes it clear why for Bradley the doctrine of internal relations as ordinarily understood is nearer to the truth, or has a higher degree of truth, than the doctrine of external relations as ordinarily understood. For it is nearer[31] to the view of reality as a supra-relational whole or Absolute than the doctrine of external relations, which, taken absolutely, i. e., as involving no degrees, entails, for Bradley, not only the complete disintegration of the unity of reality into totally independent entities, but even makes such entities impossible. So the choice, for him, is not between absolute unity and absolute plurality, but between absolute unity and nothingness. The doctrine of internal relations, conceived as involving degrees of internality, leads upward to the Absolute; for as we have seen, when we have perfect "internality" of "relations," we have neither relations nor terms (qualities), but a unity transcending qualities and relations. And this is Bradley's view of the Absolute.

---

31 For on Bradley's argument relatedness would involve internality, in contrast to externality which involves unrelatedness (what Bosanquet calls "bare conjunction").

From this it is seen that Bradley's argument that relations (taken absolutely and not as involving degrees) are self-contradictory because they cannot and do not relate, applies, strictly speaking, to the doctrine that (some or all) relations are *external* (absolutely speaking), and not against the notion of *relations* as such. It is true, Bradley uses this argument both against this doctrine and against the view that relations are ultimate; or more exactly, the view that reality consists of a system of terms in relation. And the question arises whether, thereby, Bradley is not eating his cake and having it too, or undermining his own position. For if the externality of relations involves the consequence that relations cannot relate, i. e., if the doctrine of external relations makes relations a third term or separate thing (what his critics accuse *him* of presupposing) then this doctrine will be false only if terms *can* relate, i. e., are not distinct things or third terms. But if they can relate, then no infinite regress or any self-contradiction arises, and relations will therefore be ultimately real; hence also terms (qualities) will be ultimately real, since relations and qualities go together. But if so, reality could be a system of (internally) related terms, and there is no logical need or ground for positing an underlying supra-relational unity. In other words, it seems, that for Bradley's argument against the doctrine of external relations to be valid, it has to posit the contrast between relating versus not relating as one which excludes a middle, in the sense of degrees between these two. (That would make the argument inconsistent with the doctrine of degrees of relatedness.) But then, what becomes of the transition from perfect relatedness to the supra-relational stage? It is only if relations do not relate completely or perfectly that another relation would be necessary to make the relation possible, and yet another relation to make *this* relation relate, and so on *ad infinitum*; thus making it necessary to posit an underlying supra-relational unity. But Bradley's logic leads him to hold that such a reality would be logically arrived at or entailed precisely where relations *do* relate perfectly.

We can put these points in another way. Greater and greater relatedness or internality can never logically lead to a stage which is non-relational. If degree of relatedness or internality is degree of systematization or coherence and inclusiveness, as Bradley holds, then perfect relatedness would be perfect or all-inclusive system; and a system of course cannot but be a system of terms in relation.³²

Spaulding presents the following argument against the underlying-reality theory: If we have a relation R between two things a and non-a, and U is the underlying reality which mediates the relation and makes it possible, then we have the following situation:

If a *first* U is found to mediate the relation between a and *non-a*, then, since this U is related to the complex, $a\ R\ non\text{-}a$, another U is in turn implied to mediate this relation, and so on in infinite series. Therefore, either an *ultimate underlying U is never reached*, or, if it is, then, although it is related to the complex of the *preceeding complexes*, this relation does not demand an underlying reality to mediate it. But, if there is this one exception, then *no relation need demand an underlying entity to mediate it*, and the whole theory falls to the ground.³³

It is to be noted that this argument is not affected by Bradley's assumption that relatedness is a matter of degree. For if R does relate a and b in some degree and yet, for all that, requires an underlying reality to mediate it as Bradley argues, it remains that this underlying reality will be related to the complex $a\ R\ b$; and *this* relation itself, as a relation, will also relate only in some degree, and therefore would require another underlying reality to mediate it; and so on *ad infinitum*. On the other hand, if the relation between U and the complex "$a\ R\ non\text{-}a$," although *necessarily a matter of degree*, does not require another underlying reality to make it possible, then there is no reason to suppose in the first place that the relation R between a and *non-a*, because it relates only in degree, requires an underlying reality to make it possible. If it is objected that the relation between U and "$a\ R\ non\text{-}a$" does relate perfectly or absolutely, then since this implies that there can be relations which relate perfectly (which is

---

32 For a detailed criticism of the doctrine of degrees of internality of relations, see Chapter VI.

33 *The New Rationalism*, pp. 187-188. Spaulding also presents an empirical argument. But we do not need to go into that, since the above argument seems to me to be conclusive. (Italics in original.)

contrary to Bradley's position), Bradley's argument, assuming it to be valid, would merely imply that ultimate reality must be a system of terms *related absolutely* and not only in degree—and not that no system of related terms, however closely related, can be ultimate.

It is obvious that it cannot be validly maintained that U is *not* related to the complex "$a\ R\ non\text{-}a$." For if so, U cannot be said to underly "$a\ R\ non\text{-}a$": far from underlying it, it will have nothing to do with it! And of course it may be asked how anything can make a relation possible and mediate it without in any way being related to it. (The assumption would have the further inconvenience of supposing that there can be existent things which are not related at all. For even if U is externally related to "$a\ R\ non\text{-}a$," if we grant that external relations are relations at all, the difficulty remains. For, as a relation, it would require mediation; and Spaulding's criticism would follow.)

It may be argued that we are falsely assuming that the underlying reality, U, is something set over against "$a\ R\ non\text{-}a$" and is not *the reality which underlies* "$a\ R\ non\text{-}a$": something which includes, although it goes beyond, "$a\ R\ non\text{-}a$." I. e., in terms of Bradley's metaphysics, Spaulding's criticism (the objection would say) presupposes that the phenomenal world or the world of Appearance is outside Reality or the Absolute and not a part or, rather, a manifestation *of* it. But Appearances have no existence apart from Reality, whose Appearance they are. Reality, in so far as it manifests itself, *is* its Appearances. There are not two realities, Reality or the Absolute on the one hand, *and* Appearances on the other hand. Hence the Absolute is not and cannot be *related* to its Appearances. To assume that it is or can be related to it is to assume that Appearances are a distinct entity or set of entities. "$A\ R\ non\text{-}a$" is not a distinct entity set over and against U, and therefore related to it as one entity to another. To appear is to be partial, fragmentary, not perfectly coherent. Reality is wholeness.

But does this invalidate the criticism? I do not think so. For things as perceived or thought are qualitatively and numerically differentiated and, at the same time, related. Whether we call these things Appearances or not, we cannot get over this fact. And as differentiated and related they are not and cannot be a non-relational or supra-relational unity. So far, Bradley would go with us. But if so, they are not, as such, identical with Reality or parts of Reality (for the notion of "parts" involves differentiation, and relation to that of which they are parts), and I do not see how the passage from them to the Absolute can be accomplished at all other than by a relation. But even a relation would not bridge the gap. If a relation is posited it will still be a relation between a relational whole and something else; and we cannot pass from this relational whole to something non-relational. This difficulty is no other than the perennial difficulty of all monisms: how to admit the existence of plurality and yet to pass beyond it to a unity; to admit the existence of the Many and yet to hold that this Many is somehow One. If we start with a non-relational One we cannot ever pass to the Many; if we start with the relational Many we can never arrive at a non-relational One.

We now turn to Stout's argument for the non-sufficiency of a system of interrelated terms. For though Stout rejects Bradley's arguments, he agrees with his theses. He contends that reality or the Whole, "... has a form of unity which is not, and cannot be, constituted merly by relations."[34] The reason is that—

It is a continuum, and continuous connexion, as such, is not relation in the sense in which Mr. Bradley uses the word. Relation is *between* related terms, and the word BETWEEN implies that the related terms as such are discrete. If and so far as there is continuous connexion there is *nothing* between, and there is therefore no relation.[35]

In a footnote he adds that we may call continuous connexion a relation if we like; but in that case it would be a peculiar kind of relation, since it is immediate, "... and therefore does not presuppose intervening links *between* the terms related."[36] A line is an example of a continuum. There is a relation of right and left between the two halves of the line. But these two halves "... have also a continuous connexion with each other. But the continuous

---

34 *Studies in Philosophy And Psychology*, p. 183.
35 *Ibid*., Italics in original.
36 *Ibid*., Italics in original.

connexion is not itself a relation. For it exists only at the immediate junction of the two halves. In fact it simply is this immediate junction."[37]

But if Stout's argument is valid it merely proves that, in some cases, where there is a relation between terms, there is also something over and above this which is not a relation but a "continuous connexion." Thus though the two halves are related as left to right, there is the immediate junction where the two halves meet; and this junction is not a relation. But the argument does not show that such "continuous connexions" exist or can exist *where there are no relations at all*; i. e., that there can be a "continuum" where there are no relations *whatever*. And this latter is precisely what Stout has to prove, since he wants to show that "The all-inclusive universe cannot ultimately consist in a collection of interrelated terms...."[38]

Thus in the example of the line, in order to have continuous *connection* we have to *divide* the line, conceptually or actually, into parts. The line as a whole may be a "continuum," whatever that may mean; but *connection*, immediate or otherwise, can only arise if and when we have a division of the line into *parts*. For to have connection, we have to have *discrete things*, which can be connected. And if we have such a division we cannot but have relation. Thus in the example of the line, continuous connection does not and cannot exist without there being some relation. Of course this does not preclude the possibility of there being relations without any "immediate connexion." If two lines AB and CD are separated by some distance (i. e., say B and C are two different points) then there is a spatial relation between AB and CD such that (for instance) AB is to the left of CD. Here there is no "immediate connexion."

Thus I agree with Stout that the "continuous connexion" between the two halves of our first line is the immediate junction of the two halves, and that this is not a relation. A junction is a point, and a point is not a relation. But this, as I said above, merely shows that "continuous connexion" is different from a rela-

---

[37] *Ibid.*, pp. 183-184.
[38] *Ibid.*, p. 183.

tion. It does not show that "continuous connexion" can exist without any relation. Stout goes on :

> Within the continuous line it is possible to distinguish component parts and points of junction, and relations of these component parts and points of junction, and again, relations of these relations.... The discernible relations are numberless. They do not form a sum total. But the line itself is a terminated whole. If therefore, it is to be reduced to terms and relations, it must be their sum total, and not an endless series. But since the terms and relations do not form a sum total, and do form an endless series, they cannot of themselves constitute the units of the continuous line.[39]

Now it is admitted that a line is a continuum in the sense that it is continuous, that there is no break in it as a line. Also, that as a line, there are no relations within it ; since it is not actually divided into discrete parts—though it may be related, as a whole, to other geometrical magnitudes, such as other lines, points, or surfaces. But at the same time it does not involve any "*continuous connexions*" either. The line is *divisible* into finite parts ; and if we do divide it (conceptually or actually) into portions of finite length, there will be "continuous connexion" between the parts : but at the same time these parts will be *related*. Further, the number of geometrical relations within the line, as well as the number of "immediate connexions," will be finite and not infinite. If, on the other hand, the line is conceived as sub-divided into geometrical points ; that is, into points with no finite magnitude, then we will indeed have an infinite number of relations between these parts ; but in that case we will have no "immediate connexions" at all, since these points, being without magnitude, cannot be "immediately" connected. This is another way of saying that actual lines are not composed of geometrical points. For no number of points with no magnitude at all can together make a line, which does have some magnitude. (Stout himself says that "... points are not component portions of the line. A point is an immediate meeting, and for that reason points themselves cannot meet.")[40]

---

39 *Ibid.*, p. 184.
40 *Ibid.*

This throws us back on the first alternative, namely, the subdivision of a line into finite portions. But as we have seen, the number of relations which we will have within the line, between the different portions of the line itself (for that is what matters here), will not be infinite; since a finite line cannot be subdivided into an infinite number of finite parts. The "discernible relations" will not be numberless, literally speaking, as Stout maintains.[41] And what is more, we will also have an indefinite (but finite) number of "immediate connexions," although their number would be smaller than the number of relations involved. And since the portions of the line (if and when the line is actually divided or is regarded as divisible into portions) will have some finite length and will be finite in number, the line itself will be the sum total of all these portions *in* their particular relations to one another; we will not have to "reduce" the line, at Stout thinks, to terms *and* relations. The relations are not terms; they are not magnitudes. And the terms and relations do not form an endless series. But if we think of the line as a *continuum*, Stout's conclusion that "they [terms and relations] cannot of themselves constitute the units of the continuous line" would indeed be true; but then there would be no continuous *connections* either.

Stout's attempt to show that a continuum involves continuous connections but not relations must therefore be considered unsuccessful. But even if his attempt were successful, it would not follow that reality itself is a continuum; and Stout (at least as far as this particular argument goes) does not show that it is.

On the other hand, if Stout maintains that a non-relational whole cannot be constituted by terms in relation, he will obviously be perfectly right. But that, as we have attempted to show, constitutes a major difficulty in the type of position he is arguing for, since it is an undeniable fact that the things in the world we

---

[41] If we include relations above the first order (that is, relations of relations, relations of relations of relations, and so on) in the "discernible relations," the number of relations we will have will be numberless or infinite. But these purely logical relations are not involved in the constitution of the geometrical line as a geometrical line. Only the first-order relations, between the different (finite) portions of the line, are involved here. And these are not infinite in number.

experience are relational, and therefore the passage from them to a non-relational whole (or a non-relational whole which in some sense "includes" these relational entities) is impossible.

Finally, if what Stout is concerned to show is that reality is a non-relational continuum, but that it also includes or contains related terms within it, the difficulty would then be to show how something which is non-relational can contain relations and terms which are in relation.

Our analysis, if correct, seems to show that the coherence theory of reality does not logically require and presuppose the underlying-reality theory of reality, and not merely that the attempts to show that it does require it are unsuccessful. Further support to our criticism of the arguments for the underlying-reality theory, so far as these arguments assume the doctrine of degrees of internal relations, will be found when we criticize the latter in detail in Chapter VI.

CHAPTER III

THE DOCTRINE OF INTERNAL RELATIONS (CONT'D.)

In Chapter II we mentioned the various senses of "internal relations" as listed by Ewing, and discussed the sense or senses of "internal relations" in which the coherence theory of reality is a logical presupposition of the coherence theory of truth. But there we did not raise the question whether or not the doctrine of internal relations in this sense or these senses is true, and therefore whether or not the universe is an all-inclusive system of interdependent parts. In this chapter we shall occupy ourselves with the attempt to answer these two questions by examining, first, some of the main arguments which the advocates of the coherence theory of truth present in support of the doctrine of internal relations. In doing so, we shall attempt to show that these arguments are untenable; and to support our contention positively, we shall offer, second, some arguments in support of the doctrine of external relations, i. e., the doctrine that not *all* relations are internal. But we shall not argue that *all* relations are external. The view that all relations are external, like its contrary, seems to me to be false: as we hope will become clear in the course of this chapter. What we shall attempt to show is rather that *some* (at least one, but not all) relations are external.

(1) *Some arguments in support of the doctrine of internal relations.*

The arguments brought forth by the advocates of the doctrine of internal relations are of two kinds : epistemological and metaphysical. We shall begin with the epistemological arguments and then pass to the metaphysical ones. (1) First of all, it is argued, negatively (a) that thought in its very essence aims at understanding, and understanding means the apprehension of all things as parts of an allinclusive internally-related system, where nothing is left out as in herently incapable of being included in the system. If therefore reality is not such a system, thought is doomed to defeat; and all attempts on its part to relate and systematize, are illusory. As Blanshard puts it, "... to accept a discrepancy between the structure of reality on the one hand and the ideal of thought [system] on the other is to commit thought to defeat."[1] It is true, Blanshard adds, it is not possible to disprove the view that the satisfaction we get when we think we have arrived at a solution to a problem is merely subjective, that this satisfaction merely proves that "... we happen to have a liking for working up our experience into a special kind of pattern...."[2] But if this view is accepted, we are doomed to complete scepticism and ignorance.

(b) It is argued that all science presupposes that the world is a unity. As Marvin puts the argument:

Unless the world is a unity, it is simply an aggregate of more or less disconnected worlds and some of them may be absolutely unknowable even to a perfect intellect inhabiting other systems. Unless the world is a unity, the sciences must remain more or less disconnected and it can never be understood why they are true as a group.... Now whatever postulate makes the world either unknowable or unintelligible cannot be consistently entertained by science. The pluralistic hypotheses [the doctrine of external relations] does so, therefore it must be rejected.[3]

In answer to this argument the following may be said:

(a) The possibility of knowledge does not necessitate the doctrine of internal relations. Knowledge would still be possible if some relations are external. For to know that some relations *are* external, and, still more, to know what relations, both in general and in a given case, are external, is to have knowledge. The alternative: either an internally-related system and therefore the possibility of knowledge, *or* the absence of such a system and therefore the impossibility of knowledge, is untenable. To deny that all relations are internal does not entail affirming that all relations are external. But even if *all* relations are external, a knowledge of individual, seperate things would still be possible;

---

1 N. T., vol. II, p. 449. Cf. also pp. 450, 475.
2 *Ibid.*, p. 449.
3 W. T. Marvin, *A First Book In Metaphysics*, New-York, 1920, p 91. (Marvin himself is not an advocate of the doctrine of internal relations.) Also Cf. N. T., vol. II, p. 453 ff., and the following statement by Bosanquet: "Is there any man of science who in his daily work and apart from philosophic controversy, will accept a bare given conjunction as conceivably ultimate truth?" (Quoted from N.T., vol. II, p. 454.)

although it is true that in that case we cannot pass from a knowledge of one thing to a knowledge of anything else.[4] But this fact cannot be used against the doctrine that some (but not all) relations are external, without illegitimately identifying the doctrine of external relations with the view that *all* relations are external, as Bradley for instance does.[5] If *some* relations are internal, we can pass from a knowledge of one thing to a knowledge of another thing to which the former is internally related.[6] But, of course, only if all relations are internal (in the crucial senses) can we pass from a knowledge of one thing to a (partial) knowledge of everything else in the universe.

(b) No *a priori* assumption that all relations are internal seems to be required or logically presupposed by our desire or attempts to understand the nature of reality and to arrive at knowledge, whether in science, philosophy, or elsewhere.

Now it may be that in scientific inductive generalization, and in the use of the laws of probability (whether the *a priori* or the frequency theory) we have to assume that certain events, or certain existent things, are intrinsically connected with other events or other existent things, so that if and when the former occur the latter would, or even must, occur also (the necessary-connection theory of causality). But that is different from the assumption that *all* events, or all existent things in the universe, are causally related to all other events or all other existent things, directly or indirectly. The necessary-connection theory of causality is perfectly compatible with the existence of any number of limited internally-related systems of events or of existent things, which are independent of one another. But further, even the supposition of a plurality of systems of *internally*-related events or of existent things would not follow from the assumption of the necessary-connection theory of causality, unless it is first shown that the latter implies the internality

---

[4] But to say that all relations are external does not imply that there is no relation whatever between the mind and reality, so that reality cannot be known. Unless it is proved that externality of relations means the absence of any relation, the externality of the so-called cognitive relation cannot be tantamount to scepticism.

[5] E. T. R., p. 259.

[6] Cf. I. C. S., pp. 143-144.

of the causal relations in the crucial senses of 'internal relation.' That the necessary-connection view of causality implies the internality of the causal relations in Ewing's senses eight, nine and ten of this term is true, as we shall see when we come to a discussion of causality in the latter part of this chapter. But as we shall attempt to show there, the causal relations would still not be internal in sense seven, which is the most important and crucial sense of 'internal relation.'

Apart from all this, perception does give us some knowledge of the world, and perception, to be possible, does not require an assumption of any kind. It is admitted that purely-perceptual knowledge is meager, and also that it is not knowledge in the sense in which many philosophers use the term 'knowledge.' But it is knowledge in at least one use of this term in ordinary language. Further, since we have indicated that the assumption of the necessary-connection view of causality does not logically presuppose the internality of *all* relations in our crucial seventh sense, the passage from purely perceptual knowledge to inferential knowledge by using the notion of necessary causal connection does not logically presuppose the internality of all relations.

(c) Further, the human desire for system, or if it is an innate tendency, the tendency of the mind to see things in systematic relation (assuming that it is universally true), to discover general all-inclusive principles, does not itself in any way guarantee that this desire, tendency, ideal is or can be realized; unless we assume that the universe is made to the measure of our desires and ideals. And this assumption itself would presuppose the premise that the universe is teleological: not merely that, but that it is anthropocentric. Unless this is proved, we cannot be required to accept it.

There is nothing absurd or contradictory (though it may be tragic!) in the notion that the aim of thought may be frustrated, that knowledge after all may be impossible; though the affirmation that all knowledge is impossible is self-contradictory. However, as we have attempted to show, the doctrine of external relations does not entail the desperate view that reality is unknowable. This will be further seen from the following consideration:

(d) The notion of a system of *knowledge* does not necessarily presuppose the notion that reality is an internally-related system.

This does not contradict what we have said in Chapter I, namely that the coherence theory of truth logically presupposes the coherence theory of reality. For the latter states that *truth* lies in a system of a *certain special kind*, i. e., a system where the truth of every component part depends on and results from its coherence with the rest of the system; and the truth of the system as a whole depends on and results from the coherence of its parts, and not on the correspondence of any proposition with any particular facts thought to lie outside the system. Thus though the coherence theory identifies truth with knowledge, and therefore knowledge for it is a coherent system (but of a special kind), it is because of the conception of truth as a special kind of system that knowledge, *in the same sense of 'system,'* presupposes the coherence theory of reality.

(2) It is further said[7] that the doctrine of external relations is not only false, but leads to absurdity. For if two terms are related by an external relation, then by the fact that the relation is external, the terms are independent of each other. But if so, they are also independent of the relation between them; which amounts to saying that they are not related at all. Hence, in order to relate the terms, we must have another relation to relate the original relation to its terms; and so on *ad infinitum*. If this infinite (vicious) regress is to be overcome, we must assume that terms are not independent of one another, and consequently not independent of the relation between them.

It will be noted that we have met something very similar to this in Chapter II, in connection with the discussion of the underlying-reality theory. There, however, the very notion of relations was alleged (by Bradley) to be *ultimately* self-contradictory and to lead to an infinite regress; if valid, it could therefore be urged against the view that relations are internal as much as against the view that they are external. Here, however, and as we have tried to show in Chapter II, Bradley inconsistently attempts to show that an infinite regress is involved only if relations are taken to be external. In other words what the criticism amounts to is that the

---

[7] A. R., pp. 32-33; Royce, *The World And The Individual*, New York, 1900, especially Lecture III; also Cf. Spaulding's clear and succinct presentation of this argument in *The New Rationalism*, pp. 182-183.

doctrine of external relations makes relations a third term or separate thing.[8] This position, as Ewing points out, is not held by any advocates of the external theory of relations, nor does rejection of the theory of internal relations in any of the ten senses of 'internal relation' (not even the first),[9] imply the acceptance of such a view.[10]

It is clear that the whole argument rests on the assumption that externality of relations implies complete independence in any and all senses of the term, or the absence of all relation. But as Perry has shown,[11] 'independence' as used by the modern Neo-Realists (and the same is true of other philosophers), does not mean 'non-relation'; and certainly one need not mean by 'independence' the absence of all relation. The either, or of the idealistic argument: either internal relations or no relations at all, is untenable. Indeed, Spaulding holds that the argument begs the very issue at hand, by assuming that "... *if terms are independent, they cannot be related, and that the relation does not relate them.*"[12] The argument does not prove that externality of relations is independence in the sense of the absence of all relation. And this is precisely the issue in hand.

(3) It is argued that the cognitive relation is internal, since the object cognized makes a difference to cognition; and therefore it would be absurd to suppose that cognition itself could make no difference to its object,"... that there could be a relation which was, so to speak, internal at one end and external at the other."[13] This argument, if valid, merely establishes that one particular

---

8 I. C. S., p. 143.

9 Ewing is inclined to except the first sense of 'internal relation.' But we shall attempt to show later in this chapter that rejection of internality of relations even in this sense does not imply that relations are third terms.

10 Ibid.

11 R. B. Perry, "A Realistic Theory of Independence," *The New Realism*, New York, 1922, pp. 113-114. But the whole chapter is pertinent to this issue. Also, Cf. Spaulding, who sums up what the theory of external relations holds in the words "relatedness and independence are quite compatible." (*The New Rationalism*, p. 177)

12 *The New Rationalism*, p. 183. Italics in original.

13 I. C. S., p. 144. Cf. Joachim, *The Nature of Truth*, p. 50, footnote 1.

relation—although admittedly a very important one—is internal, not that all relations are internal. But *is* this relation internal? And if so, in what sense? The supposition that the object cognized makes a difference to cognition indicates that what is assumed is that cognition is internally related to the object cognized in sense seven, such that cognition could not be what it is if the object cognized were absent or different. From this it is intended to prove that the object of cognition is internally related to cognition in the same sense; that the object of cognition could not be what it is if cognition were absent or different.

It will be remembered that sense seven of 'internal relation,' both as stated by Ewing and as we interpreted it, stated that a *relation* "makes a difference" to its terms, that its terms could not be what they are if the *relation* were absent. But is this the same as saying, or does it follow from this, that if *one* of the *terms* were different or absent, the other term would be different or absent? It is obvious that the two statements are not the *same*. Then does it *follow* (a) that if a given act of cognition could not exist if the object cognized were absent (which is true), that the object cognized could not exist if cognition were absent? Assuredly not. And it does not follow empirically either; for, according to the causal theory of perception, the existence of a given act of cognition is causally dependent on the existence of an object of cognition; and hence the object of cognition must already be existent in the first place to make the act of cognition possible. This means that the existence of the object of cognition cannot depend on the existence of an act of cognition. Further, if the existence of the object of cognition were dependent on the act of cognition in the above sense, no object can exist uncognized, which is contrary to what Absolute Idealism holds, since for it the given in cognition (perception) is not the product of the cognition or the perceiver's mind. (b) Does then the view that "the object of cognition" would be different if "cognition" were different, follow from the view that a given "cognition" would be *different* if "the object cognized" were different? The term 'the object cognized' is ambiguous. It can mean either (1) the object actually cognized in a given case, O, or (2) the object-to-be-cognized-if-possible or *cognoscendum*, C; the object as it exists uncognized or independently of cognition—if such an object exists—which may or may not be numerically identical with O. This gives us two logical alternatives : O may be (a) numerically identical with C; or (b) numerically and qualitatively different from C as a result of cognition. In (a), *ex hypothesi*, O will not be affected by its being cognized: i. e., "cognition" will not "make a difference" to it. In (b), "cognition" will "make a difference" to O, but O will be a different object from C. C itself will not be affected or modified by "its" being cognized. "Congnition" will not "make a difference" to it. Rather it, together with "cognition," will be the (partial) cause of the production of the new entity, O. In both (a) and (b), "cognition" will not "make a difference" to C. In (b), O would be different if "cognition" were different. But then, it is not O but C which "makes a difference" to the "cognition" in the sense of *determining its content* (for the *act* of cognizing itself, if present at all, is not affected or determined by the character of C, and least of all by C). In this sense of 'make a difference'; therefore, (i) C "makes a difference" to the "cognition" ; but not vice versa ; (ii) "cognition" "makes a difference" to O ; but not vice versa. In either case there is only a one-way and not a two-way internal relation between "cognition" and (put ambiguously) "the object cognized." In short, it is not true that if "the object cognized" (*the cognoscendum*) "makes a difference" to "cognition," "cognition" "makes a difference" to "the object cognized" (the *cognoscendum*).

We should carefully distinguish the object of cognition, or more precisely, the *cognoscendum* (the object-to-be-cognized-if possible) and the cognized object ; since in the case of sense-perception the two *may* be different. On almost any view but that of Subjective Idealism, the object-of-cognition-if-possible or *cognoscendum* is independent of the cognition of a particular perceiver; but according to Epistemological Dualism and Absolute Idealism (among others) the cognized (perceived) object as cognized is different (in some crucial sense or senses of 'different') from the *cognoscendum*, and is (partly) dependent on or determined by the cognition (perception) of a percipient. But note that once we make the distinction, it becomes plain that the fact (or alleged fact) that the object-of-cognition-if-possible or *cognoscendum* "makes a difference" to cognition, does not entail at all that cognition makes a difference to it. On the other hand, if cognition "makes a difference" to its "object" (leaving this indefinite), this object, by that very fact, will *not itself be the cognoscendum* or the "object of cognition" but a numerically and perhaps also qualitatively different object: and it is *this* object (not the *cognoscendum*) which "makes a difference" to cognition. If we symbolize the *cognoscendum* by "C," the "cognized object" by "O," cognition by "G," these points can be indicated as follows: (1) G depends on C; but C is independent of G. (2) O depends on G (i. e., O is different from G); but G is independent of O. Hence the dependence, in both cases, is one-sided and not reciprocal; and thus, far from it being absurd to have what the argument we are criticizing ambiguously calls "a relation which was, so to speak, internal at one end and external at the other," we here have an actual instance of it. Actually, it is not *one* such (determinate) relation that is involved here, but *two*; one of which is internal while the other is external. But this is not the logical relation called "the cognition relation" or the "cognizing-cognition" relation as we might call it; rather, it is the causal relation of cognized object to the act of cognition.

(4) Ewing mentions, among the arguments brought forward in support of the doctrine of internal relations, Bradley's conception that in "feeling" we have a unity which is non-relational.[14] This view is an aspect of Bradley's conception of Reality as a non-relational or supra-relational unity underlying things experienced in perception and conceived in thought (the underlying-reality theory). It can either be taken as a premise for the underlying-reality theory, as it actually was for Bradley, or as a deduction from it; and even in the latter case this view might be true-- even though the underlying-reality theory itself is false. But supposing it to be true, it does not serve to show that the unity allegedly apprehended in "feeling" is an *internally-related* unity, but

---

14 Bosanquet holds that, for Bradley, "diversity" (and therefore relation) is present in "primary feeling," as well as in the Absolute. (*The Distinction Between Mind And Its Objects*, p. 59.) But this "diversity" does not make either "feeling" or the Absolute itself relational in nature. It is a non-relational entity which in each case "contains" "diversity." For problems raised by this view, see chapters V and VI of the present work.

rather that it is neither internal nor external. Moreover, even if it is merely taken as an argument against the theory of external relations, as it is meant to be taken, it would merely prove that *some* (at least one) apprehended things are not externally related. But it is a fact that in ordinary perception we do apprehend things in relation. Unless it is shown that these (and other, non-perceptual) relations are all internal (which the argument does not do), the argument, if valid, would not entail that *no* relations are external : which is what we are concerned with here.

(5) Bosanquet argues that "relations are true of their terms. They express their position in complexes which positions elicit their behaviour, their self-maintenance in the world of things."[15] This seems to mean what Blanshard expresses by saying that "... everything is so integral a part of a context that it can neither be nor be truly conceived apart from that context."[16] Or, as he puts it formally, that every term is what it is by virtue of *all* of its relations to everything else.[17] This could mean that relations cause a change in their terms; but it is not what is actually meant. What is meant is that relations are internal in Ewing's seventh sense ; that at least one of the terms could not have been what it is without the relations being present. In this sense, it is certainly true that some relations are internal; namely, those relations whose presence and nature wholly depend on characteristics in their terms—e. g. the relations of similarity and difference. In these cases, both terms of a relation could not be the same if a relation between them were absent or different. But as we have attempted to show in Chapter II, this sense of 'internality of relations,' *in these cases*, is nothing but Ewing's sixth sense in disguise, since the proposition : "Terms A and B could not both be the same if a relation r between them were absent or different," logically follows from its contrapositive : "R's presence and nature are wholly determined by the presence and nature of terms A and B." And in the sixth sense of 'internal relation' it is really the terms that

---

15 *Logic*, Second Edition, pp. 278-279. Quoted from I. C. S., p. 145.
16 N. T., vol. II, p. 452.
17 *Ibid.*

determine the nature of their relations, not relations the nature of their terms.

As for relations which, as determinate relations, are only partly determined by their terms, such as spatial and causal relations, these relations are external in Ewing's seventh sense as defined by him. Whether or not the relations we just mentioned are only partly determined, *qua* determinate relation, by the nature of their terms (we shall later on endeavor to show that they are), it is I think clear that if any relation is only partly determined by its terms, a difference in the relations does not logically imply a difference even in one of its terms. The difference in the relation could always be due to a difference in or the absence of those conditions which, besides the terms, partly determine the relation. And these conditions, *ex hypothesi*, would not constitute a term of the relations.[18]

Finally, it can be readily seen that relations cannot determine their terms in the sense that they cause a change in them. (It would be true that relations can and do *logically* generate relational characteristics in their terms if we grant the existence of such characteristics. But such a determination of terms by their relations would be a trivial sense of internality of relations; and we have already touched on this.) To begin with, I have not come across any arguments by the advocates of the doctrine of internal relations which show that relations can cause a change in their terms. It is noteworthy that whenever these thinkers attempt to show that relations determine their terms—except where, unwittingly, they show instead that *terms* determine their relations—they merely show (or try to show) that relational characteristics are generated by relations.[19] Apart from this, it seems obvious that relations, even the so-called empirical, non-logical relations, such as the causal relation, are by their nature causally otiose. Ewing states the point very clearly in regard to the relation of similarity and mathematical relations.
He says:

---

18   See arguments seven and twelve in the present chapter.
19   Cf. for example, McTaggart, *The Nature of Existence,* Cambridge, 1921, vol. I, pp. 29-30, and N.T., vol. II, p. 478.

If [term] A is like [term] B in respect of a certain quality or qualities there is a relation between A and B which is internal in the sense defined [Ewing's seventh sense], namely, the relation of similarity. If A and B are similar at all, they could not have been different in quality from what they now are. Again, If A is half of B the relation is internal, since it could not have been absent without A or B being different in size from what it now is.... Yet with neither of them is it true that the relation causes a change in either A or B. And it is equally obvious that this relation... does not create, make or bring into being either of its terms. The same is clearly true of the numerous internal relations that hold between timeless universals, as in pure mathematics.[20]

The same applies, *mutatis mutandis*, to the relation of difference.

With regard to the causal relation, the question is whether or not a present causal relation r between an agent A and a patient B causally changes one or more of the original characteristics A and B possessed immediately before they entered the causal relation; immediately before A acted upon B. It might be thought that since B is the patient, and r is a causal relation, r at least changes one or more of B's original characteristics. But if we distinguish—as we must—between the causal *relation* and the causal *action* of the agent on the patient, it becomes clear that this is not the case. R itself is not the causal event, the causal action of A on B; r logically obtains as a result of the occurrence of the causal action and the production of an effect in B. We speak of A and B as *entering* into a causal relation *as a result of* causal activity. The action of A on B does the rela*ting*: the rela*tion* is a logical result of this. The relating of A to B, and *vice versa*, is an activity, but the relation is not an activity; it is a logical result of the activity of relating. The so-called "causal" relation itself is not a causal agent or causally efficacious. In the case of A, even if and when it is changed by its action on B, it is not the new and different relation s established as a result that changes A's characteristics, but B's action on A.

A word must be said here about relational characteristics. To say that a term A has the relational characteristic of being related to B by a relation r is simply, it seems to me, another way of

---

20 I. C. S., pp. 46-47. See also the opening of Ewing's discussion of his seventh sense of 'internal relations,' p. 130, and footnote 6, p. 131.

saying that A is related to B by *r* (and B is related to A by the converse of *r*). That is, there does not seem to me to be such a thing as a relational characteristic generated (logically) by a relation. This applies to any and all so-called relational characteristics, whether they are thought of as generated by the relation of difference or by any other relation. In this respect I agree with C. D. Broad, who considers such "relational characteristics" as "mere figments." To take Broad's example: "A is a lover of B" and "B is a beloved of A" are different sentences from "A loves B"; yet all three sentences express the same fact, namely the fact that A loves B.[21] If this is true, there is no need to appeal to common sense or to the law of parsimony in order to reject relational characteristics. For common sense cannot be taken as the final word in philosophy (assuming that there is such a thing as *a* common sense, the same in all men at all times), and the law of parsimony (viewed from one angle) assumes that the simpler explanation is (at least) more likely to be true than a more complex explanation: which certainly need not be the case. Further, I agree with McTaggart and Broad that the infinite regress which the positing of relational characteristics entails is not vicious.

Returning to our discussion of the relation of difference, let us consider the following argument offered by McTaggart—

When any substance changes, all substances must change. If A and B are any two substances, they must be related—by similarity and diversity, if in no other way. If A changes, then the object to which B stands in certain relations has changed. Even if B keeps the same relations to the changed A, the object to which it has them will now have a different nature, and thus the relationship will have been changed. Instead of having the relations XY to a substance with the nature PQR, it will now have them to a substance with the nature PQS. And this will mean that a derivative quality in B has changed, and therefore that B's nature has changed.[22]

McTaggart adds that "nothing does change." However, let us see what the above involves if held by the advocates of internal relations; that is, if relations are held to be internal in the seventh sense as well as in the sixth sense.

---

21 *Examination of McTaggart's Philosophy*, vol. I, pp. 93-94.
22 *The Nature of Existence*, vol. I, p. 87.

(a) If it is granted that relations generate relational characteristics, then a change in any one thing with respect to any characteristic it possesses would result in a change in at least one relation between it and something else: namely, the relation determined (in part) by the changing characteristic. The change in this relation would then result in a change in the relational characteristics which the other terms of the relation have by virtue of the relation. This change in the relational characteristics would in turn result in a change in a relation between the terms which possessed these relational characteristics, and something else to which they are related; and so on, ultimately resulting in change in everything else with respect to their relational characteristics. But as we have said before, this is of little significance for the doctrine of internal relations.

(b) However, since we have rejected relational characteristics, the nature of a thing cannot include such alleged characteristics; and further, a change in the *bona fide* characteristics of a thing, though it does result in a change in the relation between it and other things, would not affect the nature of everything else. If such a change were to affect the nature of everything else, a single change in any one of a thing's characteristics, say its color, would not only change everything else in existence with respect to one characteristic (which is sufficiently absurd in itself, since in this case the changes would not be causally produced) but would result in a series of changes which would ultimately change all the characteristics of everything in existence! Nay, since these changes will never come to an end, a single change in the universe would change everything in existence in every respect, and such changes in turn would produce other changes, and these again other changes, and so on *ad infinitum* to the end of time! Such a state of affairs would not be absurd, of course, if all things are causally related, and if these endless changes are all causal changes. But this is not the case here. Only the first change is (and has to be) causal; all the other infinite changes, though changes in the non-logical characteristics of things, such as size, volume, color, hardness, velocity, position in space, would be produced non-causally merely by a change in one single relation between two terms!

But even if we confine these infinite changes to relational

characteristics, as McTaggart does, the situation would still be hard to accept. If A changes, B will change in relational characteristics. But that would change its relation to A, and so A itself will change again, resulting in a change in B; which once more results in a change in A, which in turn results in a change in B, and so on *ad infinitum*. The same occurs with everything else in existence. No sooner is a relational characteristic generated in B by a change in A than it is replaced by another relational characteristic, which is in turn replaced by another relational characteristic, and so on; and no sooner is a specific relation (of difference, say) generated than it is destroyed by being replaced by some other specific relation (of difference), and so on. The upshot of this would be that actually no relational characteristic survives and succeeds in characterizing A or B or anything else. Moreover, since these changes are instantaneous, being logical, an infinite number of them will occur instantaneously. And if relational characteristics are supposed to form part of a thing's nature, as the Idealists hold, the nature of everything in the universe, so far as their relational characteristics go, will be in a perpetual flux beside which the flux of the most extreme Heracliteans is the height of permanence!

(7) Blanshard argues[23] that relations are determined by their terms in the same way as terms are determined by their relations: if a term were different, its relations would be different, or, relations can be what they are only if their terms are what they are. Relations are determined in this sense by the generic and the specific character of the characteristics possessed in common by their terms. For example, the north-west relation between two towns, say, is determined not merely by their occupying space, but also by their determinate spatial positions. In other words, terms determine their relations by virtue of their characteristics *qua* determinables and also *qua* determinates. To quote Blanshard:

The White House at Washington is a mile or so north-west of the Capitol. You could not infer that particular relation simply from the fact that the

---

23 N. T., vol. II, p. 482 ff.

two buildings were spatial. Could you derive it from anything else in the nature of either or both? Yes, I think you could. The argument is indirect, but it is perhaps none the worse for that, since it involves showing *both* that the terms depend on their relations and the relations on the terms.... If you can show first that *unless* the terms were thus related, they could *not* be what they are, you can then argue that their being what they are requires their being so related.[24]

With respect to Blanshard's assertion that relations, as kinds of relations, are (wholly) determined by the kinds of characteristics their terms have, there is no difficulty. Its truth is easily seen. As he points out, there cannot be a spatial relation between two things if they are not spatial themselves. The more important question is whether or not the specific character of the relation is *wholly* determined by the specific character of the terms. To this we must give a negative answer. If two objects A and B are related by a left-right relation, this relation is determined by A's and B's characteristics only in so far as they are spatial characteristics. But the *specific* characteristics of A and B, both those which are not themselves spatial, e. g., their respective masses, odor, taste (if they have the latter two), their dispositional properties, and those which are themselves spatial, e. g., their color, volume, shape, do not and cannot wholly determine that A shall be to the left of B or that B shall be to the right of A. But if these objects are manipulated by sentient beings, especially human beings, for a given end, A's and B's spatial as also their non-spatial characteristics may determine in part the left-right relation. But in no case do the specific characteristics of A and B constitute a sufficient condition for the existence of the relation as a specific relation: a causal agency is necessary, and (depending on the particular instance) the presence of certain conditions, other than the character of A and B, which are indispensable for the occurrence of the relevant causal activity itself. To take a simple example, the two books lying on the table before me as I write are related by a left-right relation relatively to me. The book to the left has an olive green color, and is about the size of the book to the right which is reddish brown. But it is not the color of these books, their size, thickness, newness or oldness which made me put them

---

24 *Ibid.*, p. 483. Italics in original.

on the table before me in this particular case, but only the fact that both are books written by Idealists, whose ideas I wanted to discuss. But nothing in these books determined me in putting them on the table in the particular left-right position. They merely happened to be causally determined in this way by the movements of my hands when I placed them on the table. The ideas in these books would have served their purpose so far as I am concerned if I had put them in some other spatial relation relatively to me.

It cannot be maintained, in order to save the Idealist's view, that the causal agency, and the conditions requisite for the causal activity concerned, are terms in the above relation. The left-right relation is plainly a relation between A and B alone. There is of course a causal relation between A and B severally, and the causal agent. But this relation itself is not spatial, though the spatial character of both A and B, and of the causal agent, is a necessary condition for the occurrence of the causal activity; further, the causal relation is not the left-right spatial relation between A and B.

Still, we have seen that in the case of the relation of similarity, the relation of difference and mathematical relations, the terms do determine their relation completely.

Blanshard states that "If you can show first that *unless* the terms were thus related, they could *not* be what they are, you can then argue that their being what they are requires their being so related." This Blanshard considers to be the way to prove that relations depend on their terms; he assumes that (i) "their (*the terms*') being what they are requires their (*the terms*') being so related," amounts to (ii) "*relations* are determined by their terms" or to (iii) "the relations' being what they are requires their terms to be what they are." But obviously, (i) is not equivalent to (iii), and therefore not equivalent to (ii). As a matter of fact, it is merely a restatement of the premise: (iv) "Unless the terms were thus related, they could *not* be what they are"; i. e., that the *terms* are determined by their *relations*; and to prove this is not to prove (ii), which is its converse (ii. being the proposition which Blanshard thinks can be derived from iv). On the other hand, if we interpret "Their being what they are requires their being so related" as (v) "The relations' being what they are requires the terms' being so related," we merely get the tautology: "The relations' being what they are requires the relations to be what they are."

Since what Blanshard does in the succeeding pages is to (try to) prove that terms are determined by their relations, and since from this the desired conclusion does not follow, Blanshard does not succeed in proving his point.

That the desired conclusion does not follow from Blanshard's premise is seen more clearly as follows:

(a) If the relation r were absent, A or B or both would be different; but A and B are not different; therefore r is not absent (i. e., it is what it is).

This is valid, and it is the argument Blanshard uses. But the conclusion is not what he wants to prove. This conclusion does not show that r is what it is as a *consequence* of the terms' (A and B) being what they are. On the other hand, if we argue:

(b) If the relation r were absent, A and B would be different; therefore r's presence (its being what it is) requires A and B to be present (i. e., to be what they are), we will be arguing fallaciously, since from $\bar{r} \supset - (A \& B)$, $r \supset (A \& B)$ does not follow.

But these points aside, we have already attempted to show that terms do determine their relations (partly or wholly, depending on the nature of the relation) in Ewing's sixth sense, but that only some relations determine their terms (leaving aside "relational characteristics") in Ewing's seventh sense.

We must now consider a further point. If terms determine their relations, *can* relations at the same time determine their terms in the same sense (which is what Blanshard appears to hold) and vice versa? Or, to put it in other words, will we not have a vicious circle if terms determined their relations and relations determined their terms?[25] That a vicious circle would be involved is what Bradley believes, and this belief is one of the reasons why he considers both relations and terms (qualities or complexes of qualities) as ultimately unreal or merely Appearance. As he puts

---

25 If A is determined by B, A depends (or is dependent) on B; i. e., one or more of A's characteristics are generated (logically or causally) by B, and, or one or more of the characteristics it possessed prior to being related to B are modified as a consequence of B's presence.

it: "Relation presupposes quality, and quality relation. Each can be something, neither with nor apart from the other; and the vicious circle in which they turn is not the truth about reality."[26] Or, each term "... has a double character, as both supporting and as being made by the relation."[27] The two aspects of one and the same term: the term as supporting and the term as supported by the relation are therefore related; which repeats the same dichotomy. And so on *ad infinitum*. To be what it is, a quality must be differentiated from others; it must be related to others by the relation of difference. Hence quality presupposes and depends on relation. But Relations too cannot exist without, and do presuppose, qualities. "Nothings cannot be related." Hence the mutual dependence, which Bradley pronounces to be vicious.

Now it is certainly true that as soon as a quality comes into existence, or by the sheer fact that a quality is what it is, it is at least numerically distinct or different from all other qualities and other types of existence. Therefore, it would be related to other things. So qualities, *qua* numerically distinct entities, require relations.[28] Similarly, relations *qua* relations require qualities—or

---

[26] Quoted from Stout, *Studies In Philosaphy And Psychology*, p. 187.

[27] A. R., p. 31.

[28] Stout (*Studies In Philosophy And Psychology*) thinks that the crucial point in Bradley's statement that "qualities are nothing without relations" "... does not lie in the bare fact abstractly considered that qualities are qualities." He thinks that "It lies rather in the fact that the qualities are partial features within a whole—within the unity of the universe. As such each partial feature must be connected with other partial features entering into the constitution of the whole. Ignore the unity of the universe as including all difference and distinction and there is no argument left. Since, however, all distinction is distinction within the universe, whatever we distinguish must be connected." (p. 188) But we have already tried to show that the unity which Stout is thinking of must be rejected. For we have attempted to show that Stout's contention "that all relations ultimately presuppose a continuity" is not valid. All continuous connection gives rise to relation, and cannot be continuous connection without relation. Continuity does not involve relation; but it does not involve immediate connection either. And if we want to pass from relational complexes to a non-relational continuum through continuous connection, the attempt is doomed to failure. Further, there does not seem to me to be any way by which we can pass from a relational complex to a non-relational continuum. There cannot be such a thing as *continuous* connection. All connection implies discrete things which are connected, and what is connected can be considered continuous only if the notion of connection does not arise.

in general, terms—which are to be related. But a particular quality, *qua* possessing a specific character, does not require just any and every relation. That is, it is capable of existing apart from certain kinds of relations. A particular patch of red, as an existent thing, will be related by a relation of difference to all other things *qua* numerically distinct. It will also be related by a relation of difference to all other qualities which are not colors, and to all colors which are not red. Also, it will be related by a relation of similarity to all other patches of red. But as a patch of *red*, it does not and cannot require the relation of "father of" or "heavier than" to other things. It requires only some relations. Further, the relations in which it is related do not make it what it is: a red patch, or an existent thing. It is because it is an existent thing having a specific character (redness) that it would be related to other things, *if other things exist*. Similarly, although a relation, to be a relation at all, requires qualities to relate, it does not require, as a relation of a specific kind (for any actual relation will be of a specific kind) any and every kind of quality, Depending on its nature, it requires only qualities of certain kinds. Thus the relation of similarity, say, in order to exist, requires at least two qualities which are the same in character. A relation of difference, on the other hand, requires at least two qualities which are different in character. So the relation of similarity or of difference requires the existence of certain specific qualities, not just any and every quality. Hence, although abstractly speaking qualities presuppose relations and relations presuppose qualities, concrete qualities need specific kinds of relations to relate them; and concrete relations need specific kinds of qualities to make them possible. So no vicious circle is involved.[29]

The fact that no vicious circle is involved in the type of situation envisioned by Bradley's argument does not preclude the possibility that the dependence of terms on relations and vice

---

29 Since the alleged vicious circle involved in the mutual dependence of terms and relations is only apparent, we have in this further ground for rejecting the underlying-reality theory. For one of Bradley's arguments in support of this theory is that qualities and relations are ultimately self-contradictory, because they cannot but depend on each other and yet cannot so depend, on pain of a logical vicious circle.

versa, in our sence seven, may involve a vicious circle. For it was not the same kind of dependence that we encounter in Bradley's argument.

Clearly, a vicious circle would be involved if a specific quality entirely depends for its existence and character on a specific relation between it and something else, and if the relation depends either entirely or partly on that quality for its own existence and character; or if the quality depends partly on its relation, while the relation depends entirely on the quality; or thirdly, if both the quality and the relation depend partly on each other. The result is that a quality and a relation cannot be mutually dependent; since dependence will have to be either partial or complete, and in each case a vicious circle would arise.

In order to avoid a vicious circle, therefore, if a relation r is construed as dependent, partly or wholly, on a quality a, a must be construed as dependent, partly or wholly, *on some other relation*, s, which does not itself depend either partly or wholly on a, nor (if such a dependence is possible) on r, whether partly or wholly. And if a is construed as partly dependent on s, it must not be even partly dependent, either on another *quality c* which is itself dependent, partly or wholly, on r, or on a *relation t*, which is partly or wholly dependent on r.

Taking complexes of qualities or things as our terms, a term A cannot be dependent, partly or wholly, on a relation r with respect to a quality a or a set of qualities axy in it, if at the same time r is dependent (partly or wholly) on A with respect to quality a, or set of qualities axy. But a term A can depend on a relation r with respect to quality a or a set of qualities axy, and r can depend on A with respect to quality b, or set of qualities bnm, assuming that b or bnm are not themselves dependent on a or axy.

Now if qualities a, axy, b, bnm are considered part of A's nature, so that A would not be itself if any one of these qualities were absent or different, then on the above analysis A would not be A if r were absent or different, and r would not be r if A were absent or different. For if (i) r were absent or different, and if it completely depended on b or on bnm, r could not be absent or different unless b or bnm were absent or different. And if b or bnm were absent or different, A would be different. Also, if A were absent as a whole, r would be absent. Similarly, r would be absent or different if A were different with respect to a or axy, whether r is completely or only partly dependent on a or axy.

(ii) However, if (a) r depends only partly on b or on bnm, then although r could not exist or be the same if A were different with respect to b or to bnm, A could exist and be A if r did not exist. For if r were absent, or were different, b or bnm could still be the same; therefore A could still be the same if and when the *other* quality or qualities on which r also partly depends are absent; when these qualities are qualities of another term B, to which A, say, is related by relation r. In this case the dependence would not be reciprocal.

(iii) (b) Also, if A were different with respect not to b or to bnm but some other qualities, r could still be present whether A itself could or could not exist if r were absent; and the dependence would not be reciprocal.

But since in (i) there is reciprocal dependence between A and r and yet no vicious circle is involved, it is logically possible to have a term dependent on a relation in Ewing's sense seven (assuming throughout that a term *can* be dependent on its relations to begin with); and the relation could at the same time be dependent on the term in the same sense, with the qualifications we have mentioned in (1), one of which is that we have to understand by "term" not a single quality but a complex of qualities; i. e., a thing in the ordinary sense of the term (although it need not be an object).

The upshot of this is that the charge of circularity cannot be urged, in this type of case, against the Idealist's view that relations "make a difference" to their terms and that terms in the same sense determine (or "make a difference" to) their relations.

(8) In argument (6) we saw that Blanshard contends that concrete things are what they are by virtue of their relations; i. e., that things are related internally in Ewing's seventh sense. In this argument, that contention is extended to qualities or attributes or "abstract characters" as Blanshard calls them. Blanshard's contention, taking things and qualities together, is that "... *terms as such or generally*, and not merely concrete existing things, are

what they are in virtue of their relations."[30] Here, as in the case of concrete things, Blanshard argues that the nature of attributes is constituted by their total context; that is, by all the relations which they have to everything else. Some of these relations are more or less essential than others; but no relation is completely non-essential or accidental. This rests on Blanshard's view that the distinction between essence, property, and accident, using these terms in their traditional technical sense, is not a matter of kind but only of degree. From these things it seems to follow that a given attribute cannot be what it is if any one of its relations were absent or different. Also—something which Blanshard brings out in his argument—it follows that no attribute (and for that matter no concrete thing or any other kind of existent) can be fully and completely known unless and until its relations to everything else in the universe are known.

A possible way of attacking this argument would be to criticize Blanshard's view that the nature of an attribute is constituted by all its relations; and this can be done by criticizing the doctrine that the distinction between essence, property and accident is a distinction in kind and not of degree. But we shall not take this line of argument here. Let us only note in this connection, as Ewing points out, that strictly speaking relations cannot form part of either a thing's or an attribute's nature; it is rather the relational characteristics which are generated in the thing or attribute by these relations that can form a part of the nature of these things (assuming that such things exist and that all the characteristics of a thing or an attribute are essential to it in some degree or other). A relation is *between* a thing and another thing, and to treat it as part of either term is to make it a quality; which is incorrect. Thus the view we are discussing must be corrected to hold that an attribute is what it is by virtue of its relations in the sense that these relations are necessary for the production in it of relational characteristics; and that these characteristics are a part of its nature.

(I) It is plain that if the relational characteristics of an attribute are considered to be part of its nature, the attribute cannot

---

30 N. T., vol. II, p. 488. Italics in original.

be what it is, as possessing these characteristics, without these same characteristics. But would it lose its qualitative nature, as an attribute, if its relations and therefore the relational characteristics generated by them were absent? Would a patch of red, say, cease to be red if the patch were to the left of a patch of green instead of to its right as it actually is at this moment? Would it be different in color if another patch of red, to which it was related by a relation of similarity, were not red but green? Surely, these *relations* (that is, spatio-temporal relations, relations of similarity, mathematical relations, such as the red patch's being twice the size of another red patch, etc.) presuppose and depend on the existence of the red patch as a red patch of a certain size, shape, intensity and hue; if you take its character as red alone, without reference to its being a patch of red of certain dimensions, intensity and hue. And we have already seen (in relation to argument seven) that relations cannot both depend on and at the same time determine a quality.

(II) Of course the red patch depends for its existence and character on certain causes. Red-headedness, which Blanshard takes as an example, surely depends causally on the nature of the organism in which it is found; and the organism in turn causally depends on other things. This, as a matter of fact, is what Blanshard bases his argument upon in attempting to show that red-headedness, for example, is determined by its relations; as the following passage will show—

Red-headedness is an integral part of an organism, and indeed is so bound up, for example, with the structure of hair-fibres, and this in turn with all manner of constitutional factors determining racial and individual differences that our common notion of it supplies scarcely more than a sign-post to its real or ultimate nature.... As we grasp these further relations, our explicit thought of the attribute is modified while our reference remains the same; we see that we are advancing toward the character as it really is.[31]

Although this is true, it does not show that red-headedness is causally determined by its relations themselves, but rather that it is determined by the causal activity of other parts of the organism.

---

31 *Ibid.*, vol, II, p. 490.

We have already dealt with this point at some length in argument (5), and need not linger on it here.

(III) It is essential to note that we have been speaking about qualities as particular existents, as this or that particular (patch of) red, or the particular red headedness of this or that particular person. We were not talking about redness or red headedness as such, as universals. Blanshard and the other Idealists, on the other hand, regard so-called particular qualities or attributes as (concrete) universals, and deny the existence of abstract universals—such as redness, red headedness, triangularity—as subsistent, unchanging entities sometimes exemplified in particular red objects, red headed persons, and the like. When Blanshard speaks of red headedness, say, as being an integral part of an organism, he is not thinking of the abstract universal red headedness, nor of a so-called particular red headedness as merely particular, but of a universal which cannot exist apart from and outside particular red headednesses and is partially realized in them. With this in mind, we can see that unless we first refute the doctrine of the concrete universal, we cannot argue, as Moore and Ewing for instance do, that the doctrine of internal relations "... cannot be applied to relations between abstract universals, e. g. the relation of equality between the pure number 4 and 2 + 2, because we cannot speak of the possibility of an abstract universal being different from what it is, but only to relations between concrete terms."[32]

That the doctrine of the concrete universal is untenable we are convinced. But we shall not attempt to prove it in the present work; fortunately the view is dispensable for a criticism of the doctrine of internal relations or the coherence theory of truth. Still, supposing abstract universals to be real and unchangeable, they can still be internally related[33] to each other; but because

---

32 I. C. S., pp. 130–131. Ewing attributes the view to Moore in *Philosophical Studies*, p. 283 ff. See also N. T., vol. II, pp. 490–491.

33 An abstract universal is not something which by its nature or by definition cannot be related, as Blanshard suggests. It would be so only if an abstract universal is, as Blanshard says, "... an *abstracted* universal, i. e., a universal considered by itself and apart from its context in nature...." (*Ibid.*, p. 491. Italics in original) As conceived by those who posit abstract universals, an abstract universal does not acquire *existence* by abstraction from things: we only conceive it by a process of (conceptual) abstraction from its particular exemplifications.

they are unchangeable, these relations would also be unchangeable. This would be the meaning of saying that they could not be what they are if their relations were different or absent. If a present relation r between universals U_1 and U_2 were absent, U_1 (or U_2) would not be U_1 (or U_2); but U_1 *is* U_1 and necessarily so (and similarly with U_2); so r is not absent, and necessarily so. Or, to express this in another way, if r were absent, U_1 (or U_2) would necessarily have been different; but U_1 (or U_2) cannot be absent or different. Therefore r cannot be absent or different.

The doctrine of internal relations does not entail that everything in the universe and the universe as a whole must necessarily be what it is and could not be different. It merely entails that if relations are thus and so, terms must be thus and so. But relations could be different, or more precisely, some other relations could have existed instead; other terms could therefore have existed instead of those which actually exist or are supposed to exist.[34]

(10) Arguing that relations cannot be external, Bradley says that "the leaving by the terms of one set of relations and their adoption of another fresh set"[35] would be incomprehensible if relations are external and if the result makes no difference to their terms. For if a change of relation makes no difference to its terms, to what can it make a difference?[36] That a term cannot meaningfully "have" a set of relations and "adopt" another if a term is completely and in every sense independent of its relations, is true enough (by the very meaning of the words 'leave' and 'adopt'). For in that case the first set of relations will not be *its* relations, nor can *it* acquire new relations. But does the doctrine of external

---

34 This is not true without qualification. It would *not* be true if the ultimate causes of these relations themselves cannot but produce certain particular relations (and terms, since relations are themselves dependent on terms according to the doctrine of internal relations) and no others; i. e., if these causes themselves are determined to act causally in a certain way. Otherwise, what we said in the body of the text above would be true. In the case of abstract universals, if we suppose that they are necessary, then from our analysis it follows that their causes (if they have any) were determined to bring them about and not some other universal or universals.

35 Quoted from L. J. Walker, *Theories of Knowledge*, London, 1924, Second Edition, p. 276.

36 Ibid., pp. 276-277.

relations hold, or need to hold, that terms are completely and in every sense independent of their relations? The majority if not all[37] of the exponents of the theory of external relations maintain that relations are internal in the first sense of 'internal relations,' that is, that relations generate relational characteristics in their terms. This entitles these thinkers to speak of relations as the relations *of* this or that term, and therefore to speak meaningfully of a term as "leaving" a set of relations and "adopting" another set. But from this it only follows that terms would be different with respect to their relational characteristics if their relations change. And if relational characteristics are considered to be a part of a term's nature then a change in a relation does change a term's nature. This is far from establishing that relations "make a difference" to their terms in sense seven of 'internal relation': which is what Bradley seems to have in mind, and which is one of the crucial tenets of the doctrine of internal relations as held by the Idealists.

But, it seems to me, it is not even necessary to grant that relations are internal in sense one, to be entitled to speak meaningfully of a term as "leaving" a set of relations and "adopting" another set. It is perfectly possible to deny the existence of relational characteristics, as the present writer does; and still speak in this fashion. For it is an undeniable fact that things are related; and whether their relations are external or internal, a specific relation obtains between a particular thing and another or other particular things. The objects before me are all related spatially; and the relation between any one of them and another is determined, in the sense of being specified, by its being between these two particular things and not between one of them and something else; or between two others. The inkpot on my table is about six inches to the left of the copper ashtray. The left-right relation is not just any left-right relation but the relation of a specific inkpot on my table to a specific copper ashtray which is six inches to its right. It is not by virtue of the relational characteristics it (allegedly) generates that it becomes or can become a relation *of* its terms; rather, it is by virtue of its being a relation of its terms in the first place

---

[37] C. D. Broad excepted.

that it (allegedly) generates relational characteristics in them. Thus it does not seem to be true that, as Ewing for instance maintains, if we deny that terms have the characteristics of standing in a given relation, we cut relations adrift from their terms.[38]

(11) Bradley further argues that comparison cannot reveal the truth about things if relations are merely external.[39] Here again Bradley is thinking of external relations as completely and in every sense independent of their terms, conceiving of them as third terms or discrete things. If relations are not thought of in this way, for example, if we consider that relations are determined both generically and (partly) specifically by their terms, the supposed difficulty vanishes. It is by virtue of the fact that terms have the characteristics they have that they can be compared; and comparison tells us something about them precisely because it is based on their characteristics. This applies whether the comparison is qualitative, quantitative, causal or otherwise. We need not add, the dependence of relations on their terms does not entail the dependence of terms on their relations, in the sense and way in which the advocates of the doctrine of internal relations understand this; hence the internality of relations in this sense is not proved.

(12) We now come to one of the most important, if not the most important argument, for the doctrine of internal relations; namely, the argument from the nature of causality. Apart from whether or not other relations are internal in the crucial senses of this term, the causal relation *seems* to afford a clear example of an internal relation. Moreover, since the causal relation seems to relate everything to everything else in the universe, the entire universe, if this view is true, is a grand system of internally-related parts. The thesis of the advocate of the doctrine of internal relations here, as Blanshard puts it, is twofold: (1) that all things are causally related, directly or indirectly, and (2) that the causal relation involves an element of logical necessity, and therefore, "... being causally related involves being *logically* related."[40] The second proposition may by otherwise expressed by saying that according to this view causality involves an intrinsic

---

38 I. C. S., p. 143, footnote 2.
39 L. J. Walker, *Theories of Knowledge*, p. 278.
40 N. T., vol. II, p. 492. Italics in original.

and necessary connection between cause and effect, such that if a given state of affairs A is present, another state of affairs B necessarly follows; and if a state of affairs B is present, another state of affairs A must have preceded it, and must have produced B. The causal connection does not consist in mere invariable sequence of states of affairs of a certain kind, as the regularity theory of causality holds. It is not merely that as a matter of fact certain events have been observed to, or do actually, precede certain other events (or even that this is universally the case), so that whenever certain events are present other events of a certain nature as a matter of fact follow them. The causal connection cannot be reduced to mere factual universal sequence or succession. The cause logically entails the effect, and the effect logically presupposes the cause. To quote Ewing, cause and effect are "... so related that one is logically dependent for its existence on the other, and... it would be logically impossible for the one to be what it is without the other existing also."[41]

On the basis of this view, Ewing holds that the causal relation is internal:

(a) in the sixth sense, i.e. it follows from the nature of its terms, in some sense of 'follow' other than that of regular sequence;

(b) in the seventh sense, i. e. it could not have been absent (in some sense of 'could not' distinct from 'never is') without at least one of its terms being different;

(c) in the ninth sense, i. e. neither could the cause have existed without the effect following nor the effect have existed without being preceded by the cause.[42]

Ewing also holds that this relation is internal (d) in the eighth sense, i. e., "... cause and effect are so related that determinate characteristics of the one could be deduced *a priori* from the other"[43]; and finally (e) in the tenth sense—

That the nature of one term is *logically* dependent on that of the other, i. e. the events which constitute the cause could not exist and be what they are if it did not produce the effect, and the effect could not exist and be what it is if it had not been produced by the cause.[44]

---

41 I. C. S., p. 171, foonote 1.
42 *Ibid.*, p. 183.
43 *Ibid.*, p. 183, footnote 2.
44 *Ibid.*, p. 183, footnote 1. Italics in original.

Since the view that the causal connection is internal involves two main propositions, criticism of the view may be attempted by attacking either of these propositions or both. It is seen that if the first proposition alone is attacked while accepting the second, the internality of causation will be admitted; but it will be denied that the universe is *a* system in which *everything* is internally related to everything else (though the universe might still be held to consist of limited internally-related systems which are externally related to one another). On the other hand, if the second proposition alone is attacked, the notion of an all-inclusive causal system is again rejected; though the all-pervasiveness of the causal connection (as an external relation) is accepted. The third alternative, of course, combines the rejections of both criticisms taken separately. But it is obvious that the second type of attack is more drastic and fundamental than the first and, indeed, it is the type of attack which the critics of the doctrine of internal relations would be expected to make. It is also not surprising that Bradley, Bosanquet, Blanshard and Ewing are most anxious to rebuff this attack. Thus Blanshard and Ewing, for instance, take great pains to try to disprove the regularity theory of causality; and also, as part of their defence, to show that the indeterminist's abolition of the notion of cause altogether is mistaken.

In criticizing the doctrine that causality is an internal relation, we shall not, however, attempt to disprove the necessary-connection theory of causation. An adequate discussion of the question whether causality involves necessary connection or only invariable sequence; or whether it involves a third thing (if a third alternative is possible), requires an amount of analysis which is beyond the scope and aims of the present work, and would carry us too far afield. What we shall rather attempt to do is something quite different: namely, to point out that even if we grant that causality involves intrinsic, necessary connection, it is *not* an internal relation in Ewing's important seventh sense of the term; so that the universe is not a system of internally related parts. This has the methodological advantage (over the criticism levelled from the standpoint of the regular-sequence theory) of assuming the premises of the opposite camp; and therefore, if successful, is more potent and compelling than a purely external criticism which the defenders of the doctrine of internal relations will not at all countenance or concede.

In order to be able to answer the question whether the causal relation is internal in the sixth, seventh, eighth, ninth or tenth senses, we must first decide what the terms of a causal relation are; whether they are things (or continuants) or events, or in different ways both things and events. Actually, the word 'cause' is ordinarily sometimes used to refer to things and sometimes to events. We speak of a car and also of its collision with a person as being the cause of the person's death. But we normally speak of events and hardly ever, if at all, of things as effects of things or of events: the victim's death and not the victim is said to be the effect of the collision (but not the effect of the *car*).[45] In order to avoid confusion, we shall here use the words 'cause' and 'effect' to refer only to events, and not also to things. But since the event called the "cause" is an event or change in a thing or things, and similarly the event we call the effect is an event or change in another thing or other things, we can (and we do ordinarily) speak of an indirect causal relation between these things; which we shall call the "agent" and the "patient" respectively, following C. J. Ducasse.

Further, since we have defined the cause as an event, we must distinguish between causes and conditions, the static circumstances which are necessary for the occurrence of the causal action, without which the causal action cannot take place.[46] These conditions include (i) the agent or agents in which the cause occurs, (ii) the patient or patients in which the effect occurs, as well as (iii) other things or states of affairs in the environment. But since we have given the names 'agent' and 'patient' to some of these conditions, we shall reserve the terms 'conditions' for the things and circumstances other than the agent and patient, which are relevant to a given causal activity in a given case.

---

45 This, plus the fact that the effect is ordinarily not thought of as a thing, seems to indicate that in ordinary usage things are taken as causally related only in a derivative and secondary sense; i. e., derivatively from the causal relation thought of as existing between given events.

46 See Arthur Pap, *Elements of Analytic Philosophy*, New York, 1949, pp. 212-213.

THE DOCTRINE OF INTERNAL RELATIONS (CONT'D.)

We must now distinguish between: (1) necessary and sufficient causes, (2) necessary but not sufficient causes, and (3) sufficient but not necessary causes.

(1) According to our analysis and terminology, a cause is necessary and sufficient for the occurrence of a given effect if (a) the effect follows from it alone, and (b) the effect would not occur if it did not occur.

The word 'alone' needs clarification. A cause which is necessary and sufficient for the occurrence of a given effect is sufficient, as an event, for the occurrence of the effect—*but only provided the requisite* environmental *conditions* (as well as the patient) *are present*.

(2) A cause which is necessary but not sufficient for the occurrence of a given effect is one without which the effect cannot occur, but which cannot produce the effect in the absence of other causes (events).

(3) A cause which is sufficient but not necessary for the occurrence of a given effect is one which (a) if present, would be followed by the effect; but (b), the effect may be present although it itself may be absent: provided, in both cases, that the requisite environmental conditions are present.

We now turn to our first question.

Those who speak of the internality of *the* causal relation do not make it clear what exactly they have in mind by it: whether they have in mind (a) the relation between the cause or causes (C) and effect or effects (E); or (b) the (triadic) relation between the environmental conditions (Co), the cause or causes, and the effect or effects; or (c) the relation between the characteristics of the agent (Cag) and those of the patient (Pag) at time T_1 which partly determine the nature of the cause and effect respectively; or (d) the agent (G) at time T_1 and the patient (P) at time T_1, which, by virtue of characteristics Cag and Pag, partly determine the effect; or (e) the relation between characteristics Cag_2 and Pag_2 at time T_2, which arise as a result of the causal activity; or, finally (f) the relation between the agent and the patient at time T_2, these being modified as a result of the causal activity.

Since the relation in (c) entails the relation in (d), and vice versa, we do not need to distinguish them for our purposes. Thus besides the relations in (a), (b) and (c) we can have two more relations (d_1) and (e_1): (d_1) will then be the relation between the characteristics or between the subjects of these characteristics, at time T_1; while (e_1) will be the relation between the characteristics or between the subjects of these characteristics, at time T_2.

Of all these relations the most important for our purposes are, I think, the relations in (a) and (e_1). However, if we have to speak of one relation as *the* causal relation, we shall limit it to the relation in (a). As for the important relation in (b), this relation as a whole is really not a *causal* relation; for though the effect is produced by the cause or causes together with the requisite conditions, the causal relation obtains directly only between the cause or causes and the effect; the conditions are involved (though very importantly), only in so far as they partly determine the effect. They do not enter into a direct relation with the effect, as the cause or causes do. Their logical status, in relation to the effect, is different from that of the cause or causes in relation to it.[47] But the conditions are already involved in (a), since the causal action of agent on patient, and so the relation between the "cause" and the "effect," cannot obtain without the requisite conditions being present.

(1) Now whether an event C or a set of events C, F, H (say) is or are sufficient and necessary, or necessary but not sufficient, or sufficient but not necessary, for the occurrence of a given effect, the relation in (a) is always partly determined by the nature of the terms (partly only because the conditions present also determine it). Since a relation is considered to be internal in sense six if the terms determine it, whether partly or wholly, the relation in (a), the "causal relation," is internal in that sense.

(2) Is the "causal relation" internal in the seventh sense of 'internal relations'? The answer seems to me to be in the negative. This is seen if we remember that the agent and the patient, or the characteristics of the agent and of the patient, or the causal event (cause), only partly determine the causal action of the agent on the patient: and consequently only partly determine the

---

[47] We cannot validly regard the so-called conditions as part of the causal event; or vice versa. A distinction has to be drawn between them.

establishment and the character of the causal relation between the causal event and the effect, or between the agent and the patient. The causal relation is also partly determined by the nature of the environmental conditions present; and these are not part of the agent or the patient, the causal event or the effect. The causal relation is a dyadic relation between the agent and the patient, or the causal event and the effect; it is not a triadic relation between the agent and the conditions on the one hand and the patient on the other hand. It is also not a triadic relation between the causal event and the conditions on the one hand, and the effect on the other hand. The conditions are indispensable for the occurrence of the causal action; but it is the action of the *agent* on the *patient*; and the conditions are not part of the agent (or the patient). To illustrate: in order that a quantity of sulphuric acid may act upon a quantity of copper, the acid should be hot and concentrated and the reagents should be under a given minimum pressure. Also the rate of reaction (which characterizes the causal relation, in any given case, as a specific relation between sulphuric acid and copper) depends at least in part on the temperature and pressure. Yet the causal action is the action of the acid on copper, and the resultant causal relation is a relation between the two alone and not between them and the given temperature, pressure and so on. This means that if the causal relation were absent or different, i. e., if the particular effect did not occur, this could very well be due to the absence of or a difference in the requisite range of temperature and pressure; or the requisite concentration of acid; not to the absence of acid or copper or both. In general, a difference in or the absence of the causal relation (if the effect is absent or different) does not necessarily imply a difference in or the absence of either the agent or the patient or both, the requisite characteristics in the agent or the agent, or the causal event. It may, rather, be due to a difference in or the absence of the requisite conditions. The situation is not materially affected by whether or not we assume the necessary-connection theory of causality. If we assume it, it merely follows that, *provided the requisite conditions are present*, a causal event cannot occur without being followed by a given effect; and a given effect cannot occur without having been preceded by a given causal event. Once more, the absence of a given causal activity and the corresponding causal relation does not necessarily imply the absence of, or a difference in, either the agent or the patient. For the causal relation to be internal in Ewing's seventh sense, the causal relation should, by its presence, *cause* a change in the agent or the patient or both. In that case its absence or a difference in it would logically imply a difference in at least one of its terms; since this causal change would then be absent. But it is impossible for the causal relation to cause a change in anything, as we had occasion to point out.

(3) Is the "causal relation" internal in the eighth sense?

In his account of causality as an internal relation Ewing defines the eighth sense of 'internal relations' as follows: "... cause and effect are so related that determinate characteristics of the one could be deduced *a priori* from the other."[48] Elsewhere he defines it as a relation which is "... such that from a knowledge of one term and the relation in which it stands to the other term we can infer with logical necessity that the other term possesses a certain determinate on relatively determinate characteristic other than the characteristic of standing in the relation in question."[49] Now if the necessary-connection theory of causality is assumed (as we are doing throughout the present discussion), the internality of the causal relation in (a), in sense eight, logically follows. If cause and effect are intrinsically and therefore necessarily connected, it would be *logically possible* to have certain knowledge of characteristics of one term from a knowledge of the other term and the determinate causal relation. Such certain knowledge, however, is not actually possible. Ewing says that the causal relation *would be* internal in sense eight "... for a being who possessed the requisite insight, if not for the human mind."[50] This seems to mean that if we have perfect knowledge of one term of a causal relation, and of the relation itself, we would be able to infer the characteristics of the other term with certainty. For the advocate of the view that reality is an internally-related system, such perfect initial knowledge,

---

48 *Ibid.*, p. 183, footnote 2.
49 *Ibid.*, p. 135, Italics in original.
50 *Ibid.*, p. 183.

at any given moment, of everything in the universe: which itself presupposes some knowledge of the entire past history of the universe up to that moment.

(4) Is the "causal relation" internal in the ninth sense, i. e., that "neither could the cause have existed without the effect following it nor the effect have existed without being preceded by the cause"?

That a given effect could not have existed without being preceded by a given causal event or "cause," follows from the view that the "causal relation" is necessary. (The presence of the effect also implies the presence of the requisite environmental conditions.) So, assuming the necessary-connection theory of causality, the "effect-cause" relation is internal in the present sense. But the converse relation—the "cause-effect" relation—is external in the present sense. For an effect (let alone one and the same effect) would follow a causal event or "cause" only provided the requisite conditions are present. Hence a given "cause" or causal event could exist without being followed by the, or even an, "effect" (except that in that case, it would not be a *causal* event, it would not be called a "cause").

(5) The same is true as regards sense ten of 'internal relation,' since the only difference between the ninth and tenth senses of this term is that the former merely asserts that the cause and effect are mutually dependent; while the latter asserts that this dependence is a logical dependence.

We now turn to the second major assertion of the advocates of the doctrine that the causal relation is an internal relation; namely, the proposition that everything in the universe is causally related, directly or indirectly, to everything else; that the universe is one vast causally-related system.

We shall begin by a brief definition of an indirect causal relation.

A and B are causally related indirectly if (a) A is the indirect or remote cause of B (symbolized by A→ X→ ...→ B); or (b) A is the indirect or remote effect of B (B→ X→ ...→ A); or (c) A and B are together (i) the proximate, or (ii) the remote, cause of C (i. (A & B)→ C; ii. (A & B)→ X→ ...→ C); or (d) A and B are together (i) the proximate, or (ii) the remote,

effect of C (i. C⟶ (A & B); ii. X⟶ ...⟶ (A & B), or
C⟶ { X⟶ ...⟶ A
      X⟶ ...⟶ B).

So much for the definition. Now since objects which are directly related causally form causal chains or lines running from the past toward the future,[51] there are four major ways in which such causal lines may be related:

(1) All the causal lines in the universe may have a common origin in one ultimate cause but may not be related otherwise; i. e., these lines may not intersect or cross one another: an object in one causal line may not act causally upon an object in another causal line; or

(2) All the causal lines may have a common origin and in addition may intersect at some moment or other in time and some point or other in space; or

(3) Some (at least two, and perhaps all) causal lines may have no common origin, but all lines may intersect at some moment or other in time and some point or other in space; or finally,

(4) Some (at least two, and perhaps all) causal lines may have no common origin, and may not be related otherwise; i. e., they may not intersect—at least those which have no common origin.

In cases (1), (2), and (3), *all* points (objects) on all lines will be causally related to all others, directly or indirectly; in case (4) *some* but not *all* points (objects) will be causally related to some other points, directly or indirectly. Since the view under consideration asserts that all things in the universe are related to all others, directly or indirectly, it falls under (1), (2) or (3), while case (4) plainly contradicts it. Hence our problem is to find out (if it is at all possible) which of these cases corresponds, or has the greatest probability of corresponding, to reality.

There is one qualification we have to be aware of at the outset. In trying to answer the question in hand we shall limit ourselves to the physical world. Our knowledge of mental processes,

---

51 See B. Russell, "Postulates Of Scientific Inference," *Procedings Of The Tenth International Congress Of Philosophy*, 1948, vol. I, part I, pp. 33-41, for some grounds on which the existence of separable causal lines are postulated.

and especially of their causal connections (if any) with physical events is at present so meager that we cannot profitably include them in our discussion. If we find that the most plausible picture we can form of the physical universe is that all things in it are causally related, directly or indirectly, that is wealth enough; it will then be more probable that all things, whether physical or mental, are causally related to all other things in reality, than that some things are not. For then, if we can find even a few causal connections between mental and physical phenomena, that will be enough to give us the presumption that other mental phenomena are indirectly, if not directly, related to the entire physical universe.

There is, fortunately, one empirical hypothesis that simplifies our problem to some extent; and that is that all physical bodies in the universe attract one another gravitationally. This, I think, is one of the best-established of scientific theories, and we can safely take it as true. At any rate, we can do no better. This means, I think, that irrespective of whether or not we regard all causal lines as radiating from a common causal origin, all the causal lines in the universe intersect at least so far as the gravitational pull is concerned. This enables us to disregard or eliminate alternatives (1) and (4) on our list, and leaves us with (2) and (3).

William James, in *Pragmatism*, in the course of speaking about the problem whether relations are external or internal, puts the issue between what are alternatives (2) and (3) on our list—at least with regard to the question of the convergence or non-convergence of causal lines toward a common origin in the past—in the following words:

All these systems of influence or non—influence may be listed under the general problem of the world's *causal unity*. If the minor causal influences among things should converge towards one common causal origin of them in the past, one great first cause for all that is, one might then speak of the absolute causal unity of the world. God's *fiat* on creation's day has figured in traditional philosophy as such an absolute cause and origin. Transcendental Idealism, translating 'creation' into 'thinking' (or 'willing to think') calls the divine act 'eternal' rather than 'first'; but the union of the many here is absolute, just the same—the many would not *be*, save for the One. Against this notion of the unity of origin of all things there has always stood the pluralistic notion of an eternal self-existing many in the shape of atoms or even of spiritual units of some sort.[52]

---

52 New York, 1928, New Impression, pp. 138-139. Italics in original.

This at first sight seems to render it impossible to settle the issue in hand without lengthy speculation concerning the existence or non-existence of God. But actually, even if we do believe in God's existence, the convergence of all causal lines towards a common origin does not necessarily follow from it as James seems to think. Even if the universe was created by a single act of will or thought, it is still conceivable that what was thus created was not a single body or state of affairs from which all the plurality of things we find in the universe arose or radiated. It is perfectly possible that a number of bodies—nebulae, galaxies, or what not, composed of an infinitely large number of atoms or molecules, came into existence simultaneously through divine *fiat*, and therefore that the causal lines which they initiated were discrete from the very start. Also, and to my mind the more important point is that, if we are to try to settle this issue, however tentatively, on the basis of knowledge and not of sheer speculation, we have to take as data what science has to tell us about this problem. But as might be expected, the current scientific cosmogonies are highly speculative; and none has any overwhelming evidence either in its favor or against it to make it possible to pick out any one of them as probably more true than the rest.[53] Astronomers are far from agreed upon any one account.[54] So our question must remain open so far as present knowledge is concerned. However, even if solar systems, galaxies, and nebulae ultimately originated from a single source, this does not mean that the process was started by a single causal event. For instance, if the first nebulae resulted from, say, a gigantic explosion (as some older theories held), the exploding gaseous mass could have been, and probably was, a vast mass composed of an astronomical number of atoms

---

53 For instance, Herbert Dingle writes: "... we have no settled ideas about the history of cosmic bodies previous to the earliest giant stellar stage. An attractive case can be made out for the evolution of a nebula of some kind into stars... It is useless at present to speculate on the possible parentage of a nebula." (*Modern Astrophysics*, New York, 1927, p. 396.)

54 See for instance, Fred Hoyle, *The Nature Of The Universe*, New York, 1950; Herbert Dingle, *Modern Astrophysics*; and Sir James Jeans, *Astronomy And Cosmogony*, Cambridge, 1929, Second Edition, and *The Universe Around Us*, New York, 1930.

and molecules; and the explosion could have started simultaneously in different parts of the gaseous mass. In that case the causal chains would still be distinct at their origins.

With regard to our particular problem, these things mean that we have no sound empirical grounds which enable us to choose between alternatives (2) and (3) on our list. But even if we take alternative (3), which excludes universal relatedness so far as direct causal relatedness is concerned, there would still be indirect universal relatedness; if the gravitational attraction between bodies is assumed to have come into existence with the existence of the first bodies in the universe.[55] According to (3), the members of all the different causal lines will *become* causally related, directly or indirectly, only when all causal lines in the universe intersect; which may be at different times. Therefore, so far as (3) goes, there could be a time when at least some and perhaps all physical things in the universe were causally unrelated, either directly or indirectly—not however, if gravitational attraction obtains between bodies as soon as they come into existence. In the latter case the intersection of causal lines or, rather, of what in time become causal lines, takes place at the very origin of the various causal lines, between the first (physical) causes themselves. If new causal lines originate at later periods (i. e., if creation is continuous as Sir James Jeans, for instance, holds) their original causes, and therefore also the other members of these lines, will become causally related to all other things already in existence.

---

55 But Cf. Sir James Jeans' view; "Jeans has found... that the observed differences in the rates of motion at different parts of the arms of nebulae cannot be explained in terms of known forces. He suggests a modification of the normal law of gravitation or the existence of some force of which we have as yet had no experience." (Herbert Dingle, *Modern Astrophysics*, p. 335, footnote 1) Still, this, if true, does not logically affect our general conclusion. For Jeans' position still calls for some force operating between nebulae or the stuff from which they are supposed to have evolved. But even if no forces whatever are posited as operating there and then, the causal lines originating from the nebulae or from the primeval stuff would still intersect (though not at their origins); and hence these nebulae, or the original stuff, would be indirectly related causally to everything else in the physical universe. For gravitational forces would still operate at later stages (the existence of gravitational forces being a scientific fact).

So whether we accept alternative (2) or alternative (3) it seems probable that everything in the *physical* universe is causally related to everything else in it, directly or indirectly; at least so far as gravitation is concerned. But since our analysis of the causal relation (the relation between the causal event and the effect) seems to show that this relation is external in the crucial seventh sense, we must reject the doctrine that the universe (even the physical universe) is an internally-related system, causally speaking, in that sense of 'internal relation.' Similarly with regard to the other kinds of relations we have discussed, except the relations of similarity and difference.[56] Consequently we must reject the view that the universe is, causally or otherwise, an internally-related system in sense seven.

So far our discussion of the doctrine of internal relations has been negative. We have argued that it is false that *all* relations are internal, though we have agreed that *some* relations (in some senses of 'internal relation') are internal. But we have not offered positive arguments for the doctrine of external relations. To that task we must now turn.

II. *Some arguments in support of the doctrine of external relations.*

As in the case of our discussion of the arguments for the doctrine of internal relations, the arguments we shall now discuss do not pretend to be exhaustive or complete. This applies to any kind of argument we use in this work, elsewhere as well as here. Moreover, we shall present and discuss only those arguments which we have not already met in our criticism of the arguments for the doctrine of internal relations; although some of the arguments we shall present may be related to this criticism.

(1) Spaulding [57] offers a twofold proof that some relations are external: (a) that the view that all relations are internal itself presupposes the externality of some relations, and (b) that it can be inductively established that some relations are external.

(a) Suppose that any two terms do affect each other. These

---

[56] But we have tried to show that the supposed internality of these relations in Ewing's seventh sense is really a case of internality in his sixth sense.

[57] *The New Realism*, p. 178 ff.

then will be complex. As complex, they will consist of parts which are related. These parts, by the same hypothesis, will affect each other, and will therefore be complex; and so on *ad infinitum*. Ultimately there must be simple terms which make this complexity possible; and these will not themselves be complex. But they are nonetheless related. Hence these simple terms do not modify each other; that is, they are externally related. Examples of such ultimate simple terms are points and instants. The former are related to form space, the latter, time. It follows that the analysis of space and time requires the theory of external relations.

Leaving aside the causal relation, in which at least one term (object) does change the other term with respect to original characteristics, the doctrine of internal relations, so far as the modification of terms by one another is concerned, need only assert that a thing effects a change in another by generating one or more relational characteristics in it. It might be argued that even then the thing concerned will be complex in the sense that it now becomes composed of $(n+1)$ characteristics; where n is a finite number higher than 1 in the case of objects, and is the number of characteristics the object possessed before it entered the relation. Yet it does not follow from this that the thing is divisible into parts, if we mean by 'parts' spatial parts.

Further, suppose we take two simple characteristics, such as two colors. These are related; consequently, each of the terms acquires a relational characteristic. But this relational characteristic will not be a second characteristic added to the original characteristic and on a level with it: it will be a characteristic of the original characteristic, or a second-order characteristic, so to speak. It will be the characteristic of the original characteristic's being related in a certain way. As a characteristic of a characteristic, it will be related to the original characteristic; and this will result in the generation of a third order relational characteristic in each of its terms; and so on, so that the original and each of the relational characteristics becomes increasingly more complex, *ad infinitum*. (This complexity is not acquired *in time*, though the language we use to describe it gives that impression. Since at least all but one of the original relations and of the relational characteristics acquired are logical, they do not involve a lapse of time.

As soon as the original relation comes into existence (with the existence of both terms) all relational characteristics and relations come into existence).

The question whether or not such infinite complexity or such an infinite series of characteristics and relations is vicious, we have discussed elsewhere. But even if it is, the argument under discussion does not direct its criticism against it. And unless this infinite series is vicious, there is nothing in the situation which contradicts the supposition that the relations modify their terms. Also, the criticism of the view that relations modify their terms in the sense discussed because it involves an infinite series of relations and characteristics, would affect not only the doctrine of internal relations but equally all those positions which envision the existence of relational characteristics; including positions which do not countenance the doctrine of internal relations.

The truth of Spaulding's conclusion rests on the fact that the original characteristics, which make all the complexity possible, are not determined, as characteristics (i. e., as a specific color, shape, texture, etc.) by the original relation and therefore, also, by any of the relational characteristics and relations resulting from it. On the contrary, there must be original characteristics to begin with in order that relations and relational characteristics may be at all possible. These characteristics, being logically prior to their relations, cannot be determined by them. Otherwise, we will have a vicious circle and neither terms nor relations will be possible. In other words, at least one kind of relation (the original relation between the original characteristics) is external in the fifth sense.

Further, the doctrine of internal relations holds that the original, simple characteristics could not be what they are if the relation between them were absent (seventh sense of 'internal relations'). But where does complexity enter here? Even if Spaulding's argument is valid against the view that relations modify their terms, in some sense of 'modify,' it would not be valid against this particular sense in which relations are said to modify their terms.

Finally, the examples given, i. e., points and instants, as ultimate simple terms, indicate that the term 'parts' is taken in a quantitative sense. But I do not see how it follows from the supposition that relations modify their terms (or, as the argument puts it, that each term modifies the other), that they must be composed of quantitative parts—ultimately, of indivisible parts. In the conclusion of the argument, "Ultimately, there must be *simple terms* that make all this complexity possible, but that are themselves not complex," 'simple' is taken to mean indivisible (quantitatively speaking), while 'complex' is not taken to mean the opposite of 'simple' in this sense; rather, it is taken in the sense that terms modify each other. From the "simplicity" of the terms in the above sense it follows of course that they are not "complex" in the same sense (i. e., quantitatively), but not in the latter, different sense.

(b) The second part of the argument: that we can find by empirical (conceptual) analysis that some relations do not "modify", their terms, is true, in the relevant sense or senses of 'modify' we have discussed in connection with the doctrine of internal relations; and therefore we need not pursue this here.

(2) Perry[58] contends that terms, when they are simple entities, are independent (i. e., are externally related) (a) of each other, and (b) of the complexes of which they are members. Also, terms, when they are complexes, are independent of each other with respect to their simple constituents.

Perry distinguishes three kinds of cases where entities are dependent: a is dependent on b if (i) a contains b (whole-part dependence); or (ii) "... a is the cause or effect of b in a system which exclusively determines a"; or (iii) a implies b, or a is implied exclusively by b.[59]

(a) "*All simple entities are mutually independent.*"

Simple entities are mutually independent in the whole-part sense, since they cannot be wholes composed of parts. They cannot also imply or be implied by each other, since these relations are "... confined to propositions or combinations of propositions."[60]

---

58 "A Realistic Theory Of Independence," *The New Realism*, pp. 118-119.
59 *Ibid.*, p. 117.
60 *Ibid.*, p. 118. This is of course true if "implication" is used in the formal logician's sense. But it is not true if the term is used in the wider sense in which

Perry also denies that they can be causally related, "... because they cannot be values of variables, since this again would belie their simplicity."[61] Since Perry does not give examples of simple entities in his sense, it is difficult to determine whether he includes the notion of qualitative uniqueness in the idea of simplicity. If so, simple entities obviously cannot be values of variables, and since Perry thinks of causation in terms of laws and systems which these laws describe, simple entities cannot be causally related. But if the necessary-connection theory of causality is held, as the Idealist advocates of the doctrine of internal relations do, causal interaction would be possible even among unique entities; since then causality will be an intrinsic connection between two or more entities, and the notion of recurrence of entities of the same kind at different times would not be involved or be necessary. In the latter case causal interaction between simple (unique) entities will be possible, and therefore according to Perry's own analysis of "independence," these entities will be mutually dependent. However, if simple entities are conceived of as individual characteristics, it will be true that single characteristics do not interact, but only sets of characteristics in conjunction.

(b) *"Simple entities are independent of the complex of which they are members."*

Perry's argument here is that a complex cannot be a part of one of its components, and so the latter cannot be dependent on the former as whole to part. But can they not be dependent on the complex as parts of the complex, i. e., can there not be part-whole dependence? Perry's answer is that this is not possible. He illustrates his contention by the example of the respiratory system. The respiratory system cannot be a part of the living organism *qua* living organism without its relation to the whole organism. This, however, is not the dependence of the part on the whole,

---

the Idealists use it to apply also to *things*, as when they say that a given object or characteristic (or event) implies another causally, in the sense that if the former exist the latter must also exist and follow it in time. For entities may be simple and yet may conceivably be causally related. But concerning this, see the body of the text above.

61 *Ibid.*

but rather the dependence of the whole on the part. The respiratory system is dependent on other *parts* of the organism, such as, perhaps, the digestive system. But it is the organism as a whole which depends on the respiratory (and the digestive) system. The organism is what it is by virtue of its relationship to its parts.[62]

The advocates of the doctrine of internal relations will reply that the dependence is reciprocal: the respiratory system is dependent for its existence and character on (its relation to) the whole organism, as much as the latter depends for its existence and character on (its relation to) the former. The respiratory system cannot exist in the absence of (its relation to) the living organism. I. e., part and whole are mutually dependent in (Ewing's) sense seven of 'internal relation.'

However, assuming that there is a reciprocal dependence involved, the dependence cannot be of the same kind in both cases. For though the respiratory system or, rather, the respiratory organs cannot function as respiratory organs except in a living organism, the dependence here is not on the organism as an organic whole (for this organic whole would not be an organic whole, or would not exist as an organism, without the functioning of the respiratory system) but on the causal relations between the respiratory organs and the other bodily organs. And this is dependence of part on part, not of part on whole. The organism as a whole is nothing but the parts in causal and other relations; it has no separate existence over and above or apart from these parts in relation. To say that the respiratory system cannot be what it is without the entire organism being what it is, is to say in a roundabout way that it depends on that which itself depends on the digestive system, the circulatory system, etc., including the respiratory system itself. In short, the respiratory system as a living, functioning thing depends on the nature of the respiratory digestive, circulatory and other *organs* and on the way they causally interact.

If therefore there is no part-whole dependence in the case of complexes with complex parts, there cannot be part-whole dependence where the parts are simple, since the argument above is not dependent on the supposition that the parts are complex, but only

---

62 *Ibid.*, pp. 108-109.

on the nature of the logical relation between a part and the whole of which it is a part.

As in (a) above, Perry argues that simple entities, because of their simplicity, cannot enter into causal relations or relations of implication; this time with the complexes which include them. Our remarks in (a) concerning causation and implication apply equally here.

(c) *"Complexes are mutually independent as respects their simple constituents."*

This is derived by Perry from (b): If the constituents of a complex do not depend on the complex, the latter may be destroyed without affecting them. Hence where two complexes have some (numerically identical) constituents in common, they will not be interdependent.

The constituents of a complex do depend on their relation to the complex as a whole in so far as they acquire a relational characteristic in common (if we assume the existence of such characteristics). But apart from this, the destruction of the complex as a complex would not affect the constituents, if what was said in (b) is correct—if the constituent parts of the complex do not depend on one another causally. If they do, and the complex is destroyed, the relation between the parts—at least between any two parts—will be destroyed.

If the relations between the parts are causal, and the complex is destroyed, these parts will be modified, so far as they are the *effect* (in different respects) of each other. But since the destruction of the complex is compatible with the destruction of only one relation between two of its parts, the numerically identical parts of the two complexes can still remain the same even when the complex is destroyed. So if the conclusion of Perry's argument does follow from the independence of the simple constituents of a complex from the complex, it would be true even if we assume that simple entities can be causally related. But on Perry's grounds the situation is even simpler, since Perry holds that they cannot be causally related.

But Perry's conclusion will be true whether or not the simple constituents depend on the complex of which they are parts. For

THE DOCTRINE OF INTERNAL RELATIONS (CONT'D.) 89

each of the complexes according to Perry (and I think rightly), is dependent on its constituents. And since some of these constituents are, *ex hypothesi*, common to both complexes, these two complexes depend on their common constituents. In addition, since they are directly dependent on the same thing, they will be logically related, but not by a relation of interdependence. The reason is that one of the complexes can be destroyed without the consequent destruction of the other, if and so long as its destruction is not a result of the elimination from the complex of the constituents common to both complexes. If *that* is the cause of the destruction of the one complex, then the other complex too would be destroyed, even if it is assumed that the simple constituents of a complex do not depend on it.

Does Perry's conclusion follow from *his* premises? To answer this question, let us assume the contradictory of his basic premise and see whether or not the two complexes will then turn out to be interdependent. If constituent a, which is the (and the only) common constituent in complexes A and B, is dependent on the complexes of which it is a part, it will be dependent on both A and B. But will that mean that A and B will be interdependent? Suppose A is destroyed as a complex: that will result in the destruction of complex B only if A's destruction is the result of the destruction of a. If a is destroyed (assuming that simple entities can be destroyed) B will also be destroyed, since B is dependent on each and every one of its constituents. *In that case*, B would be dependent on A (and vice versa) in the sense that B could not exist if A did not exist; which means that the relation between them is internal in the ninth and tenth senses of this term; or in Perry's terminology, A and B would be interdependent. However, this would not follow if A were destroyed by the destruction of some other constituent than a. In that case B would still remain intact. And we must assume that A and B have some other characteristics in addition to a; since otherwise they would not be two complexes but one, and the whole issue would become meaningless. Perry's conclusion is therefore true, and his argument does prove it, in those cases where the destruction of either complex does not result from the destruction of one or more of the constituents they have in common. Such complexes are independent so far as their non-common characteristics are concerned. But in so far as they are dependent for their existence, *qua* these particular complexes, on their common-constituents; that is, in so far as they possess common characteristics, the relation between them *is* internal in the seventh,[63] ninth, and tenth senses of this term.

So far we have assumed that the complexes Perry envisions have some numerically-identical characteristics in common. But we can also think, and more readily, of complexes which have qualitatively but not numerically identical characteristics in common; e. g., two red roses. Here the situation is somewhat different. Suppose A and B to be two complexes possessing characteristic a_1 and a_2 respectively, these being qualitatively identical but numerically distinct. A would be destroyed if a_1 is changed, or if one or more of its other characteristics (b, c, d, etc.) are changed. (A will not be less of a complex for that; but it will be a different complex, even though, qualitatively, it may not have changed appreciably.) In either case B would remain unchanged. Hence B would be independent of A, so far as the particular situation we are concerned with goes; that is, A and B would be externally related in the ninth and tenth senses. But since A and B have a in common, qualitatively speaking, they will be related to each other by a relation of similarity with respect to a. And as will be remembered, the relation of similarity is internal in the sixth sense.

(3) Moore argues that the defenders of the doctrine of internal relations maintain that "... if P be a relational property which belongs to A, then P is internal to A both in the sense (1) that the absence of P entails qualitative difference from A; and (2) that the absence of P entails numerical difference from A."[64] He maintains further that neither (1) nor (2) is true. Put in terms of Ewing's ten senses of 'internal relation,' Moore's position is that a relation is not internal to its terms in sense seven (as Ewing

---

63 Only as far as *one* of the terms is concerned, if we assume that "simple entities" cannot be destroyed but can only be eliminated from a complex. On this assumption the other complex may still retain the characteristic concerned and so remain intact.

64 *Philosophical Studies*, London, 1922, p. 286.

understands this). For if a term has a relation *r* to some other term by virtue of which it has property P, and if the absence of P entails that A would be different, qualitatively and numerically, then the absence of *r* would make A qualitatively and numerically different. What Moore argues for is that "... it may be true that A has in fact got P and yet also true that A might have existed without having P."[65] He continues: "And I say that this is equivalent to saying that it may be true that A has P, and yet *not* true that from the proposition that a thing has *not* got P it *follows* that that thing is *other* than A—numerically different from it."[66] The defenders of the doctrine of internal relations confuse the true proposition (1) "... that if A has P, and *x* has not, it does follow that *x* is other than A..." and the false proposition (2) "... that if A has P, then from the proposition with regard to any term *x* that it has not got P, it *follows* that *x* is other than A...."[67] (2) is equivalent to saying that no relations are external, and therefore if (2) were equivalent to (1), or if it followed from (1), then all relations would be internal. To illustrate—

> To maintain external relations you have to maintain such things as that, though Edward VII was in fact father of George V, he *might* have existed without being father of George V. But to maintain this, you have to maintain that it is *not* true that a person who was *not* father of George would necessarily have been other than Edward. Yet it is, in fact, the case, that any person who was not the father of George, *must* have been other than Edward. Unless, therefore, you can maintain that from this true proposition it does *not* follow that any person who was *not* father of George *would necessarily* have been other than Edward, you will have to give up the view that Edward might have existed without being father of George.[68]

What Moore seems to be asserting is that the doctrine of internal relations involves that everything is necessarily what it is, i.e., that nothing but what *is* could have existed. Whereas he maintains that the existence of a certain thing A rather than B is only a matter of fact. Thus he says—

---

65 *Ibid.*, p. 289.
66 *Ibid.*, Italics in original.
67 *Ibid.*, Italics in original.
68 *Ibid.*, p. 290. Italics in original.

What the dogma of internal relations asserts is that in every case in which a given thing actually has a given relational property, the fact that it has that property is a necessary truth; whereas what I am asserting is that, if the property in question is an "internal" property, then the fact in question will be a necessary truth, whereas if the property in question is "external,' then the fact in question will be a mere "matter of fact."[69]

If A's possession of P is merely a matter of fact, A could have existed (i. e., could have been what it is) without P; while if A's possession of P is necessary, then if P were absent, A could not have been the same.

In order to deal with Moore's argument, it is important to distinguish between two different things which are easily confused: the proposition (i) that if A, which has characteristics a, b, c, exists at time T, nothing else which is numerically distinct from A could have existed instead of A at time T (e. g. B, having characteristics w, n, x): or, that the existence of a thing rather than another is necessarily determined or is necessary; and the proposition (ii) that if A exists at time T—and has characteristics a, b, c,—*it itself* could not have been the same if it lacked any one of its present characteristics, such as characteristic a.

Now the advocates of internal relations certainly assert proposition (ii), because they hold that the nature of a thing is determined and constituted by *all* of its characteristics: by its original and relational characteristics. This, as was mentioned before, follows from their view that the distinction between essence, property and accident is only one of degree. (The latter, as a matter of fact, seems to me to be one of the fundamental bases for the view that all relations are internal.) In the light of this it is seen that proposition (ii) follows from the *definition* of a thing A. If A is constituted by all its characteristics without exception, then A could not be A if it lacked any one of these characteristics. And the latter would be the case if A lacked a relation (and hence a relational characteristic) it actually has. Since we shall discuss the view of essence alluded to in Chapter VI, we shall here leave the foregoing without comment.

But does the doctrine of internal relations logically entail, as Moore thinks it does, that nothing in the universe could have been

---

69 *Ibid.*, pp. 302-303.

different; that the entire history of the universe, past, present and future must *be* what it is? That is, does it entail proposition (i)? The answer seems to me to be No. It is true that according to the defenders of the doctrine of internal relations, everything in existence is necessarily determined by its own cause or causes. But what this view amounts to is that everything in the universe at all times is ultimately determined by the first cause or causes of the universe. If the first causes are such and such, then everything in the universe, past, present and future will necessarily be such and such. But that leaves open the question whether the first causes are necessarily (logically) what they are, or whether they are what they are merely as a matter of fact. And it is clear that the doctrine of internal relations has nothing to say on this point and is compatible with either position. This goes to show that the doctrine of internal relations is not disproved by showing that the existence and character of things is contingent and not *logically* necessary.

The view that a thing's nature is constituted by all of its characteristics involves the position that if a thing A, which has a property P, *does as a matter of fact exist,* it could not be A if P were absent. It does not assert that A must necessarily exist and have P, i. e., that a thing A_1, which lacked P, could not have existed instead of A. But the whole point is that Moore wants to assert that A *itself* could have existed without having P. This would be logically possible only if A is defined in such a way as to exclude P from its definition. If this is not done, given that A has P, it cannot follow that A itself could have existed without having P; otherwise it would be the case both that A cannot be A without P and that it can be A without P. Hence the assertion that if A has P it would not have existed if P were absent (otherwise it would have been numerically different), follows simply from a particular definition of A, and not necessarily from the notion that A (and everything else) is *necessarily* what it is. But the converse is true: from the notion that everything is necessarily what it is it does follow that a thing A which has P could not have existed without having P, if P were absent. For then the contradictory of the consequent would be logically impossible. The proposition that A could have existed without having P would mean that the existence of P is contingent, and so A's being A (its possessing P) would be contingent: which contradicts the initial supposition.

Moore holds that the doctrine of internal relations entails the Identity of Indiscernibles; namely, according to him, that things which are qualitatively identical *must necessarily* be numerically identical, or that numerically distinct things cannot be qualitatively identical.[70] But actually this doctrine[71] follows from (1) the conception that relational properties form part of a thing's nature, and (2) that no two numerically distinct things in the universe *can* have identical relations to everything else. For, from (2), it follows that no two numerically distinct things can have identical relational characteristics: and therefore, from (1), that they cannot have the same nature; that is to say, they must be qualitatively different. *A fortiori*, the same would be true if relations are supposed to modify the (original) qualities of their terms, as well as to generate in them certain relational characteristics.

We had occasion to mention before that the doctrine of internal relations can be construed as holding either or both of two distinct views:

(a) that a thing's relations are internal to it in the sense that they generate relational characteristics in it: relational characteristics being regarded as constituting part of the thing's nature; or

(b) that a thing's relations are internal in the sense that they modify the original qualities of their terms, and therefore that *none* of these qualities could be what it is if the relations were absent; that a difference in them implies a difference in at least one of their terms (sense seven); that a term in a relation could not exist unless the other term existed and was related to it by

---

70 Moore is not concerned with the less stringent interpretation of the doctrine of Identity of Indiscernibles, namely, that *as a matter of fact*, all numerically diverse entities in the universe *are* qualitatively diverse. Nor is this view important for our purposes here.

71 But only in one of its two possible forms (see discussion on p. 95): if it is taken to assert that no two numerically distinct things in the universe can have qualitatively identical *relational characteristics* though they can have identical *qualities*.

the specific relations with which it is actually related (senses nine and ten); and so on with the other senses of 'internal relation.' We also had occasion to mention that the sense in which relations would be internal in (a) is trivial, and that the doctrine, if it is to be of any importance, must be taken as asserting (b).

It is easily seen that the doctrine of internal relations involved in (a) follows from proposition (1) above; hence, the doctrine of Identity of Indiscernibles cannot be a logical consequence of the doctrine of internal relations taken in sense (a), since (1) is also one of the premises on which the doctrine of Identity of Indiscernibles rests. On the other hand, the doctrine of internal relations, taken in sense (b)—which is the crucial form of the doctrine and is what we want to criticize—is independent of (1) above, and could be true even if (1) is false. Also, the doctrine of Identity of Indiscernibles *does* follow from the doctrine of internal relations in sense (b), together with (2) above. For if no two numerically distinct things in the universe can have identical relations, (1), and if relations modify their terms with respect to their original qualities, (b), then no two numerically distinct things in the universe can have qualities which are identical in nature: which is the other and more important possible form of the principle of Identity of Indiscernibles.

My view is that both forms of the principle of Identity of Indiscernibles are false. (I am assuming, of course, that this principle is empirical and not analytic, though, naturally, it could be made analytic by defining 'qualitative' and 'numerical diversity' in the appropriate way.) In its first form the principle is refuted if it is shown that relational characteristics do not exist: which we have already tried to do. In regard to its second form it is enough to show that relations are not internal in the required sense. It may be thought that if the second form of the doctrine can be refuted on other grounds than by refuting the premises from which we here derived it, the theory of internal relations itself, in the requisite sense, would be refuted. Unfortunately this is not true; if the doctrine is disproved, it will have been proved that *either* the theory of internal relations is false *or* proposition (1) is false, but not necessarily both. To show the falsity of the former it is further necessary to prove that (1) is *true*. But the simplest way of refuting the principle of Identity of Indiscernibles (and perhaps the only feasible one) lies in disproving either the doctrine of internal relations, or proposition (1); or both. And even if it is possible to refute the doctrine of internal relations (which is our main concern here), indirectly, by disproving the doctrine of Identity of Indiscernibles on independent grounds, and also proposition (1), this disproof would be so lengthy and circuitous that it is better left untried. At any rate it will not be attempted here, to avoid overlengthening an already-lengthy discussion of internal relations.

(4) We shall end our criticism of the doctrine of internal relations by giving a direct argument of our own against the coherence theory of reality. So far we have been attempting to show that the coherence theory is untenable by criticizing the doctrine of internal relations; for obviously the former cannot be true if the latter is false. Yet as our previous analysis toward the end of Chapter II (pages 39-41) seemed to show, the coherence theory of reality involves more than just the internality of all relations, even in Ewing's crucial seventh sense. Even if all relations are internal in this sense, the view that reality is an all-inclusive internally-related whole might still be false. This will be clearly seen as we proceed.

It will be remembered that in our discussion of the minimal conditions required by the coherence theory of reality, and indirectly, by the coherence theory of truth (Chapter II, pp. 39-41, and p. 42, respectively) we stated—without criticism—that the former would be true if either of two conditions is true:

(1) (a) That a change in any term (object, characteristic, event, etc.) in the universe involves a change in its relations to every other part of the universe; and

(b) That a change in these same relations involves a change in all the other terms in the universe;

or alternatively,

(2) (a) That a change in any term in the universe involves a change in all the other terms in the universe; and

(b) That the same change in that term involves a change in all the relations in the universe.

We now want to discover whether or not these conditions are in fact true.

Let us begin with (1) (a). This condition is readily seen to be unobjectionable. Relations, as we already have had the occasion to mention, are wholly or partly determined by the nature of their terms. So if a term changes in any way (qualitatively, quantitatively, in spatial location, etc.), *all* its relations would change to some extent as a consequence, at least *qua* specific relations if not also as kinds of relations.

Passing to (1) (b), we notice that this condition can mean either of three different things:

(i) That relations, by obtaining between two or more terms, generate relational characteristics in the latter; consequently, that if a relation changed, its terms would change with respect (and only with respect) to the relational characteristics generated in them by the relation, since now these characteristics would be eliminated; or

(ii) That a change in the relations logically *presupposes* a change in *all* their terms; in which case a change in the relations would logically imply a change in all the terms; or

(iii) That a change in the relations causes a change in all the terms of the relations.

Of these, (i) is true—if we assume the existence of relational characteristics to begin with. But this sense of (1) (b) above is a trivial one and would not satisfy our conditions. (ii), on the other hand, is only partly true. It is true in so far as some terms wholly determine some of their relations. But from this it only follows that a change in a relation necessarily presupposes or implies a change in *one* of its terms. And even this is not true if the determination of a relation by its terms is only partial. In both cases—where the determination of the relations by the terms is complete and where it is only partial—change in *all* the relations does not necessarily presuppose a change in *all* the terms.

Finally, (iii) is unqualifiedly false, as shown earlier in this chapter.

The upshot is that (1) as a whole is false, since one of the two terms of the logical conjunction of which it consists (i. e., (1) (b)), is false as a whole.

Let us now take (2) (a). For a change in a term to involve a change in all the other terms, the former term, in changing, must act causally on all the other terms and change them; whether by directly acting upon all of them, or by directly acting on some and causing them, through the change produced in them, to act upon the rest. This seems to be perfectly unobjectionable as a sheer logical possibility; if we assume with the Idealists that causality is universal. But when we come to the actual universe, logical possibility is not enough. What is required is evidence that this always actually happens. But as a matter of fact, there seems to be very considerable scientific evidence to the contrary. Even granting, as we are here doing, that causality is universal, it does not follow merely from this that any change in the universe would result in a change in the rest of the universe. As we have mentioned before, the occurrence of any given causal activity requires the presence of certain specific or relatively specific environmental conditions; and it is perfectly possible—nay, extremely likely—that all the conditions necessary for the direct or indirect action of any given entity in the universe on everything else are not simultaneously or even successively present, at the moment when the first change occurs, or for short or long periods after that. The effect of any given change in any one thing in the universe, if an effect does at all occur, may very well be confined to a large or small but nonetheless limited portion of reality.

We need not linger on (2) (b). This logically follows from (2) (a), and would be true if a change in any one term caused a change in at least all but one of the other terms in it. And this we have already discussed.

The upshot seems to be that (2), as actually applicable to the universe, is empirically not well-founded; and we are forced to regard it as untenable unless and until the advocates of the coherence theory of reality advance convincing evidence in its support. Since we have already attempted to show that (1) as a whole is untenable, it follows that the universe is not, as the advocates of the coherence theory maintain, an internally-related system. With this we come to the end of our discussion of the coherence theory of reality and the doctrine of internal relations.[72] In this discussion,

---

[72] For other arguments which have been advanced in support of the doctrine of external relations, see for instance W. T. Marvin, *A First Book In Metaphysics*, pp. 93-95.

it will be remembered, we have attempted to show that the doctrine of internal relations is untenable. We have analyzed various kinds of relations, such as the relation of similarity, the relation of difference, and the causal relations. In doing so we argued that the relations of similarity and difference are internal in Ewing's sixth and seventh senses. However, an attempt was made to show that the internality of these relations in the latter sense is only a disguised form of internality in the former sense, and not a new type of internality over and above it. As for the crucial "causal relation," this relation, we maintained, is external in Ewing's seventh sense. On the other hand, assuming the necessary-connection theory of causality, the relation between causal events and their effects, and the converse relation, were admitted to be internal in Ewing's eighth sense. But the "cause-effect" relation (though not its converse, the "effect-cause" relation), was held to be external in Ewing's ninth and tenth senses. We have also admitted that at least the physical universe is a network of terms related causally, directly or indirectly; but since we have argued that the "causal relation" is external in the seventh sense, we have concluded that the physical universe cannot be regarded as an internally-related system even causally speaking. In addition to the foregoing, we have attempted to criticize some major arguments offered in support of the doctrine of internal relations; and to strengthen our criticism, we presented and discussed various arguments which have been advanced for the doctrine of external relations (as well as one argument of our own against the coherence theory of reality).

If our criticism of the doctrine of internal relations and our direct criticism of the coherence theory of reality is valid, the latter theory must be regarded as untenable. Further, since we have also attempted to show (Chapter II) that the theory that coherence constitutes the nature of truth (and as we shall see later, the theory that it constitutes the test of truth) presupposes the coherence theory of reality—and hence the doctrine of internal relations—our criticism of the latter two doctrines seriously weakens the former doctrine. In the following three chapters we turn to a discussion of the view that coherence constitutes the nature and also the test of truth, on its own merits, in order to show that on those grounds too the theory is inadequate and must be rejected.

CHAPTER IV

COHERENCE AS THE CRITERION OF TRUTH: A CRITIQUE

In this chapter our main objective is to criticize the view that coherence constitutes the criterion of empirical truth. The advocates of the coherence theory themselves regard coherence as also the criterion of the truth or falsity of mathematical statements,[1] which they regard as synthetic and not analytic. But, for one thing, since this is contrary to what many present-day thinkers hold, we shall disregard these kinds of statements in our criticism of the coherence test, though we shall occasionally mention them in the course of our discussion. At any rate, whether mathematical statements are analytic or synthetic, we have a wealth of material to deal with without having to add to it by considering these kinds of statements, especially in the limited space at our disposal. In order to criticize the coherence test, we shall merely examine the main arguments offered by its advocates; we shall not be concerned to offer an alternative criterion or criteria of truth and falsity. Some positive results, however, will emerge in the course of the

---

1 It well be noticed that I sometimes use the term 'statement,' while at other times I use the term 'judgment.' My policy is to use the latter whenever the coherence view is being expounded and, less frequently, when it is being criticized. For the latter purpose, and in general when I am expressing my own views, I use 'statement' instead. I do not want to imply by this that 'judgment' as used by the Idealist advocates of coherence is synonymous with 'statement' as I use it. But for the advocates of coherence judgments are what are true or false, and they are what is asserted by verbal forms like 'The table is narrow,' 'Caesar crossed the Rubicon,' 'John is taller than Peter,' and so on. Similarly, in my use of 'statement' (which, following P. F. Strawson [see Chapter VI, footnote 25], I define as a sentence in use) a statement would be what is true or false, and also what is asserted by verbal forms like 'The table is narrow,' 'Caesar crossed the Rubicon', etc. Also I speak of 'The table is narrow,' and 'Caesar crossed the Rubicon' themselves as statements, while Blanshard, for instance, would speak of these as judgments, using the terms 'statement' and 'judgment' in a looser sense, perhaps, than in the above uses.

discussion, which may be considered as a more or less preliminary exploration of a more positive approach.

The contention of the advocates of the coherence test is that the criterion of the truth or falsity of any and all judgments (always understanding by "judgments" empirical judgments in this work) is their coherence or lack of coherence with the system of knowledge, ultimately with the ideal system of knowledge which embraces all the facts in existence in one comprehensive whole. Whether we are dealing with judgments of perception, such as "The patch before me is green," judgments about sensible objects, such as "The table before me is green," empirical generalizations, such as "All crows are black," empirical laws, such as Boyle's Law, or scientific and philosophical theories, such as Einstein's theory of Relativity and the coherence theory itself, respectively, the criterion is always—it is alleged—coherence and not correspondence with facts, self-evidence, or any other so-called criterion of truth or falsity. But a great deal of confusion and misguided criticism has resulted from the assumption of some critics that coherence, for its advocates, means nothing but logical consistency—despite the continued protests of the defenders of the theory against such an interpretation; their constant reiteration that consistency is only part of what they mean by 'coherence.' Part of the confusion, no doubt, is due to the admission of the defenders of the theory that no perfect positive definition of coherence can be given because perfect coherence is a never-realizable ideal, and no actual system which may be mentioned as an example of a "coherent" system is perfectly coherent. These remarks about the meaning of 'coherent' and 'coherence' should be kept in mind in the following discussion.

Before we examine the claims of the coherence view in some detail, we have to be clear about a few important points. The first of these is the question of what the advocates of the coherence test mean by 'criterion' or 'test' in speaking of coherence as *the* test of truth. To this question no explicit answer is given by the advocates of the view. But we can gather the following from their writings: (a) that coherence is held to be *the* and the *only* common feature or element involved in the testing of any and every empirical proposition: whether it is a judgment of perception, a judgment about sensible objects, an empirical generalization, or some other kind of proposition; (b) that 'feature' or 'element' in (a) does not mean or include the awareness or immediate insight that coherence does or does not obtain in any particular case—I mean the awareness that a given proposition or set of propositions which is to be tested coheres or does not cohere with the system of knowledge which is taken as the actual (in contradistinction to the ideal and ultimate) standard. This, despite the fact that immediate insight would be a universal feature of the testing of all propositions if coherence is the test of truth. Thus Ewing says that this immediate insight—

> Is not itself based on a further argument from coherence, otherwise the criterion would not be applicable to anything at all. But such an admission might still leave coherence in the position of the sole criterion, for the immediate insight would consist simply in seeing whether a proposition conforms to this criterion and so is true, or contradicts it and so is false, and the essential force of the coherence theory would not be impaired at all. To use any criterion we must be able sometimes to see whether a given object conforms to it or not.[2]

It is to be noted that in the above quotation Ewing implicitly makes a distinction between the criterion of truth and what we do or may have to do in order to use this criterion. But he does not tell us on what grounds coherence is regarded as the only feature which calls to the description of 'criterion' and not also, say, the immediate insight he talks about; since, on the coherence theory itself, both are universal features involved in testing any and all propositions. For (c) the advocates of coherence speak of coherence as *the* (sole) test of truth because they think of it as the only criterion which is involved in testing any and every proposition of any kind.

We might just mention here that if immediate insight is involved in the testing of all kinds of propositions (assuming that the coherence test is valid), or even if it is involved in the case of only some kinds of propositions, its exclusion from the "criterion" of truth would be inconsistent to some extent with Blanshard's

---

[2] I. C. S., p. 241; Cf. also Ewing's review of *The Nature Of Thought, Mind*, Vol. LIII, No. 209 (January, 1944), p. 81.

view that the distinction between essence, property and accident is only one of degree. On that view coherence would, at most, be only the most essential part of the criterion of truth; while immediate insight (if not also some or all of the procedures, say observation, which are at least sometimes involved) would be only a less essential part of the criterion. But even this will not do perfectly, if the coherence test cannot be applied without the appeal to immediate insight; in such a case immediate insight should by rights be regarded as essential a part of the criterion as coherence itself.

There is another kind of distinction which is of importance for our present discussion: the distinction between a criterion *simpliciter* and an "ultimate criterion." The advocates of coherence regard coherence as the *ultimate* criterion of truth, in the sense that it is logically foundational; that it is what logically terminates the possible process of testing.

The second point we want to make is this: if coherence is the ultimate test of truth then all other tests, if they are or can ever by actually employed, will logically presuppose it. But it itself will not logically presuppose any other (kind of) test. Hence it is important to distinguish between (i) a test or the tests we actually employ in a given case to verify a given proposition or a set of propositions, whether or not we know its correct nature, and (ii) what other kinds of *tests* the test we actually employ may logically presuppose. We should also distinguish between the latter and (iii) what the test we employ logically presupposes, or entails, concerning the *nature* of truth, the truth or falsity of other propositions than the one to be tested, and concerning the nature of the universe as a whole.

With these preliminary remarks we turn to a discussion and criticism of the view in hand. We shall first deal with the theory in relation to individual propositions, whether singular, particular or universal, whether about sense perceptions or about objects. Later on we shall deal with scientific laws, together with scientific theories. But our remarks and criticisms here will apply, *mutatis mutandis*, to scientific laws and theories, as we shall have occasion to point out when we come to the latter.

There is one central point which runs through the arguments

of the defenders of the coherence theory: that there is no such thing as a "solid fact" or a "bare given," which we apprehend completely detached and isolated from all judgment and inference (inference being alleged to occur in all judgment). It is not denied that there is a "given" in sense experience and in introspection. But it is contended that—

As soon as we attempt to say *what* is given, we find ourselves thrown back upon coherence anyhow. The solid piers of fact, supposed to be standing there in broad daylight as the bases of our structure of theory, are illusion.... The 'facts' that were to support our system are themselves relative to the system. In short, the coherence of judgements within a system is our test, and our only test, of any truth or fact whatever.[3]

There are two important points which we have to bear in mind concerning the given if confusion is not to ensue. The first is that the ontological status of sensible qualities, or of perceptual subjects as a whole, is irrelevant to the question whether or not what is perceived (the "given") can or cannot serve as evidence for the truth or falsity of judgments about sensible objects. Whether what each of us perceives is public or private, existentially subjective (to borrow a phrase from A. O. Lovejoy) or existentially objective, mental or physical, is irrelevant to whether or not appeal to the perceptually given can be made in verifying judgments. Even if what is perceived is private and subjective, so that the external world,[4] if known at all, is indirectly known, the essential point remains that we do perceive things through our senses, and so far as we know different percipients have similar if not identical perceptions. These perceived things can be and are appealed to in verifying empirical judgments. Their subjectivity and ideal character, if they are subjective and ideal, would not in any way detract from or destroy the fact of their givenness. This applies to so-called "wild" as well as to so called "veridical" perceptions; except that in the case of some kinds of "wild" perceptions, such

---

3 N. T., vol. II, pp. 214-215. Italics in original.
4 I. e., the world of objects which are partially responsible, causally, for the production of perceptual objects in us, and which are causally and existentially independent of the individual percipient.

as hallucinations, the fact that they are not experienced by the majority of men militates against their use in public verification.

From this it is seen that the attempt to discredit the "given" as a basis of verification by relegating it to the private world of the individual percipient it doomed to failure. I have H. H. Joachim in mind[5] who, in his *Logical Studies*, attempts to prove that the given in perception is not "immediate"; that is, that "... it is not the direct awareness of an independent fact; of a solid constituent of reality, presenting itself, entire and complete, to the passively accepting observer."[6] To put the matter briefly, he attempts to show that in any given perception, say of a flash of lightning, the perceived datum is private; and in order to prove this he marshalls some of the arguments which are the stock-in-trade of the Epistemological Dualist, such as the relativity of what is perceived to the spatio-temporal perspective and to the perceptual mechanism of the individual percipient. He concludes:

The 'real flash' is that which all the observers postulate on the ground of the 'appearing flashes' or presentments.... It is the product of an inexplicit and confused thinking, a thinking immersed in and inseparable from sensation. It is the hybrid offspring of that blend of sense and thought which

---

5 Similarly Blanshard is mistaken when he argues that because hallucinatory data are as much given as "veridical" ones, if verification consists in correspondence of judgments with the given, the judgments of people having hallucinations about what they see will be as true as our judgments about veridical data; whereas of course (so Blanshard says), the former are illusory. We may attempt to differentiate between two kinds of givenness; "... but to do that one must go beyond givenness as a test. And then one has abandoned the theory" (N. T., vol. II, p. 234). Our reply is that whatever may be the nature of the given—whether "veridical" or "wild"—its givenness remains. So far forth, judgments asserting the existence of these data will be as true as judgments asserting the existence of veridical data. The "wildness" or "veridicality" of the data is irrelevant. In both cases, the test of the judgments involves the appeal to these data. It is only when the deluded percipient asserts that what he perceives is "objective," e. g., is a *snake* or a pink *elephant* in the ordinary sense of these words, that his judgment will be false. Of course, we do have to "go beyond" the mere given; we have to interpret it in terms of other givens: those of the percipient himself and those of others, in order to distinguish between "subjective" and "objective" data. But such "going beyond" the given does not preclude the appeal to the given as part of what is involved in verification.

6 *Ibid.*, p. 80.

goes by the name of 'sense-perception.' And its hybrid character stares us in the face. For 'sense-perception' is a form of 'knowledge,' a 'cognizant experience,' in which the mind thinks sensuously. There is 'thought' in sense-perception, but not thought free and explicit—not 'thought' which the percipient controls, or of which he is even aware *as* 'thought.' And in sense-perception the percipient 'sensates'; but, in sensating, his mind instinctively interprets the *sensa*, 'forms' or 'constructs' them, analyses and (in analysing) synthesizes them.[7]

And so on in the same vein.

The trouble with this passage is that it is confused and commits a palpable *non sequitur*. The conclusion which Joachim sets out to establish by proving the causal and existential subjectivity of the given in perception: that the "real objects," so to speak, which are supposed to be "immediate" are a blend of sense and thought, does not follow. The "real flash" which is "postulated" on the basis of the private perceptions of individual percipients is not and cannot be an object of perception (or sense) at all if Epistemological Dualism is right. It is wholly an object of thought and is known, if at all, only indirectly, through an examination of our private, subjective perceptions. On the other hand, what we do originally perceive[8] or is an object of sense (which according to Joachim's argument is subjective and private) is only an object of sense and not a blend of sense and thought—at least Joachim's argument does not and cannot serve to show that it is such a blend. But it is precisely this that has to be shown, as Blanshard and Ewing for instance do attempt to show, if a case for coherence as a test of truth is to be made.

The second main point we want to note is that the "given" which is relevant for the verification of judgments of fact (judgments of perception, judgments about sensible objects, empirical generalizations) is not the given devoid of *all* mental accretion. It is only the given devoid of a certain type of mental "accretion"; namely, the given as it exists apart from and independently of judgments in the ordinary sense; i. e., of conceptual elements which are not or have not become perceptual in the sense-experience of adults. Textbooks of psychology are full of examples of elements

---

7 *Ibid.*, p. 83. Italics in original.
8 The so-called "given" in perception.

in adult perception which are (believed to be) absent from the perception of the newborn child; in short, elements of interpretation which seem to pass into and become a part of what is (later) perceived. I mean such things as the perception of objects as three-dimensional, the perception of distance between separated objects, the perception of the size of objects, and so on.[9] But these elements are as much a part of what is literally perceived, sensed, or given in adult life as the perception of color or texture or shape, which presumably are given even in the perception of the infant when it first begins to perceive. Hence when we (adults) make judgments about the perceptual world (unless we are philosophers or psychologists concerned with finding out what part of our perceptions is originally given and what part is "added" by the mind in the sense discussed), our judgments are generally about the "total" objects *qua* "composed" of the originally-given plus the psychically-added. Still, even if and when we, in our capacity as philosophers or psychologists, make judgments as to what is originally given in a newborn's perception and what is "acquired," the situation is logically no different from the case of the testing of any other judgment about objects, or of judgments of perception. These judgments are testable by appeal to the facts of perception as psychology gives them to us (and the rules of language and its vocabulary) though the question whether or not it is possible to discover *all* that is "acquired" in perception and therefore to discover exactly what a newborn's perceptions are like is a moot and perhaps insoluble question. But that stems from the nature of the particular problem, and not from any defect in any particular test which may be applied to verify or disverify these judgments.

All this is meant to indicate one thing: that the admission that an adult's perceptions include "acquired" elements (and we are not denying it) does not in any way deliver one into the hands of the coherence test.

In what sense then is interpretation or judgment involved in experience, perceptual and other, in a way which makes it relevant to the question whether or not appeal to experience involves appeal

---

[9] See for instance F. Goodenough, *Developmental Psychology*, New York, 1945, Second Edition, Chapter XIV.

to coherence? The answer is: interpretation or judgment which is not or has not become a part of what is actually perceived or, in general, experienced. It is the interpretation of *what* is experienced, or judgment *about* it. In what follows we shall understand by "experience" and the "given" what remains if this conceptual element is stripped off. Consider a simple proposition like "There is a green patch before me." This proposition goes beyond anything given in sense-experience at the moment it is framed. Even when we merely point to an object and say 'green patch,' or merely 'green,' we have gone beyond the given by classifying it as a specific color. And in the case of a proposition like "That is a cardinal-bird on the branch yonder," and still more, in the case of, say, "All philosophers are talkative," much more than mere classification is involved. In all these cases, appeal is made at least (a) to a specific language, here English, and (b) to the past experience and knowledge of the person making the proposition. Suppose we now want to verify the relatively simple proposition "That is a cardinal-bird" (hereafter called X) accompanied by pointing. In order to do so, we look in the direction indicated and observe the supposed cardinal-bird. We observe its characteristics; but these characteristics, as such, do not and cannot verify or disverify X. In order to be capable of serving as evidence for or against X, the given has to be interpreted; and this again involves at least an appeal to language and to the verifier's past experience and knowledge. Suppose these form a system, which we shall call S. If therefore we accept the view that the interpretation of the given in verifying X involves a reference to a *system* and not to a set of detached propositions, the coherence view would be right that coherence is involved in testing X. Now the process of verification in any actual case is very complex if traced out in all its actual detail. But the logical process involved seems to me to be fairly simple, and seems to be essentially the following: (1) "If S, and if S is correctly applied, 'cardinal-bird' means a small, scarlet, North American bird..."; (2) "If S and if S is correctly applied, then if anything is what we call a cardinal-bird, it is what we call small, scarlet, living in North America... etc. (i. e., it possesses characteristics A, B, C, D... etc.)"; (3) Coming to the given located in the direction indicated by the person making X, we observe certain characteristics, which we shall indicate by $\alpha, \beta, \lambda, \gamma, \varphi, \omega$... in order to be able to refer to them (these symbols do not stand for names); (4) We interpret $\alpha, \beta, \lambda, \gamma, \varphi, \omega$... in terms of S, and we form a conditional proposition: "If S, and if S is correctly applied, then α is an *instance* of the *kind* of characteristic we call smallness (A); "If S, and if S is correctly applied, then β is an instance of the kind of characteristic we call scarletness (B); and so on with the other observed characteristics; (5) We now have (i) "If S and if S is correctly applied, then if anything is what we call a cardinal-bird it has the kinds of characteristics called A, B, C, D, etc." (ii) But "The given has characteristics of the kind we call A, B, C, D, etc."; therefore, "The given is *probably* a cardinal-bird"; (6) But "If the given is probably a cardinal-bird, X is probably true."[10] In actual testing, the logical process involved can be broken down into a chain of conditional arguments of the kind we have stated in (5); but the same logical process as the present one is involved in each case. In the case of every conditional argument in the chain appeal is made to S, and the correctness of its application is assumed.

The following conclusions can I think be drawn from the foregoing:

(a) Without appeal to (what we assume here to be) a system, the given cannot serve as evidence for or against a given proposition about objects of experience.

(b) The appeal to system in interpreting the given consists in classifying the latter as an instance of a kind. The classification is made in terms of a specific language; but this classification may be itself based on scientific knowledge; for example on zoology in the case of X. But that the given is an instance of one kind rather than of another, a member of one class rather than another in this classification, depends not only on the nature of the classification but also on the nature of the given.

(c) The propositions we may make in interpreting the given to be this or that given, if made by a correct application of S, cohere with S, since they are made by applying S to the given.

---

[10] I am disregarding, for the sake of simplicity, the problem of the spatial location of what is observed.

But both where the given-as-interpreted confirms, and where it disconfirms, the proposition to be tested, the same principles of interpretation are used; in both cases the propositions made about the given, assuming that S is correctly applied, cohere with S. What then makes the proposition to be tested cohere or not cohere (according to the coherence theory) with these propositions about the given and therefore with the system S implied? The answer seems to me to be: what the proposition to be tested asserts, together with what the propositions about the given assert. If the proposition to be tested is "There is a cardinal-bird on the tree yonder," and the propositions we arrive at in and by interpreting the given are, say, "That *is* a cardinal-bird," "That (in the same region) *is* a tree," "The cardinal-bird *is* on that tree," etc. etc., the latter propositions together would imply[11] the former proposition, and vice versa. In other words, they would cohere. On the other hand, if the propositions about the given are, say, "That is a humming-bird," "That (in the same region) is a tree," "The humming-bird is on the tree," etc. etc. the conjunction of these propositions, and the proposition to be tested, would not cohere. Similarly if the propositions about the given we arrive at are those of our first example but the proposition to be tested were, say, "That is a mocking-bird on the tree yonder." But what determines the coherence or lack of coherence? Surely it is in part the nature of the given. And the given, whether *qua* interpreted or *qua* uninterpreted, is not and cannot be part of system S or of any other system of propositions, since it is a quality, a set of qualities, or an object, not a proposition. Hence in so far as there is an appeal to something other than system (i. e., appeal to the given) in testing the proposition in hand, coherence or appeal to system cannot be the sole or whole criterion of its truth or falsity. This applies, *mutatis mutandis*, to all other propositions about objects of experience, if and when interpretation of some given is involved at any stage in the process of verification.

The propositions constituting the interpretation of the given

---

11 I shall disregard for the sake of simplicity the fact that it is a conjunction of an indefinite number of propositions about the given, and not any limited number of them, which implies and is implied by the proposition to be tested.

can serve to test a particular proposition by the latter's coherence or lack of coherence with them precisely because they are based in part on the nature of the given. From the truth of S and from its correct application, alone, it does not follow either that "That is a cardinal-bird yonder" is true, or that it is false. The truth of S and its correct application are presupposed *both* in those cases where "That is a cardinal-bird yonder" is found to be true, and where it is found to be false. Consequently, something more than appeal to S is required in order that it may be possible to decide whether in a particular case "That is a cardinal-bird yonder" *is* true, or whether it *is* false; and *that* is the nature of the given in any particular case. In other words, in the conditional argument we outlined, the *conditional* proposition (first premise) is determined wholly by the system; but the second premise, which *asserts* the consequent or denies it, is determined not only by the system (by the interpretation of the given) but also by the nature of the given (i. e., by the nature of the object of interpretation). That is, the second premise is determined by the given-as-interpreted. And a conclusion one way or another results only when both premises are there and not just one premise.

Let us approach these points from a slightly different angle. The truth of the conditional proposition depends on S and on the correctness of its application. If now the truth of the second premise, say "The given is small, scarlet, bird-shaped, etc. etc." (T) (where the proposition to be tested is true), or say "The given is large, grey, bird-shaped, etc." (T') (where the proposition to be tested is false), also depends solely on the system in the sense that its truth is *consequent upon* and not merely *presupposes* the truth of S, we will get the following disconcerting result: "If S, and if S is correctly applied, then T"; "If S, and if S is correctly applied then T'"; "Therefore if S, and if S is correctly applied, then T and T'; therefore if S is (or can be) correctly applied, S cannot be true."

Secondly, if a given proposition is tested wholly and solely by its coherence or lack of coherence with a system S, the question arises as to how S itself is to be verified. If S is not identical with the entire system of present human knowledge (assuming that present human knowledge does form a system), it can be verified, according to the coherence theory, by its coherence or lack of coherence with the latter. But whether or not S is identical with the system of present human knowledge, the next question is how the latter itself is or can be verified: on what grounds do we regard or have regarded it as knowledge (i. e., as true) in the first place. We cannot appeal to the ideal system, since we do not and can never have it; so if coherence with a system is to be at all a test or the test of truth of any given proposition, there must be some other way of testing the most comprehensive actual system we possess. If coherence is assumed to constitute the *nature* of truth, then the extent of this system's coherence in and by itself, independently of its relation to some other system, might constitute the test—or at least a test—of its truth or of the extent of its truth. But the thesis that coherence constitutes the nature of truth has to be proved first before the present difficulty can be (if at all) solved.

The same problem arises, though perhaps in a milder form, if coherence is taken only as *a* test or as part of the test of truth. For our analysis seems to show that the testing of a proposition about objects of experience does depend, though not wholly, on the appeal to a system of propositions (we are again assuming that interpretation of the given involves appeal to a system; and a system of propositions is either true or false, and so raises the question of verification.

We said earlier that in testing a proposition about objects of experience by appeal to a system S, the correctness of S's application to the given by way of interpreting it is assumed. This raises the question of how the correctness of such interpretation, in any given case, may be tested if we are in doubt about it. In other words, how can we find out (in terms of the coherence theory) whether or not the judgments made about the given cohere with S: or in ordinary language, whether or not they themselves are true. For unless they cohere with S, or are true, in any particular case, the test employed will give us an incorrect result. In terms of the coherence theory, the coherence or incoherence of the proposition to be tested with these propositions will not mean that it is true, or false, respectively, if they themselves are not correctly made in terms of S, and therefore do not cohere with it. For (again in terms of the coherence theory) the proposition to be tested may really cohere with S though not with the propositions about the given; and vice versa. Well, here again, appeal to S and to the given is necessary. We have to check our propositions against S, say concerning the concepts involved in these propositions; and we have to check these against what is given. Suppose I want to verify "That is a cardinal-bird," and I see an object which I interpret as being a mocking-bird. If I want to be sure that it is a mocking-bird and not a cardinal-bird, I may appeal to the English language by, say, looking up in a dictionary. I find that a mocking-bird is not a scarlet bird, while a cardinal-bird is scarlet. I again observe the bird before me, and recalling what I have been taught or learned in the past as to what color 'scarlet' names, I conclude that the bird observed *is* scarlet, and therefore not a mocking-bird but a cardinal-bird.

The upshot of this is that at every logical step in the process of interpreting the given in verifying a proposition about objects of experience, the correctness of the interpretation and the truth of propositions made have to be tested, if we want to do so, by appeal to experience as well as to the system of interpretation involved. Here again, the test is not coherence alone but coherence together with experience.

But we now come against what may seem to be a formidable argument against what we have hitherto said. The advocates of coherence argue[12] that the appeal to experience is itself justified by the coherence theory. Our appeal to experience, they say, is justified by the fact that such an appeal results in greater coherence than the appeal to fancy and fiction. The method of appealing to experience is valid because the result of appealing to any other method would be less coherence. "We use, that is, in interpreting our experience those principles the consistent employment of which leads in general to the greatest coherence, or at least that is the only way in which our use of any principles can be logically justified."[13]

---

12 I. C. S., pp. 239-240. Ewing quotes Bradley, E. T. R., p. 213. He presents this as one of the arguments given by the advocates of coherence, and he himself accepts it. We might add that Ewing himself regards coherence as the test of truth.
13 *Ibid.*, p. 240.

The first question which arises is why greater rather than less coherence should be aimed at—why coherence at all should be aimed at in the first place. If our aiming at coherence is the result of a psychological desire on our part, or even an innate and universal tendency of the mind, what justifies us in assuming that the satisfaction of such a desire or tendency would give us truth? For that is the important point here. The only logical justification for aiming at coherence (within the framework of the coherence theory as a whole),[14] seems to me to be the assumption or view that coherence itself constitutes the *nature* of truth. If truth does not lie in coherence, then I do not see why, so far forth, we should aim at achieving it, and therefore use those principles whose use leads in general to the greatest possible coherence. But to assume that truth lies in coherence prejudges the issue, since the thesis that coherence constitutes the nature of truth has to be proved first in order to make the above argument plausible. (This is especially important since Blanshard uses the thesis that coherence constitutes the test of truth—which he attempts to prove before attempting to prove that it constitutes the nature of truth—as one of the chief arguments in support of the latter thesis.)

Furthermore, in saying that the appeal to experience, to memory and to the testimony of others results, in general, in greater coherence than otherwise, Ewing means by 'coherence' "coherence with experience." But it is a truism that if we appeal to experience what we will get will be coherent with experience (whatever that means). However, if we *interpret* our experience in accordance with principles whose application in general leads to coherence in the sense of reciprocal implication (or, at least, one-way implication), then indeed coherence and not experience would be taken as determining the *truth* of propositions. And that would bring us again to the thesis that coherence contitutes the nature of truth. But suppose we want to *test* a proposition by appealing to experience: in what sense is this justified by the coherence *test*?

---

14 For if this framework is abandoned, it might be argued that though truth does not lie in coherence, the appeal to coherence is justified by the (supposed) fact that true propositions cohere with one another; consequently that coherence can, at least sometimes, be taken as an *indication* of truth—and hence as a test, or part of a test, of truth.

The answer seems to be that appealing to experience-as-interpreted (not experience as such), or to the propositions we make about experience in testing a proposition, logically means appealing to the system in terms of which the proposition in hand is actually being tested. For the propositions about what it experienced are themselves made in accordance with, by applying, the system; hence these propositions cohere with it. Consequently, a proposition which coheres with these propositions coheres with the system, and one which does not cohere with them does not cohere with it. And coherence or lack of coherence with the system is the test of truth of falsity, respectively. But if so, is the thesis that appeal to experience can be justified by the coherence test an *argument* in support of the coherence view, as it is taken to be by Ewing, or is it an interpretation of the testing situation in terms of it? I think it is the latter. For we can say instead that the interpretation of experience in terms of a system is designed to make the testing of a proposition by experience possible, to make experience serve to test the proposition; and that it is the appeal to experience which is the test of truth or falsity. Both ways of looking at the matter would I think be equally right in a sense; since as we have tried to show, the testing of propositions of the kind we have been talking about involves appeal both to experience and to (what we are assuming to be) a system. The error of the advocates of coherence seems to me to lie in taking coherence with a system as *the* test of truth, while actually the appeal to "system" (in the sense of interpretation of the given) can only be regarded as part of the test of truth. Appeal to "system" (in the sense of interpretation) and to experience are logically on the same plane: both are equally indispensable in testing propositions about objects of experience. Hence to limit the use of the term 'criterion' or 'test' to coherence would be inconsistent and arbitrary. So far as our discussion goes, we can argue that a true proposition coheres with judgments about experience and therefore with the system in terms of which these judgments are (in part) made because it is true; and that truth lies, say, in the *correspondence* of the proposition with the experiences about which the judgments are made. If a proposition corresponds with an experience it asserts something about, then it will cohere with (imply or be implied by, or both) judgments which truly express this experience. If there is a cardinal-bird yonder, then, according to our account, the proposition "There is a cardinal-bird yonder" will be true, and will imply and be implied by a conjunction of an indefinite number of true propositions about the characteristics of the cardinal. Since the advocates of the coherence test regard coherence as *the* test of truth, the appeal to experience is regarded by them as at best only a means (though a necessary means) to applying this test. That is why Ewing says that appeal to experience can be *justified* by the coherence theory. If on the other hand the opposite and equally extreme view is held, if appeal to experience is regarded as *the* test of truth, then appeal to system (supposing a system to be involved) in interpreting the proposition to be verified and the experience which is to test it, would be regarded as only a means (but a necessary means) to appealing to experience. In that sense appeal to system would be justified in terms of the test in hand. The problem in part depends on how much or how little we include in the notion of "criterion" or "test." If it is taken narrowly, as the coherence view and the above hypothetical view take it, then what the one regards as the test of truth may be regarded by the other as only a necessary condition for or even as only a means to the employment of the test of truth; and what the one regards as such a condition or means the other may regard as the test. But as we have already said, taking "criterion" or "test" narrowly in either way is logically unjustified, at least in the case of the testing of propositions about objects of experience.

So far we have assumed with the advocates of coherence that the interpretation of a proposition to be tested and of the given involves an appeal to a system. We shall now attempt to criticize this view. That the testing of propositions of the type discussed involves appeal to the verifier's knowledge, both his knowledge of language and of the nature of matters of fact, we have already admitted. But the advocates of coherence do not show that the knowledge involved in verification in any given case itself implies the entire body of human knowledge or even the verifier's entire knowledge; nor do they show that human knowledge forms even a partially coherent system in their sense of 'coherent.' True, as we know, they attempt to show that all actual and possible knowledge *would* form one single coherent system, primarily by attempting to show that the universe is an internally-related system. But we have already attempted to show that this is false. Leaving this point aside, is it true that language, which is certainly appealed to in verification, constitutes a system—or more precisely, that the different languages we have constitute one system or even a number of different systems?

A detailed discussion of the nature of languages is beyond the scope of the present work and beyond the competence of the present author. But the following remarks are pertinent in relation to our question.

(a) So-called formalized logistic systems, which are "... determined by rules which refer exclusively to symbols and expressions, regarded in abstraction from any specific interpretation"[15] e. g. the various symbolic deductive systems, mathematical and logical, which have been devised, are partially coherent systems in the sense that from a set of postulates and rules of derivation the rest of the system is derived. They are not perfectly coherent systems (I am using the term 'coherent system' in the sense in which the advocates of the coherence theory use it) because, for one thing, the postulates of each are logically independent of one another. But in our present discussion we are not concerned with such systems; rather, we are concerned with natural languages, since we are concerned with the question of testing propositions; and propositions are expressed or expressible by statements in some natural language or another. Looked at abstractly, natural languages are determined by certain syntactical and semantical rules. The former refer to expressions in the language, whereas the latter are concerned with the relations between the expressions and their referents (when they have any). This means for our purposes that the framing of any well-constructed and meaningful sentence in a given language L is achieved by applying some of the syntactical and semantical rules of L. But so far as we know, the semantical if not also the syntactical rules of any natural language L (say

---

[15] R. M. Martin, "Symposium: What Is A Rule Of Language?", *Science, Language, And Human Rights*, American Philosophical Association, Eastern Division, Philadelphia, 1952, vol. I, p. 105.

English or French) are logically independent of, though probably consistent with, one another. The semantical rule ' "B$_1$," designates in L Blue' is logically independent of ' "H" designates in L Human' and ' "C" designates in L Chicago';[16] and so on with any other of the indefinite number of semantical rules in English. However, even if semantical rules entail other semantical rules and syntactical rules entail other syntactical rules, it seems to me that semantical rules do not entail syntactical rules; and vice versa; which means, again, that the rules of language do not form a single, unified system. Secondly, so far as our knowledge of the historical genesis of various natural languages goes, natural languages have not sprung from the minds of men in the form of fixed and explicit semantical and syntactical rules which were subsequently applied. Temporally speaking, linguistic practice is prior to reflection on and the framing of rules about our practice. "We frame rules in the light of our study of our practice."[17] Our reference to the gradual, piecemeal, largely unconscious and constant growth of natural languages is meant, for one thing, to bring out the point that natural languages do not have the clear-cut logical simplicity and systematic character of mathematical systems and systems of logic. Of course, this is not in any way inconsistent with, nor does it show, that the rules of natural languages do not or cannot form a logical system. But it does mean, I think, that it would be extremely surprising if the rules of language did form a logical system, considering the way languages arise and grow. Also, so far, we have assumed that natural languages do have clear-cut, rigid and fixed rules which might form a logical system. But actually this is not true. As Strawson says—

Our linguistic practice is a very fluid affair. If we are to speak of rules at all, we ought to think of them as rules which everyone has a licence to violate if he can show a point in doing so. In the effort to describe our experience we are constantly putting words to new uses, connected with, but not identical with, their familiar uses; applying them to states of affairs which are both like and unlike those to which the words are most familiarly

---

16 These rules are quoted from N. L. Wilson, "Symposium: What Is A Rule of Language?", *Ibid.*, p. 90.

17 P. F. Strawson, *Introduction to Logical Theory*, London, 1952, p. 230.

applied. Hence we may give a meaning to sentences which, at first sight, seem self-contradictory.[18]

Apart from this, words or expressions, even in their "ordinary" or familiar uses, may be what Strawson calls "logically ambiguous (have different logical uses)." Further, whether or not a given word or expression is "logically ambiguous," many concepts used in ordinary language (and in science) have what F. Weismann calls an "open texture," or are not completely defined in all directions.[19] Also, many ordinary words or expressions are "vague"; that is, there are boundary-cases where it is not possible to decide whether or not a given word applies. In other words, there are not fixed rules appeal to which can unequivocally decide whether or not a given expression applies in any specific situation which may arise. A rule determines a range of uses of a given expression; but this range, in the case of most ordinary expressions, is not fixed and sharply delimited as in the case of expressions and concepts used in mathematics for instance, or in the physical sciences. (But as Weismann shows, even concepts and therefore, derivatively, expressions used in the physical sciences suffer from an "open texture.") We might add that the distinction between the literal and figurative senses of given words, and between one sense and another, is also often not sharply defined.[20] To quote Strawson again:

The formal logician now aims at an exact and highly systematic logic, comparable in these respects with mathematics. But he cannot give the exact and systematic logic of expressions of everyday speech; for these expressions have no exact and systematic logic.[21]

Again:

The logician... manufactures the elements of a language of his own, which, unlike ordinary language, is subject to rigid and systematically connected rules, and some of the symbols of which exhibit logical analogies to familiar expressions of ordinary speech, as these expresions are commonly, though not always, used.[22]

---

18 *Ibid.*
19 "Verifiability," *Essays on Logic and Language*, edited by Antony Flew, Oxford, 1951, *passim*.
20 P. F. Strawson, *Loc. cit.*, p. 231.
21 *Ibid.*, p. 57.
22 *Ibid.*, p. 58.

The foregoing admittedly very inadequate and sketchy discussion of our problem seems to me to indicate that natural languages—or the rules of ordinary language—do not form a logical system.[23] This, if true, means that in the case of the verification of propositions like the one we have discussed earlier, and in every kind of case where interpretation by appeal to language is involved (i. e., in the case of all propositions and sets of propositions), the appeal to language does not involve an appeal to a system. However, even if the rules of language do form a logical (partially coherent) system, the advocates of the coherence test do not, as far as I know, present any arguments to show that this is the case. Hence their view that the interpretation of the given (and therefore verification) involves appeal to system, must be regarded as dogmatically held so far as language is concerned.

So far we have talked about the verification of simple propositions about sensible objects. But I think it is not difficult to see that in the case of the verification of propositions about sensible qualities, such as "I see a green patch," the same two elements: the appeal to the given on the one hand, and to language, past experience, knowledge and sometimes the testimony of others, on the other hand, are involved. The same applies, *mutatis mutandis*, to empirical generalizations like "All philosophers are talkative" or "All crows are black," though such propositions involve appeal to experience only indirectly. The problem of the confirmation or disconfirmation of such propositions as "All crows are black" logically boils down to the problem of the confirmation or disconfirmation of as many as possible of the singular propositions (in this case about the blackness of individual crows) which are entailed by the general proposition. The confirmation of "All crows are black" can never be complete or certain since, for one thing, the proposition entails an indefinite number of singular propositions like, "This is a crow and it is black," "That is a crow and it is black," "X is a crow and it is black," and so on; while only a

---

23 For a detailed analysis of the divergence between purely logical systems and ordinary language, the reader is referred to Wittgenstein, *Philosophical Investigations*, Oxford. 1953, translated by G. E. M. Anscombe, and, especially, P. F. Strawson, *Op. cit.*

finite number of them can be confirmed (or disconfirmed). But the foregoing shows that the verification of empirical generalizations like "All crows are black" (I am assuming here of course that crows are not black by definition) also involves the two elements we have already discussed; since the singular propositions they entail are all about individual objects, events, sensible qualities or psychological experiences. And in the case of the verification of propositions about any and all of these, it can be shown that the two elements we have discussed earlier are involved. That is, in these cases, too, our remarks concerning the question whether or not coherence is *the* test of truth seem to hold.

With these hasty remarks we pass to a discussion of the coherence test in relation to the verification of empirical laws and theories.

Before we examine the question of the testing of laws and theories, we must explain what we mean here by 'laws' and 'theories.' It is important to be clear that in speaking about laws and theories I am not necessarily committing myself to the view that laws are fundamentally different in nature from theories. I merely follow here the distinction made by many scientists and philosophers of science. Also, I am not committed to any particular view of the nature of theories; either to the view that they are conventions, or to the view that they are sets of empirical propositions, propositions about matters of fact (sensible things, or unobservables such as atoms and electrons), or to some third view. But since the question of the verification of theories arises only if these are either true or false; which can be the case only if they are sets of empirical propositions (unless we are to think of them as analytic), and since this is the view held by Blanshard and the other Idealistic advocates of the coherence test, I shall assume for the purposes of this discussion that they are empirical. Since the words 'empirical law' and 'theory' are used in different ways be different philosophers, I shall explain what kind of thing I shall mean by each by some examples. By a law I have in mind such things as Boyle's Law, Charles' Law, Snell's Law; by a theory such things as Newton's theory of gravitation and Einstein's theory of relativity.[24]

---

[24] In the present discussion I am not distinguishing 'theory' from 'hypothesis,' for the sake of convenience.

Blanshard,[25] in accordance with his general conception that coherence constitutes the test of truth, holds that the verification of hypotheses consists in the insight that a hypothesis coheres with relevant fact. In other words, the elaboration of the implications of a hypothesis and the comparison of the implications with fact are two aspects of the same insight, the insight into coherence. The only difference between the two processes is that in the first case we work forward from the hypothesis to its logical consequences; in the latter case we work backward from certain judgments of fact: "... we take certain judgments of fact as pointing backward to our hypothesis. The two processes are the same process looked at from different ends."[26] In support of this contention, Blanshard first tries to show that in some cases one or other of the two processes may be missing, in the sense that the two processes coalesce into one process: elaboration may at the same time constitute verification; or vice versa. To illustrate the first type, he says:

A child who concludes that seven times eight are fifty-six may wish to make sure about this, and reasons that if it is correct he should also be able to arrive at it by adding eights to each other. He tries this and succeeds. Here the process of verifying is swallowed up in the elaboration. The elaboration consists of conceiving fifty-six as a sum of eights; but that is also the verification.[27]

This example is unacceptable, and does not at all show what Blanshard claims it shows. For one thing, "the process of squaring with fact is missing" precisely because arithmetical statements are not empirical (or synthetic) but analytic, and there is no question of verifying them by appeal to experience. To "verify" any arithmetical statement we have to turn to definitions of numbers, to the axioms, and to arithmetical operations. In the case of the child, the "verification" consists in using a different arithmetical operation, addition, instead of the one used in arriving at the result, namely multiplication. (But of course multiplication itself

---

25 N. T., vol. II, pp. 212-215.
26 *Ibid.*, p. 213.
27 *Ibid.*

is reducible to addition.) The reasoning involved is this: "If seven times eight is equal to fifty-six, then seven eights added together should give us fifty-six; but seven eights added together do give us fifty-six; hence seven times eight is equal to fifty-six." So "verification" is distinct, even here, from elaboration, and takes the form of appealing to the nature of the arithmetical operation of addition. That elaboration may be "swallowed" up by verification is also not shown by Blanshard's other example, that of inserting a piece in a picture puzzle accompanied by the awareness that it is the right one. The fact that this perception occurs almost instantaneously is no proof that no process of If-Then reasoning is involved. As a matter of fact, Blanshard himself implicitly suggests the right answer when he says: "If the data we begin with are so complete as virtually to surround the gap in our knowledge, the right suggestion when it occurs may be seen at once to be the wanting element...."[28] It is because the data are so complete that the process of reasoning takes place almost instantaneously and proceeds almost unconsciously. But it is still there. Again, the example Blanshard gives to show that neither elaboration nor verification may in some case be distinguished as separate steps, as in recalling a name accompanied by the awareness that it is the right one, does not prove its point. Here there is no hypothesis whose implications may be drawn and then verified: unless we take as our hypothesis the *judgment* that the name recalled is the right one. But in that case it is not the awareness that it is the right name that verifies the judgment but, say, the appeal to various memories or to the testimony of others, which shows that it is actually the name of the particular person, object, etc. it is judged to be.

The second and more important type of argument Blanshard resorts to prove that elaboration and verification are in essence the same process, even when they are both present and distinguishable, is the same as the one he resorts to in attempting to show that in the case of ordinary judgments of fact the test is coherence: that is, that the given with which the implications of the theory are to be compared is not a bare fact, but a judgment

---

28 *Ibid.*, pp. 212-213.

or a set of judgments. But we have dealt sufficiently with this point. Here we shall merely emphasize that the elaboration of the implications of a hypothesis and the verification of these implications are not logically the same process merely looked at from different angles. The reasoning involved in elaboration is: "If hypothesis H is true, then C and D and E, etc. must be true." Verification then consists in discovering whether C, D, E, etc. are in fact true or not, by appealing to facts. If they are thus found to be true, then the argument proceeds: "But C, D, E, etc. are true; hence H is (probably) true." The comparison (to use Blanshard's term) of C, D, and E, etc. with fact is not a logical but an empirical matter; and I do not see how this, and the consequent *logical* assertion: "Hence H," is the same logical process as "If H then C, D, E, etc." The important question, however, is how and why a particular fact or set of facts can serve to verify a given hypothesis. In the case of empirical generalizations, the answer is simple: the given fact or set of facts will be an instance or a set of instances of what the generalization asserts. There the relation between the generalization and the *statement* of fact is one of coherence only in the sense that the latter follows from the former as a singular proposition subsumed under a general proposition. But the relation is not symmetrical. The general proposition does not follow deductively from the singular proposition or any set of singular propositions, and can only follow inductively from a number of them (as many of them as possible, assuming that no negative instances are encountered). In the case of theories the relation between a theory and the verifying facts is indirect, as we have seen, and must be established through the logical elaboration of the consequences of the theory before verification can become possible.

So far, we have spoken about the testing of a theory as if the implications which are tested by observation are derived wholly from the theory itself. But this is not true. It is only with the help of already-established empirical laws and theories that this can be and is actually done in scientific practice. This means (a) that where predictions based on a theory T (with the help of accepted laws and theories, S) are fulfilled, i.e., where the consequences of T and S are found to be (probably) true, the whole complex composed of T and S, and not T alone, is confirmed with some probability; (b) that where the implications drawn from T and S together fail to square with observed fact, we can only infer that either T or S, or both, are false. From any one such test we cannot tell which of these is the case. This raises the problem whether a theory can at all be disconfirmed by such empirical testing as outlined. Pierre Duhem puts the matter in these words:

In sum, the physicist can never subject an isolated hypothesis to experimental test, but only a whole group of hypotheses; when the experiment is in disagreement with his predictions, what he learns is that at least one of the hypotheses constituting this group is unacceptable and ought to be modified; but the experiment does not designate which one should be changed.[29]

And again:

Physics is not a machine which lets itself be taken apart; we cannot try each piece in isolation, and in order to adjust it, wait until its solidity has been carefully checked; physical science is a system that must be taken as a whole; it is an organism in which one part cannot be made to function without the parts that are most remote from it being called into play, some more so than others, but all to some degree. If something goes wrong, if some discomfort is felt in the functioning of the organism, the physicist will have to ferret out through its effect on the entire system which organ needs to be remedied or modified without the possibility of isolating this organ and examining it apart.[30]

Duhem sums up this view in the statement: "A "crucial experiment" is impossible in physics."[31]

So far as the *confirmation* of a theory goes, there is no serious problem. If the implications of a group of theories are found to agree with experience, the component theory which is to be tested *is* confirmed in some degree, alongside the other theories in the group. A theory is not less confirmed because in confirming it

---

[29] "Physical Theory and Experiment," *Reading in the Philosophy Of Science*, Edited by H. Feigl and M. Brodbeck, New York, 1953, p. 240.
[30] *Ibid.*, pp. 240-241. Cf. also A. Pap, *Elements Of Analytic Philosophy*, pp. 360 ff.
[31] *Ibid.*, p. 241.

other theories are confirmed as well. In admitting this, we are also conceding an important point to the advocates of the coherence test; namely, that a theory cannot be confirmed in isolation, in the sense that the process of confirmation requires the use of other theories as logical premises. It is also conceded that, given one theory, none of its components can be confirmed in isolation. The view that an (*any*) isolated statement cannot be confirmed (and for the advocates of the coherence test it also cannot be disconfirmed) in isolation from a system, is in fact one of the major arguments of the advocates of the coherence test against the correspondence test. For it is alleged that the correspondence test logically requires that a judgment be capable of confirmation or disconfirmation no matter what else may be the case, i. e., in "isolation." A similar view is held by W. V. Quine. He writes:

The notion lingers among empiricists that to each statement, or each synthetic statement, there is associated a unique range of possible sensory events such that the occurrence of any one of them would add to the likelihood of truth of the statement, and that there is associated also another unique range of possible sensory events whose occurrence would detract from that likelihood....
  The dogma of reductionism survives in the supposition that each statement, taken in isolation from its fellows, can admit of confirmation or infirmation at all. My countersuggestion... is that our statements about the external world face the tribunal of sense experience not individually but only as a corporate body.[32]

And again, "The edge of the system must be kept squared with experience; the rest, with all its elaborate myths or fictions, has as its objective the simplicity of laws."[33] If all this is true, how can a given theory, or any component part of a theory, be at all disconfirmed? If the answer is in the negative, would it not follow that the method of testing theories we have outlined breaks down so far as disconfirmation is concerned? Would we not be thrown back upon some form or other of the coherence test at least whenever the implications of a theory fail to square with facts?

---

32 *From A Logical Point Of View*, Cambridge, Massachusetts, 1953, p. 41.
33 *Ibid.*, p. 45.

In actual scientific practice the difficulty is "solved" quite readily in many cases: certain elements in the complex which includes the theories to be tested are taken as well established and, if not beyond dispute, at least as possessing a high degree of probability. So, where the implications drawn from the complex fail to square with facts, the elements other than these favored one are generally held suspect and are modified or abandoned altogether. The elements in the complex whose modification or abandonment would cause the least disturbance in the complex and in the body of scientific knowledge as a whole, that would overthrow as few of the accepted theories as possible, are modified or abandoned. And if the theory to be tested is, as far as we know, independent of these accepted theories, it is even more readily dispensed with. (Other pragmatic factors which are taken into consideration —such as simplicity, economy and logical elegance—are too well-known to need discussion.)

But this practical, pragmatic way out leaves untouched the theoretical problems raised by the above situation. If the theories which are generally accepted are left untouched, the question of how they are themselves confirmed in the first place still remains.

Our problem then is whether the whole body of laws and theories, (i) constituting a given science, and (ii) constituting science as a whole, is implicated in the confirmation and disconfirmation of any and every scientific theory. But before we deal with it, one thing is clear at the outset: even if the entire body of theories and laws, whether within one given science or in science as a whole, is implicated in the confirmation or disconfirmation of any and every scientific theory, this does not necessarily mean that coherence is or must be the test in the sense of the sole and whole test of the truth or falsity of theories. Even where the consequences of a theory do not agree with experience, the discovery that at least one (which one we do not know) of the theories in the complex is false as a whole is based on the testing of the consequences of this complex by appeal to facts;[34] and this involves

---

[34] Here and throughout the present work I use 'facts' interchangeably with 'matters of fact' and not in any special technical sense. I mean by these terms such things as an actual event or a set of events, an actual object or a set of

coherence only in so far as facts have to be interpreted. The facts-as-interpreted (which are not propositions) are also involved in testing these consequences. Thus coherence is only part of the test here. The question now is whether coherence can enable us to determine *which one* of the theories in the complex is responsible for the discrepancy between the implications of the complex and facts.

That coherence cannot be *the* test even here is seen by considering that (1) the theory T to be tested may be logically consistent with the rest of the complex, A, though the consequences of (S & T) may not square with facts. If T is consistent with S, from this and from the fact that the consequences of (T & S) do not square with facts, we cannot infer that both T and S are false. In a set of mutually-consistent propositions, some propositions may be true while the others may be false. For example, the subaltern of a universal proposition is consistent with the latter, and yet the former may be true while the latter may be false (though not the other way round). (2) On the other hand, if T and S are mutually inconsistent, and hence if S does not imply the rest of the complex, and vice versa, we can only infer that either T or S is false but not that both are false, if the consequences of (T & S) do not square with facts; which one is false we cannot tell from the fact that they are mutually inconsistent. Of course, a theory cannot be true as a whole if some of its parts are inconsistent with the rest; and a theory which is internally consistent cannot be true if it is inconsistent with a *true* theory. But inconsistency cannot serve as a test of falsity unless we already know that some proposition or theory with which a given proposition is inconsistent, is itself true. (Similarly, consistency cannot serve as a test of truth unless we already know that some proposition or theory with which the proposition to be tested is consistent, is itself true.) And that is precisely the issue here. (3) If T is logically deducible from S, whether it has been formulated independently, or has been actually derived from it, S or any of its components cannot

---

objects, an existent sensible quality or a set of qualities, an actual experience or experiences, a thought or thoughts, as the context may require. In short, I mean by them a specific existent or existents, something that is the case.

be used in deriving the testable consequences of T. For T itself, *ex hypothesi*, is a logical consequence of S. Unless we proceed *ad infinitum*, the theories which are used to derive the testable consequences of T must ultimately be ones which do *not* imply it, although of course they could be consistent with it. *A fortiori*, S cannot be used in the verification (here disconfirmation) of T if it both implies and is implied by S—which is the very opposite of what the coherence test requires; since coherence consists (in this case) in the reciprocal derivability of theories.

But is it true, first, that the disconfirmation (and also the confirmation) of any theory implicates the entire body of accepted theories and laws in the entire field of science? The answer appears to me to be a definite No. Suppose we assume for the moment that each of the sciences—physical and other, as we have them now or at any given moment in history—is a logically systematic whole; in the sense that from one or a few of the laws and/or theories in it all the remaining, generally accepted theories and laws can be deduced. Physics, say, would be a system in this sense if from Einstein's general theory of relativity, for instance, all the other generally accepted physical laws and theories can be deduced. Even in that case it would be false that all the sciences actually form one such system. Nor is there any likelihood that such an all-embracing system will ever be achieved once for all; though an all-inclusive system seems to be, at least *prima facie*, theoretically possible. But further, even if it is theoretically possible to have an all-inclusive system such that every scientific theory or law will imply and be implied by the entire system, this is not *actually* the case.[35] Physics, chemistry, biology, psychology, and

---

35 Note that even if we do succeed in arriving at a systematization of all science, this mammoth system has to be tested by discovering indirectly whether or not it conforms to facts, as is the case with any limited system, since such a system will not exhaust the nature of reality. True, this would require the use of other theories, which are not part of the system—theories which, *ex hypothesi*, we do not have at that moment. But since such a system does not exhaust the entire universe, it is theoretically possible to discover the requisite theories at some future date, making the actual testing of the system in hand possible. Only in the case of the ideal system which embraces the entire universe (assuming that it is meaningful to speak of such a system), will such testing not be possible; since *ex hypothesi*, such an ideal system will embrace all the kinds of facts and principles which will ever exist in the universe, even in the remotest future.

the other sciences are at present still isolated to some extent from one another. The testing of any biological or chemical theory, say, does not in fact require for its elaboration all the theories of physics or astronomy; the testing of such a theory does not stake the truth or falsity of the law of gravitation, Maxwell's equations, the general theory of relativity, the nebular hypothesis, and the like. But the various sciences are not completely isolated, self-enclosed bodies, cut off from one another; nor, necessarily, is it the case that the sciences cannot, even in principle, be unified. What we are saying is merely that they *are not* completely unified and interrelated. Furthermore, even within any one science, the science's entire corpus is not implicated in the elaboration and testing of every theory. Such a situation prevails, if at all, only in the most "advanced" science, namely physics. Even this is not completely true: present-day physics is not completely systematic: note for instance the gap between the general theory of relativity and quantum theory. Even here, and more so in the other sciences, especially in biology and psychology (let aside the social "sciences") some theories and laws, so far as our knowledge goes, are isolated and rest on independent grounds. It is true that this independence may be, and perhaps is in many cases, only apparent, a reflection of our ignorance. But the crucial point is whether or not it is possible to have, or to discover, independent grounds for at least some of these theories; on the basis of which the theories have first been formulated, and in terms of which they may be tested. And what we have said seems to indicate that the answer is in the affirmative. H. Feigl says:

Science would be in a sorry condition if its theories could not be stated in terms of logically independent postulates. It is precisely for the sake of systematic examination through empirical testing that we must unravel the knowledge claims of a theory into a maximal number of independently confirmable postulates. For example, only after disentangling the various components in the principles of special relativity can we say which experiments confirm which laws. The experiments of Michelson and Morley (Trouton and Noble) confirm one component, the observations on double stars by de Sitter another; and for the confirmation of auxiliary hypotheses the measurements of aberration and the experiment of Fizeau are equally indispensable.—A view that maintains that the whole body of a scientific theory (if not of all science) confronts experience and that modifications may be required in *any* part of the system if it does not "fit",—such a view obscures dangerously what is of the greatest importance for the progress of science: the successive testing and securing of parts of science—at least in the sense of an approximation. Naturally, no part can be considered as established with finality—but this insight which impresses the pure logician should not blind him to the recognition of the methods of successive confirmation.[36]

Note that even if "the whole body of scientific theory... confronts experience," it does not necessarily follow that "modification may be required in *any* part of the system if it does... 'fit'," as Quine holds. What follows, as we have seen, is merely that if the implications of a theory do not square with facts, *either* the theory in hand *or* the other premises used in the derivation of these implications, *or both*, are false. But this is quite another thing from the patent fact that in so far as the complex of theories is a logical system, a modification in *any* part may make the implications of the theory square (or approximately square) with facts. The possibility of making such modifications solely with the purpose of preserving the systematic character of the theories in hand, does not affect the fact that one specific part of the complex may be *true*, and another part may be false: and therefore that if we are concerned with discovering the truth, and not merely with preserving a logical system, the complex should be modified in the parts which are, as a matter of fact, *false*; and the parts that are kept intact should be the parts which, as a matter of fact, are *true*.

If the existence of independent grounds for different *sets* of theories, if not for individual theories, is accepted, we can solve the problem which we set out to solve; namely the problem of discovering what part or parts of a complex of theories whose implications do not square with facts, is or are false, and has or have to be modified. To illustrate, suppose we have a theory H which we want to test. For that purpose we make use of theories S (which, *ex hypothesi*, will not be the entire body of scientific theories). From H and S as premises we draw the implications which for simplicity we may lump together as C. Then we test C, and find that it conflicts with facts. We conclude that either H

---

[36] "Confirmability and Confirmation," *Readings In Philosophy Of Science*, Edited by P. Wiener, New York, 1953. p. 528. Italics in original.

or S or any one or more of the theories comprised by S, or both H and S, are false. In order to find out which one of these alternatives is the case, we try to draw the implications of H with another set of theories T; we reason in this way: (H & T) ⊃ Y. Suppose now we find that Y squares with facts. That would mean that (H & T) are probably true; which means that H is probably true. Since we found that (H & S) are probably not both true, and H was found to be probably true, we can conclude that S is probably false. However, it may be that Y, like X, does not square with facts. In that case we cannot tell whether or not H is true; we have to look for the implications of H drawn with the help of still other theories, until we discover some implications which do square with facts. Again, both H and S may be false; in that case we will have a different picture. For example: I. (i) (H.S) ⊃ X. $\bar{X}$. ⊃ -(H. S); (ii) (H. R) ⊃ Y. $\bar{Y}$ ⊃ -(H. R); (iii) (R. W) ⊃ Z. Z. ⊃ [probably] (R. W); (iv) Therefore R (from iii.); (v)-(H.R). R. ⊃ $\bar{H}$ (from ii. and iv.); II. (vi) (S. T) ⊃ N. $\bar{N}$. ⊃ -(S. T); (vii) (T. U) ⊃ V. V. ⊃ [probably] (T. U); (viii) Therefore T (from vii.); (ix) Therefore $\bar{S}$ (from viii. and vi.); (x) Therefore $\bar{H}$. $\bar{S}$ (from v. and ix.).

Let us try to be clear about the meaning of "independent grounds of a theory." To say that different scientific theories or sets of theories have independent grounds is to say that these theories or sets of theories are logically independent of one another, which means either (a) that these theories do not logically imply each other (either by weak or by strong implication), or (b) that one of these theories or sets of theories does imply the rest, but that each of them can be tested by appeal to different sets of evidence or different experiences. (a) does not present any problem. In the case of (b) we will have the following situation: Suppose theory A implies theory B; hence the evidence for theory A is also evidence for theory B (and vice versa with probability). This does not make the *evidence* for A *qua* evidence for A cease to be independent of the evidence for B. The matters of fact *abcdef*... which constitute evidence for A may be causally or in some other empirical way related to the matters of fact *klmnop*... which constitute evidence for B; and if the advocates of coherence are right, they will also be logically related. In the latter case, *abcdef...* and *klmnop...* will depend in their nature on each other. But *abcdef...* and *klmnop...* can still serve as evidence for one theory or another by virtue of their being *abcdef...* or *klmnop...*, and not by virtue of their causal and logical relations to each other; though their being *abcdef* and *klmnop*, respectively, depends on these relations.

If the implication between A and B is reciprocal, the evidence for or against the one theory also serves as evidence for or against the other theory in a straightforward way.

We have already mentioned that at least some scientific theories, even physical ones (such as quantum theory and the general theory of relativity) are independent of one another in sense (a), so far as their present form is concerned.[37] We have also seen how, if there are more than two such independent scientific theories, especially in the same science, their independence can be utilized in the disconfirmation of theories.

That some (at least one) scientific theory must be independent of other scientific theories in the above sense—though, of course, it could be, and if they are all true, it must be, consistent with them—if scientific verification is to be at all possible, can be shown by the following consideration. Suppose all the theories we have at a given moment are theories A, B, C, and D; and A implies B, B implies C, C implies D. Since A implies B, A cannot be of any use in elaborating the implications of B in order to test the latter theory. For to test B through its implications we have to compare the latter with new facts not used or involved in the framing of theory B itself. This cannot be done by using A. So in order to test B we have to use a theory other than A, say C or D, which does not imply (or is not implied by) B. If such independent theories do not exist, verification of B or of any of the other theories becomes impossible. Consequently, unless we are

---

[37] Sometimes, theories which at first seem to be different are later found to be equivalent, that is, to imply each other. An example is Heisenberg's and Schrödinger's versions of quantum theory. (W. Kneale, "Induction, Explanation, and Transcendent Hypotheses," *Readings in The Philosophy Of Science*, Feigl and Brodbeck, p. 367.) But we are here speaking about theories which are not equivalent.

prepared to deny that scientific verification does or can take place by the elaboration of a theory and the verification of its consequences, we have to assume the actual existence of at least one independent theory. It is interesting to note that the advocate of the coherence theory cannot object to this by denying the actual occurrence of verification by appeal to fact in the manner we have earlier outlined. He does concede that we do test a theory by comparing its consequences with facts: the only, but crucial, difference is that he interprets this comparison differently, as we have already seen. But this difference in interpretation does not affect what we have said about it; and so, what we have said about the existence of independent theories.

(2) The defender of the coherence test has a ready answer to all that we have said in (1). He will point out that we have merely indicated that present scientific knowledge does not from one coherent system in which every theory or law is implied by (and for Blanshard, implies) the rest of the system. This, the advocate of the theory concedes. But the crucial point, he will say, is that *scientific* knowledge would form one vast coherent system if we only knew enough; if we had perfect scientific knowledge. The independence of theories would then be seen to be only apparent. In the perfect system, the confirmation or disconfirmation of any part of the system would entail the confirmation or disconfirmation of the entire system. The truth of the implications of any part of the system would presuppose the truth of the rest of the system, such that if these implications do not square with facts, any and every part of the system could logically be the cause of the discrepancy and therefore in need of modification. What part it is which needs modification is something which cannot be discovered by further tests of the same kind. That is, appeal to experience cannot serve as a test of falsity in such a case; and if there is or can be any test of falsity, it must be coherence—or in this case, the lack of coherence.

Now it is granted that in the case of the ideal system—if we can legitimately speak of *the* ideal system—neither confirmation nor disconfirmation by appeal to experience would be possible, since by the nature of the case there can be no *new* (kinds of) facts which can be used to test its implications; or—which follows from this same assumption—there cannot be any *other* principles or theories outside this system, which could be used in the elaboration of its implications in order to test it.

But what assurance do we have that a perfectly coherent and comprehensive system would be true, whether perfectly or otherwise? For unless this system "represents" reality, to use Bradley's term, or "coheres with facts," to use Blanshard's term, its coherence would merely be a matter of logical implication; and since comprehensiveness without coherence does not constitute truth, the system's all-inclusiveness would not make it true. The answer of the advocates of coherence is that the perfectly coherent and comprehensive system would be (perfectly) true because (a) such a system is identical with (for Bradley, is an aspect of), its object, reality, and (b) reality is an internally-related system. Coherence (reciprocal implication) constitutes truth because of this particular relation between thought and its object, (a), and because the object of thought is itself an internally-related system; and the most coherent system is (and has to be) at the same time the most *comprehensive* system possible, because only the universe as a whole is and can be a perfect internally-related system; and vice versa.

That the universe is not an internally-related system we have already attempted to show in Chapter III. In the following chapter we shall criticize the view that thought and its object are (completely) identified in the perfectly coherent and comprehensive system (and in the case of actual systems, that they are identified in various degrees). If that criticism turns out to be correct, it will mean, among other things, that perfect coherence and comprehensiveness cannot be the ultimate *test* of truth. Only if the perfectly coherent and comprehensive system is *true* will the coherence of actual systems and propositions with it entail their truth, and their lack of coherence with it entail their falsity. But if the imperfect coherence and comprehensiveness of actual systems and propositions would not entail their partial truth, then degrees of truth will not correspond to (for the coherence view, constitute) degrees of coherence and comprehensiveness. But waiving the question of the identification of thought and its object, and assuming that coherence with the perfectly coherent and comprehensive system is in principle the ultimate test of truth, our text question is whether such a test can actually be applied to actual systems and propositions—to scientific theories, laws, and individual propositions in our present discussion.

That the test of coherence or lack of coherence with the ideal system itself cannot be applied is clear from the fact that we do not, and can never, actually have the ideal system to begin with. (Further, if we did have it, the whole problem of testing propositions and systems would not arise.) The question therefore becomes whether or not the actual imperfect coherence and comprehensiveness which actual systems exhibit can be taken as an indication of truth, and of the extent of this truth in any given case.

The answer to this question seems to be in the affirmative if the extent (for the advocates of coherence, the degree) of truth of a limited system is determined by the extent of its coherence and comprehensiveness. In that case, the extent of the latter will be an indication of the extent of the truth of the system, and therefore will serve as a test of this truth. In other words, the answer will be in the affirmative if the view that truth lies in coherence is assumed. Otherwise, I do not see any reason why a more coherent and comprehensive system should be more true, or nearer to the truth, than a less coherent and a less comprehensive one. It might be said that the more coherent and comprehensive system is *more likely* to be true, or is more likely to be more true than a less coherent and less comprehensive system. But I do not see why even this should follow, unless coherence is held to constitute truth. For though all true propositions are consistent with one another, and some true propositions entail and/or are entailed by some other true propositions, it does not follow that if we have a system in which propositions do entail and/or are entailed by other propositions, either singly or together, these propositions or the system as a whole would be true, however comprehensive the system may be. Both systems, the one which is more coherent and more comprehensive, and the one which is less coherent and less comprehensive, may be false. And this applies, it seems to me, to all systems which are coherent and comprehensive to varying extents.

Our conclusion is that if the coherence and comprehensiveness of actual systems are to be taken as the test of their truth, it must be shown first that truth lies in coherence. However, in the following chapter we shall try to show that truth does not lie in coherence. And if *that* is true, the coherence test, in the case of actual systems, would lose its logical grounds.

A word about the role which logical consistency and inconsistency play in testing a theory is in place here. A theory can be legitimately regarded as probably false if it is inconsistent with the body of theories which are accepted as true at any given moment; provided that the latter have sufficient grounds for being regarded as true in the first place. But from the mere fact that a theory (and the same applies to individual propositions) is inconsistent with a body of accepted theories we cannot conclude that the latter is false. It might very well be that the former is false and the latter is true. This holds even if a *single* proposition conflicts with the most comprehensive and logically systematic or coherent system we may have short of the ideal system. We are not, logically speaking, constrained to reject a proposition or theory and to accept its contradictory as true merely on the ground that it is inconsistent with a system, even the most coherent and comprehensive system. Bosanquet puts the coherence test of truth in the form of "Either this or Nothing,"[38] which for our purposes here may be stated as "Either you accept the contradictory of a proposition inconsistent with the system which purports to be true, or you destroy the whole system and are left with nothing." This can only be valid if the system concerned is true and we know that it is true (at least if we have some evidence that it is probably true). Bosanquet envisions this criterion as ultimately resting on the distinction: "Either this or you destroy the whole ideal system of truth or knowledge." For a proposition is false for Bosanquet (as also to the other advocates of the coherence test) if it is inconsistent with the ideal system of truth or knowledge. And it is true that a proposition which is inconsistent with the ideal system would be false, because the ideal system itself is *true*. However, if we are actually to use the rule "either this or nothing" as a test of truth, we have to use it in cases where the "either/or"

---

[38] *Implication and Linear Inference.* Bosanquet uses this notion extensively throughout the book. Cf. also Ewing, I.C.S., pp. 236-250.

involves not an actual proposition or an actual theory on the one hand and the ideal system on the other, but only actual, limited systems on both sides so to speak; or an actual proposition on one side and an actual system on the other. But however comprehensive a system we may have on one side, "This or Nothing" cannot serve as a test unless the comprehensive system is known to be *true* (or probably *true*). Hence "This or Nothing" cannot be the ultimate (in the sense of what is logically foundational or basic) test of truth.

On the other hand, the consistency of a proposition or theory with another theory cannot be a test of the truth of the former even if we assume that the latter is true. For a false proposition or theory can be consistent with a true one, since we have attempted to show that reality is not an all-embracing internally-related system.

Finally, the fact that a proposition or theory q is implied by proposition or theory p can only serve as a test of truth if p is already known to be true; and though p itself may be known to be true because it is implied by a true proposition or theory r, clearly we cannot proceed in this way, on pain of infinite regress, without finally coming to a proposition or a theory whose truth is known on other grounds than its being implied by another proposition or theory.

But what about the confirmation of two or more theories through "mutual support"? Is it not the case that theories which have no antecedent evidence acquire a degree of probability through their being found to cohere with each other in the sense that the one is found to be consistent with the other or others, or to imply or be implied by them? The answer, to my mind, is No. Unless these theories—and the same applies to individual propositions—have some degree of probability on independent grounds, their coherence with each other would not lend them any degree of probability; though, if they do have some initial probability, their coherence with each other would make them more probable than before. Such initial probability cannot ultimately rest on the coherence of the theories concerned with other theories: one of the theories at least must rest on other grounds—viz, on correspondence with facts, before it can serve to lend probability to theories which cohere with it.

Now suppose we have the following situation, outlined by Arthur Pap in illustrating what he calls "coherence" or "reciprocal confirmation." This is not what the champions of coherence mean by "mutual support" but it seems to be relevant here. Different methods of computing a given constant involved in a given number of different theories are found to yield consistent results: for instance the computing of "... the mass of the earth from the acceleration of falling bodies near the surface of the earth (and thus indirectly perhaps from the period of a pendulum of known length) and from the acceleration of the moon...."[39] The consistent results obtained serve to confirm the laws of falling bodies and the laws of the pendulum, among others. Indeed, Pap holds that this kind of confirmation is the only kind possible in physics.[40] And this he calls "reciprocal confirmation."

A little reflection shows that this does not affect what we have said so far. From Pap's example it is seen that what Pap means by the term 'consistent results' is results which are either the same, or are nearly the same. The mass of the earth computed in different ways is found to be approximately if not exactly the same. This, indeed, lends support to the laws from which the result is obtained. It also shows that these laws are at least mutually consistent. But what exactly lends them support is not their consistency with each other (or if one of them implies the other, or they imply each other, these implications), but rather the obtaining of the same results *despite the fact* (or the assumption) *that they are different and logically independent theories.* The rationale of this is that it would be improbable that this "consistency" should be purely accidental. More precisely, the rationale is that it is unlikely that these results should be the same unless they are true, *if the theories are logically independent*;[41] especially as different

---

39 *Elements Of Analytic Philosophy*, p. 361.
40 Ibid., p. 362. See also Philipp Frank, *modern science and its philosophy*, Cambridge, Massachusetts, 1950, pp. 102, 107-108.
41 Note that this is necessary if the "consistency" of the results obtained is to be taken as "reciprocal confirmation" of the theories involved. If these theories imply one another, the "consistency" of the results obtained would be logically equivalent to the confirmation of one and the same theory by the empirical testing of *different implications* drawn from it.

empirical facts are used in obtaining them. This presumption is strengthened if further results independently obtained by means of other aspects of the two theories coincide; as the further application of the theories makes accidental coincidence still more unlikely.

We have been arguing that at least some scientific theories have independent grounds, that not every scientific theory implies or is implied by the whole body of actual scientific knowledge. Our discussion in Chapter III gives this view further support. As we have attempted to show there, the universe, even the physical universe, is not a network of internally-related parts. This implies that scientific knowledge cannot be—even ideally—a logical system in which every statement and every theory or law implies and is implied by the rest of the system. *A fortiori*, it is false that all actual scientific theories and laws we have at any given time imply and are implied by one another; i. e., at least some scientific theories have independent grounds.

Concerning the relation between the coherence test and the coherence theory of reality, Ewings says—

> Even if coherence were not *the* criterion but *only one* criterion of truth, it is difficult to see how we could possibly be justified in supposing that because a proposition fulfilled the coherence test it was true unless we assumed that the real was coherent. If something might be real and yet incoherent, why should a coherent view be more worthy of acceptance, more likely to be true, than an incoherent?[42]

My only objection to this way of putting the matter is that Ewing considers the rejection of the coherence theory of reality as implying the assertion that reality is *incoherent*, i. e., chaotic, disorderly, inconsistent or self-contradictory; which is certainly false. As we have tried to show in detail in Chapter III, the rejection of the coherence theory of reality need consist only in the assertion that at least some (kinds of) relations are external. And there is nothing self-contradictory about the nature of reality which this view involves. Hence also, our attempt to show that coherence is not *the* test of truth does not commit us to the view that reality

---

42 I.C.S., p. 250. Italics in original.

is *in*coherent in the sense that it is inconsistent or self-contradictory. Of course, as Ewings says, if reality is incoherent (in the sense explained), coherence could not be even *a* test of truth. But the view that reality is incoherent (in the sense explained) is not a necessary condition for the rejection of the coherence test. That the coherence test logically presupposes the coherence theory of reality can be seen briefly as follows: The coherence test of truth implies that when we make a true proposition, we implicitly assert an indefinite number of other propositions (all other propositions which can be truly asserted about reality); and when we make a false proposition, we implicitly assert an indefinite number of other propositions (all other possible propositions which are false). This presupposes the premise that for any proposition to be true, an indefinite number of other propositions must be true; or the truth of any proposition implies the truth of an indefinite number of other propositions. Similarly, *mutatis mutandis*, with false propositions. (Hence it is that for the coherence test a proposition stands or falls with the entire possible system of true propositions, the ideal system: a view succinctly expressed by Bosanquet's "This or nothing.")

But all true propositions cannot be logically related in this way, unless the facts which these propositions assert are themselves logically related, such that no fact could be what it is unless every other fact in the universe is what it is. This is precisely the view that reality is an internally-related system (in Ewing's senses seven to ten which we have discussed).

This gives us a further ground for rejecting the coherence test of truth in general, whether in connection with particular propositions, empirical generalizations, empirical laws, scientific theories or philosophical doctrines: the doctrine of internal relations, we have attempted to show, is false; therefore the doctrine that coherence constitutes *the* test of truth is untenable.

To sum up our results in this chapter: We have examined the doctrine that coherence is the (sole and whole) test of empirical truth, in the case of various kinds of individual empirical propositions and in the case of empirical laws and theories. Our examination seemed to show that coherence is not *the whole test* of truth in the case of any kind of empirical proposition or sets of propositions we discussed, including empirical laws and theories. We have found that consistency, inconsistency and implication are some of the tools used in specific kinds of situations to test propositions and sets of propositions. In that sense they can be considered as part of, or even as the entire, test of truth in specified kinds of situations; as the case may be. But unless some proposition is assumed to be true in a given testing situation, logical facts like the above-mentioned cannot be of any actual use: an appeal to experience, to empirical facts, is ultimately necessary. Without such a reference to experience or facts somewhere or other, logic is hepless in the testing of empirical propositions or sets of them. And the appeal to facts or experience, though it does involve the appeal to language, our past experience, our knowledge and, sometimes, the testimony of others, also involves an appeal to something which is outside any system of propositions; namely, that which is interpreted—the experience or the facts themselves.

CHAPTER V

COHERENCE AS THE NATURE OF TRUTH: A CRITIQUE

In the previous chapter an attempt was made to criticize the view that coherence is the (or the sole) test of truth. In the present chapter we shall attempt to criticize the view that coherence constitutes the nature of truth, as the advocates of the coherence theory maintain. But before we begin our main discussion, we have to answer a question which arises in relation to chapter four. The question is this: Granted that the problem of the nature of truth is a distinct problem from that of the test of truth, what is the logical relation (if any) between the nature of truth and the test of truth? More precisely, does one's commitment to a given theory of the nature of truth logically commit one to a certain theory of the test of truth (or vice versa)? And since we are here interested primarily in the coherence theory: Can the view that coherence is the test of truth be false (as we have attempted to show that it is) and yet the view that coherence constitutes the nature of truth be true?

In answering these questions, and especially the last one, it is well to state the views of some of the advocates of the coherence theory on the matter. According to Blanshard, the acceptance of coherence as a test of truth commits us logically to accepting coherence as the nature of truth. If we take coherence as the test of truth and yet take something else, say correspondence, as the nature of truth, we will find that we cannot intelligibly hold that coherence is the test of truth. What is more, nothing else then can serve as the test of truth.[1] "In the end, the only test of truth that is not misleading is the special nature or character that is itself constitutive of truth."[2] On the other hand, Ewing accepts coherence as the test of truth but rejects it as the nature of truth; which implies that he does not accept the view that acceptance of

---

1 N. T., vol. II. pp. 267-268.
2 *Ibid.*, p. 268.

coherence as the test of truth requires the acceptance of coherence as the nature of truth, or that the rejection of coherence as the nature of truth precludes its acceptance as the test of truth.[3]

Now it is true that no definition of 'truth' or of 'true'—whether that of the coherence, the correspondence, the semantic, the pragmatic, or any other theory—furnishes us, as Carnap rightly says, with any criterion or criteria for testing truth or falsity, understanding by the criterion or criteria (some or all of) the actual procedures, logical or empirical or both, actually employed or employable in testing propositions or sets of propositions. The only thing which the definition of truth furnishes us in this connection is the ultimate objective or aim of the employment of the various procedures of verification. For example, if truth is defined as a relation of correspondence between a proposition and a matter of fact, then the end or objective of verification becomes to discover whether such a relation holds or does not hold in the case af any given proposition. Thus, assuming that there are no difficulties concerning the meaning of a statement such as "The bird singing

---

[3] With regard to the more general logical position which this view implies, namely, that a given view of the nature of truth does not logically determine a given (corresponding) view of the test of truth, or vice versa, we may mention Arthur Pap and Rudolf Carnap. Pap writes: "It is quite conceivable that the coherence theory is a description of how the truth or falsehood of statements comes to be known rather than an analysis of the meaning of "true".... One might agree that a given statement is accepted as true in virtue of standing in certain logical relations to other statements; still it would not follow that in calling it true one *mean*s to ascribe to it those relations." (*Elements of Analytic Philosophy*, p. 356. Italics in original) As a matter of fact, Pap accepts Tarski's semantic theory as an analysis of the meaning of 'truth' or 'true,' and (at least in the case of empirical hypotheses and laws) what he calls "coherence" or "reciprocal confirmation" (see Chapter IV, p. 139 of the present work) as the test of truth. And Carnap: "We must not expect the definition of truth to furnish a criterion of confirmation such as is sought in epistemological analyses. On the basis of this [Tarski's type of] definition the question regarding the criterion of truth can be given only a trivial answer, which consists in the statement itself. Thus, from the definition of truth we can conclude only, e. g.: The statement "Snow is white" is true if and only if snow is white. This conclusion is surely correct... But the question of the criterion of confirmation is thereby left unanswered." ("Truth And Confirmation," *Readings in Philosophical* Analysis, New York, [1949], edited by A. Feigl and W. Sellars, p. 120)

outside is a mocking-bird," this statement can be verified by an empirical observation or a series of observations designed to discover whether or not what I am hearing now is a mocking-bird. The logical outcome of these procedures is the discovery of whether or not the truth-relation exists in this case. But the kind of observations I or another would and, more importantly, *can* make to verify the given statement, depends not only on the alleged matter of fact—the alleged mocking-bird's song—but on all sorts of other things involved in observing this alleged mocking-bird's song. The final end of testing such a statement is to discover whether the alleged relation between a statement and an alleged matter of fact exists. For that end, the existence or non-existence of the alleged matter of fact is ascertained. Since the term 'test,' though vague and often employed in different senses, does not include in its meaning, either in ordinary discourse or in philosophy, the end or objective of the procedures (thus we speak of the end or objective *of* a test or we say that a criterion is a criterion *of* truth), we cannot properly speak of the test of truth as being logically determined by the nature of truth. But there is a sense in which the nature of truth does determine *in part* the nature of the test or tests of truth: namely, in the different sense that the nature of the state of affairs which is asserted by a proposition to be tested determines in part the *kind* of procedures which can be employed in testing the proposition.[4] This we have already seen to some extent in discussing the methods of testing propositions about sensible objects, empirical generalizations, and empirical laws and theories. But it should be emphasized that it is only the kinds of procedures which are thus determined; also that this determination is only partial.

However, in the case of the coherence theory of truth the situation is different—not that the coherence view of truth is an exception to the above—but because of a peculiar relationship between coherence as the nature and coherence as the test of

---

4 Of course the particular logical content of the proposition to be verified, i. e., in this case the nature of the state of affairs which makes the proposition true or false, may determine in part the *particular* procedures to be employed in verifying it. But we are not concerned with that here.

truth, on the one hand, and the coherence view of reality on the other hand. As we have seen in Chapters I and II, coherence as the nature of truth logically rests upon the coherence theory of reality; similarly we have seen that the coherence test of truth logically rests upon the coherence theory of reality. This establishes an indirect logical relation between coherence as the nature of truth and coherence as the test of truth which seems to be absent in the other types of theories of truth mentioned above. This logical relation does not entitle us to infer either that if coherence constitutes the nature of truth it must also be the test of truth, or its converse. But we are entitled to affirm that if the coherence theory of reality is false, then coherence cannot be either the test of truth or the nature of truth. As will be remembered, we have already used this line of argument in the case of the coherence test of truth in Chapter IV. Here we may complete our argument. Coherence as the nature of truth cannot be true unless the coherence theory of reality is true; but we have attempted to show that the latter is false; hence coherence does not seem to us to constitute the nature of truth.

Obviously, however, we cannot rest satisfied with one argument against the theory that coherence constitutes the nature of truth. As in chapters three and four, we shall devote the remaining part of this chapter to criticizing the negative and positive arguments presented by the defenders of the view, and to supporting our contention further by offering some positive criticisms of the theory itself.[5]

---

[5] It is to be noted that the advocates of the view assume that the term 'truth' (and 'true'), at least as used in relation to statements, has only one meaning; that it signifies a property which is common to all statements which are said to be true. This, of course, does not prevent the advocates of the view from admitting, or holding, that 'truth' and 'true' may have different, distinct uses in different linguistic contexts; unless they were to maintain (which they do not) that 'use' and 'meaning' are synonymous. I think they would rather maintain that all the different uses, assuming that different uses exist, involve the same signification— the property called "truth."

For the view that 'true,' as applied to statements, has different, distinct uses, and for an analysis of some of the chief of these uses, see for example, P. F. Strawson "Truth" (*Analysis*, vol. IX, no. 6 (June, 1949), pp. 83 ff.). But note that Strawson confines his analysis to the word 'true,' which refers (at least directly) to statements, and does not analyze the uses of 'truth,' which has different uses from 'true.'

One objection with some *prima facie* plausibility, which might be raised against the view under consideration, is derived from linguistic usage. It may be said that the coherence view is false because the term 'truth' does not, in ordinary usage, mean coherence. When we say: "The weather is cold to-day," we do not mean that this statement coheres with a system of truth or knowledge, that it entails and is entailed by every other true statement, jointly or even singly (Joachim, Blanshard).

Now the coherence theory, or rather, the advocates of the coherence theory, do not contradict ordinary usage in calling any actual statements false which at the same time are generally accepted as true because they seem in some sense to "agree" with or "correspond" to facts (though the advocates of the coherence theory would interpret this "agreement" differently); for instance, in the case of accepted scientific propositions.[6] We may therefore suppose that by the term 'truth,' in such statements as "The truth of a statement is...," they purport to designate[7] the same referent, "truth," which the term ordinarily designates, assuming that it does ordinarily designate anything at all. If the defender of coherence is willing to hold this, the objection takes the form of an assertion that the coherence view is mistaken in attributing to true propositions the alleged defining characteristic, "coherence."[8] The task of the defender of the view would then consist in showing that true propositions do possess coherence as the defining characteristic; that coherence, to use traditional terminology, is the essence of truth. And the task of his critic would be to show that this is not the case. The former is in fact what the advocates of coherence, such as Bradley, Bosanquet and Blanshard, seem to be doing—though they would not describe what they are doing in the way we have done—in offering arguments for the coherence view and against its rivals.

---

6 The defenders of coherence would say that such propositions possess only a degree of truth and are not merely not certain. But this is immaterial here.

7 Using 'designate' in a wide sense and not, for instance, in the sense of Lewis' 'denotation.' As a matter of fact, what the term 'designate' refers to here is Lewis' "comprehension."

8 The objector might be willing to hold that coherence is a property or a set of properties possessed by true statements; but he might deny that it defines 'truth' as ordinarily used.

Another way of stating this account of the contention of the coherence view would be that if 'truth' is ordinarily used with the signification the critics claim for it, then 'truth' does not and cannot mean (in the sense of refer to) anything actual or real, or perhaps even anything possible; since there is, and perhaps there can be, no such thing as a relation or the absence of a relation of "agreement" or "correspondence" between statements and independent facts—or anything else which the critics of coherence may construe the referent of 'truth' to be. For the defender of coherence the word 'truth,' in the sense in which the critics understand it, would then have the same logical status as 'Centaur' or 'golden mountain,' if not 'square circle' or 'circular triangle' (i. e., it would either denote nothing or comprehend nothing, in Lewis' sense of 'denotation' and 'comprehension').[9]

Leaving aside this extreme view, and assuming that the coherence view purports to give the correct analysis of the meaning of 'truth' (in the requisite sense) as ordinarily used, the task of the defender of coherence lies in proving this point. This he attempts to do by offering arguments that coherence constitutes the nature of truth or constitutes the meaning of 'truth.' Since we do not accept this view, we might show its falsity by giving a positive analysis of the meaning of 'truth' as it is ordinarily used. But this we shall not attempt to do here. We shall, rather, criticize the coherence view itself; making use, however, of some of the things which are involved in the meaning of 'truth' (in the requisite sense) as it is ordinarily used.[10]

---

9 Both our hypothetical critics and the advocates of coherence assume that 'truth,' as applied to statements, does have a referent (comprehension). But if 'truth' does not have a referent at all, as some would hold, the coherence theory and the above type of reply would fall to pieces.

We might imagine that the advocate of coherence wants to *legislate* that we use 'truth' to mean coherence, whether 'truth' (in the requisite sense) as ordinarily used does designate something other than coherence, or whether it does dot designate anything at all. I do not think, however, that this is what the advocate of coherence is really trying to do.

10 In this chapter and throughout the entire present work, I am using 'true' and 'truth' in relation to statements and judgments or propositions, except where otherwise indicated.

One of the central tenets of the present doctrine is the view that judgments cannot be either true or false except within the system of knowledge—ultimately, the ideal system of knowledge; since individual judgments cannot have any meaning or be judgments at all except in so far they as cohere (partly or fully) with the ideal system. Truth is a characteristic of the ideal system of knowledge and only derivatively of individual judgments, in so far as they cohere with it. Truth or falsity is not and cannot be a property of isolated judgments, and so cannot consist in, say, a relation of correspondence or the absence of correspondence, respectively, with independent matters of fact. The advocate of coherence is willing to say that in a sense (relatively) true judgments "agree" with or "reflect" reality; but he maintains that this does not constitute their truth. True judgments would "reflect" reality in so far as and because they cohere with the ideal system of knowledge rather than that they are true because they "reflect" or "agree" with reality. Similarly with false judgments. However, the advocate of coherence would probably consider this way of putting the matter misleading and inexact.

Now according to the coherence theory perfect coherence or perfectly coherent knowledge is an ideal which is actually never fully realized. But Blanshard, though he agrees with Ewing that a fully satisfactory definition of this ideal cannot be given, does give a definition of it. He states: "Certainly this ideal goes far beyond mere consistency. Fully coherent knowledge would be knowledge in which every judgment entailed, and was entailed by, the rest of the system."[11] Further on he adds that in "a completely satisfactory system... no proposition would be arbitrary, every proposition would be entailed by the others jointly and even singly...."[12] (In a footnote he adds in effect that coherence can be defined without the phrase "even singly.")

Joachim formulates the notion of coherence, though he admits that his formulation is rough and provisional, as conceivability:

Anything is true which can be conceived. It is true because, and in so far as, it can be conceived.... To 'conceive' means for us to think out clearly and

---

[11] N. T., vol. II, p. 264.
[12] *Ibid.*, p. 265.

logically, to hold many elements together in a connexion necessitated by their several contents. And to be 'conceivable' means to be a 'significant whole,' or a whole possessed of meaning for thought. A 'significant whole' is such that all its constituent elements reciprocally involve one another, or reciprocally determine one another's being as contributory features in a single concrete meaning. The elements thus cohering constitute a whole which may be said to control the reciprocal adjustment of its elements, as an end controls its constituent means.[13]

In short, "... 'conceivability' means... *systematic coherence.* ..."[14]

Bradley writes:

Truth is an ideal expression of the Universe, at once coherent and comprehensive. It must not conflict with itself, and there must be no suggestion which fails to fall inside it. Perfect truth in short must realize the idea of a systematic whole.[15]

Taking Blanshard's definition of fully coherent knowledge, which is the most definite and explicit of the ones just given, we may say that 'coherence' is taken by the advocates of the theory to mean the relation of reciprocal entailment. Now if coherence —and so truth—consists in a logical relation, then any proposition in the ideal system is true because it has that relation to the rest of the propositions in the system. But a logical relation, like any other kind of relation, is not and cannot be part of the nature of a proposition. We have already had occasion to point out in Chapter II that relations cannot be said to be a part of their terms. On this emendment, if truth is identified with the relation of coherence, individual propositions even within the ideal system will not possess truth except in so far as they have the *relational characteristic* of being true (or cohering). Similarly the ideal system (and every partial system) will be true only in the sense that it includes relations which constitute truth.

What, now, is the relation between coherence and reality? If truth is a logical relation of entailment the question arises as to whether a system of coherent propositions and ideally the perfect

---

13 *The Nature of Truth*, p. 66.
14 *Ibid.*, pp. 67-68. Italics in original.
15 E. T., p. 223.

system of coherent propositions, reflects or agrees with reality. For the advocates of coherence themselves speak of a coherent system as "representing" reality. Blanshard, speaking of Bradley, writes—

> Bradley, for example, speaks of our judgements as 'representatives' of reality which are true 'just so far as they agree with, and do not diverge from', the real. Again, 'truth, to be true, must be true of something, and this something itself is not truth. This obvious view I endorse.'[16]

Indeed, any account of truth, to be adequate, must involve reference to what true judgments are about, namely reality; since such a reference is involved in the meaning of the words 'truth' and 'true' as ordinarily used; though such a reference is probably only implicit, and not a part of the explicit meaning of 'truth' or 'true' (i.e., it may be that 'true' does not *mean* "agreeing" or "corresponding" with or "reflecting" reality).

But if so, what justifies us in asserting that what is "true" according to the coherence view is true of reality? Or, but less misleadingly and using Bradley's own term, that a coherent system represents reality? Is coherence ("truth") a *logical consequence* of its representing reality? Or is coherence always, as a matter of fact, *accompanied* by the representation of reality? Or is coherence the *logical ground* for the representation of reality? But is not the representation of reality at least a part of what is involved in the meaning of 'truth' and 'true'? If it is not, or at least, if the advocates of coherence do not think so, why are they anxious to show that a coherent system represents or is representative of reality? True, Bradley's notion of representation of reality, for instance, is not what the correspondence theory of truth, for instance, takes it to be. But at least it involves some notion of a relation with reality which is analogous to that envisioned by the correspondence theory. Is not this eagerness on the part of the advocates of coherence on this point a result of their desire not to depart from the ordinary meaning of 'truth' and 'true'? For obviously, if what they are actually doing is to stipulate a totally

---

16 N. T., vol. II, p. 273. Blanshard, in footnote two on the same page adds a further remark by Bradley: 'If my idea is to work it must correspond to a determinate being it cannot be said to make.'

different meaning for 'truth' and 'true,' their use of the words 'truth' and 'true' would merely serve to confuse us by making us think that they are talking about the same thing we talk about in using 'truth' and 'true.' Also, if they are stipulating, the issue between the advocates of coherence and those who give an analysis of the meaning of the ordinary words 'truth' and 'true' will be only apparent. The two groups will not be giving different analyses of the same but, rather, of different meanings.

Bradley's above-quoted statement that our judgments are true "just so far as they agree with, and do not diverge from," the real seems to indicate that for the advocate of coherence the latter ("agreement" with or "representation" of reality) is a logical condition of the former (coherence of truth). But it might also be thought that the latter is rather a logical consequence of the former. In other words, that judgments "agree" with or "represent" reality as a consequence of and to the extent in which they are coherent. Both of these views, however, the advocate of coherence would reject as setting up a false antithesis and dichotomy between coherence and "agreement" with reality. True, he would say, there cannot be coherence without "agreement" with reality; and vice versa. But this is because coherence and "agreement" with reality are one and the same thing looked at from different angles. The false antithesis and dichotomy arise only because a coherent system of judgments is thought of as something different in nature from reality (its object); something which is set over and against it and is related externally to it; something which may or may not "agree" with reality. Hence the problem of fitting coherence and "agreement" with reality together does not arise. Coherence and "agreement" with reality are two sides of one and the same coin. The false opposition between judgments and reality is based on a false dualism between mind or thought and an external world which is supposed to be different in kind from it—which is material, or at any rate, is non-mental,—a self-sufficient and self-enclosed world. On the contrary, perfect truth *is* reality; or more precisely, one aspect of reality: a judgment is true in so far as and in the degree in which it is real, and the perfect system of truth is reality itself conceived ideally, reality manifesting itself in the form of ideas. But note that for Bradley, strictly speaking, truth can become perfect truth, or pass completely into reality, only when it ceases to be ideal and so ceases to be a system and hence truth. The ultimate identification of truth or thought and reality is arrived at only by the suicide of thought, the passage of truth into something which is not truth but which includes, though it transcends, truth. Ideas, says Bradley, "represent" reality. By this he means—

> That less or more they actually possess the character and type of absolute truth and reality. They can take the place of the Real to varying extents, because containing in themselves less or more of its nature. They are its representatives, worse or better, in proportion as they present us with truth affected by greater or less derangement.[17]

He adds: "We may put it otherwise by saying that truths are true, according as it would take less or more to convert them into reality."[18] Bosanquet states with great clarity his view of the nature of truth and its relation to reality. I quote:

> Truth seems to me to have no meaning unless (1) it is reality; [and in a footnote he adds: "The phrase "it is *about* reality" suggests that its quality depends on representing something outside it. But this is upside down; it is reality which becomes truth when it takes ideal form."] (2) is in the form of ideas. It is the form which reality assumes when expressed through ideas in particular minds. It is unintelligible if this unity is broken up. If you suppose a course of ideas inexpressive of reality, or a reality which has no expression in ideal form, you have destroyed the essence of truth. This is the only way of understanding the paradox about the making of truth and its discovery. You can hammer upon either side of this antithesis for ever; but you cannot possibly make sense without both. Certainly truth comes to be when we find it out; the very determinations in which it consists, the selection and connection of things and relations, had for all we know no emphasis, no distinguished place in the scheme of the universe before or apart from our mental operations. But no less certainly it was true before it was found out; if it was not true before it could not be true when it was found out. It is of no use to deny either of these paradoxes; they naturally affirm themselves if we insist on dismembering an essential unity.[19]

Similarly, he says:

> You cannot have truth except as reality in ideal form. And you cannot know reality except by apprehending the ideal form in its concrete spirit

---

17 A. R., pp. 362-363. Quoted from N. T., vol. II, p. 273.
18 *Ibid.*
19 *Implication And Linear Inference*, pp. 148-149. Italics in original.

and all its detail. This does not mean that reality is qualified as or by a series of psychical events. The qualification of reality by ideas is from the beginning a qualification by meanings. This is the significance of thought, which is in its essence an effort to define the universe by meanings adequately conditioned; to reconstruct the unity of the real in ideal or discursive form.[20]

For Blanshard, as we have seen in Chapter I, the relation between thought and its object is that of a purpose partially realized and a purpose fulfilled completely. "Thought, we have insisted, *is* its object realized imperfectly, and a system of thought is true just so far as it succeeds in embodying that end which thought in its very essence is seeking to embody."[21] The relation between thought and its object is like the relation "between seed and flower, or between the sapling and the tree."[22] Such a relation cannot be called a relation of correspondence or anything approaching correspondence.

This view of the relation between thought and its object takes us to the heart of Idealist metaphysics on which it is based. The specific metaphysical grounds involved here are (a) that the objects of thought—and specifically the so-called external world—are ideal in nature. Sensible objects, which constitute the external world—since the Absolute Idealist denies the existence of a world of unperceived and unperceivable non-mental objects which are (partly) the causes of sensible objects—are ideal in character. They are not the products of the perception or experience of the individual, finite percipient; the sensible world transcends the experience of any individual percipient at any given moment; it is not a series of private psychic events. Nevertheless, sensible objects are composed of and are nothing but universals. They exist only as the experience of some subject, primarily of the Absolute. As a matter of fact the sensible world is a fragmentary and partial manifestation or appearance of the Absolute in our experience or consciousness; it is an abstraction if taken apart from the larger context in which alone it (and the finite human selves) can exist—the Absolute or Reality. Nor is there a so-called material substance or substratum underlying the sensible qualities and their relations,

---
20 *Ibid.*, p. 149.
21 N. T., vol. II, p. 273. Italics in original.
22 *Ibid.*

a substratum in which these qualities and relations may be supposed to inhere. To quote Calkins, "Qualities and relations are the only discovered factors of objects as known. The inferred object[23] itself must, therefore, consist in relations, in sense qualities, or in a combination of the two; or else it is an object of unknown nature."[24] Watson, "the Canadian Hegelian," says:

> In the ordinary view of correspondence... a dualism is assumed between the idea in the mind and the object of which it is supposed to be a copy. Now... an idea of the kind supposed is a pure fiction.... There are not two things —an idea of sensation, as Locke calls it, and a sensible object—but what is called an idea of sensation is simply the consciousness of a sensible object.[25]

This quotation does not point out the important notion that the object which we apprehend in the form of an "idea" is more than this "idea." And it is precisely this notion that the object is always more than our apprehension or experience of it; that the ideal expression of reality always falls short of the fullness of reality; that the 'what' always falls short of and hence is discrepant with the 'that' (to use Bradley's expression), which is

---

[23] This does not make clear, nor are the Absolute Idealists in general always clear, about the distinction between (a) the notion of a substratum in which sensible qualities themselves inhere, something of which sensible qualities form a part, and (b) the different notion advocated by Epistemological Dualism, of objects which may have some of the qualities (the so-called primary qualities) sensible objects possess, but which are numerically distinct from sensible objects and are in part the causes of the production of these objects in the mind or the brain, as the type of Epistemological Dualism involved may be. It is true that, generally speaking, Epistemological Dualism conceives of sensible objects as nothing but a complex of sensible qualities, i. e., it denies the existence of a material substratum in which sensible qualities inhere. It is also true that those who believe in the existence of a material substratum underlying sensible qualities reject Epistemological Dualism; that is, reject the existence of objects numerically distinct from sensible qualities and the underlying substratum. But the two notions are nonetheless different and should not be confused or identified with each other.

[24] "The Idealist to The Realist," *The Journal of Philosophy, Psychology And Scientific Method*, vol. VIII. no. 17 (August, 1911), p. 454.

[25] Quoted from L. P. Chambers, "A Defence of Monism," *Journal Of Philosophy*, vol. XXXII, No. 5 (February, 1935), p. 114. Note that here Waston is rejecting Epistemological Dualism, i. e., the view of objects discussed under (b) in footnote 23.

crucial for us here. Bradley states this point concisely in the following way:

> I mean that its [the presented object's] detail always goes beyond itself, and is indefinitely relative to something outside. In its given content it has relations which do not terminate within that content; and its existence therefore is not exhausted by itself, as we ever can have it. If I may use the metaphor, it has always edges which are ragged in such a way as to imply another existence from which it has been torn, and without which it really does not exist. Thus the content of the subject strives, we may say, unsuccessfully towards an all-inclusive whole.[26]

(b) The second main metaphysical ground is the Idealist's account of judgments. Judgments are not private psychic occurrences in individual minds, or the act of judging itself, but rather that which is judged, the meaning entertained: and this is not private or subjective. But on the other hand, judgments are not what the Platonic Neo-Realists call "propositions"; they are not self-subsistent entities outside and independent of individual minds but which may be "exemplified" in thought. Nor are judgments composed of abstract subsistent entities or abstract universals. The Idealist rejects the notion of abstract universals and substitutes for it the notion of the concrete universal. The concrete universal is conceived as existing or as partially realized *in* particulars—in concepts and in sensible objects. As a matter of fact, only ultimate reality or the Absolute fully realizes the concrete universal, is a concrete universal in the fullest sense.

This shows that a full criticism of the conception of the relation between judgments and their objects embodied in the coherence theory of truth requires a criticism of at least (a) and (b). This we cannot do within the scope and limits of the present work. We do hold that the external world is not ideal in character, that it is not an abstraction, and that the notion of the concrete universal is mistaken. But we shall not and cannot support our views in the present work. Fortunately we can still criticize the coherence theory with regard to the point under discussion without showing that the external world is not ideal or that the notion of the concrete universal is mistaken.

---

26 A. R., pp. 176–177.

(1) Assuming that the external world or reality as a whole is ideal, and that judgments, whether true or false, are not self-subsistent entities, it still remains that sensible objects or, in general, the objects or facts with which judgments or systems of judgment are said to "agree" or not to "agree," are and remain numerically and qualitatively distinct from judgments (thought). The absolute distinction is not eliminated or obliterated if both are conceived to be ideal. In the latter case the only difference would be that the distinction is and has to be drawn within an ideal reality. Judgments do not have the sensible qualities their objects possess; they are composed of concepts, while objects are not concepts or congeries of concepts. Judgments and concepts are not green or yellow or hard or extended; sensible objects are perceived and not conceived (when we conceive a sensible object, the conception is not the sensible object itself but the apprehension *of* the object; it is the thought of it or a thought about it). Even granting that the space in which sensible objects are experienced is ideal, i. e., does not exist apart from some consciousness (though this may be the consciousness of the Absolute), concepts and judgments are not in that ideal space or in any space at all.[27] If this is admitted, the question of the "agreement" or lack of "agreement" of the ideally coherent system of *judgments* with this (ideal) sensible world still remains. Unless the Idealist advocate of coherence gives evidence that an ideally coherent system does "agree" or "correspond" with reality—and he does not offer any (positive) evidence for it—we must pronounce the contention of the theory unfounded and thereby reject it.

But even supposing that an ideally coherent system does "agree" with or "reflect" reality, the relation between this system and reality will not be what the Idealist conceives it to be—an identification of thought and its object, the full actualization of thought. If thought (judgments) and sensible objects are and remain qualitatively and numerically distinct (even if ideal), the view that thought is the full *actualization* of its object or that a given judgment is its object *potentially*, becomes meaningless. The

---

[27] The difference remains even if we hold a relational or relativist conception of space; since we would still have extended sensible objects on the one hand and non-extended concepts and judgments on the other hand.

seed can be said (if at all) to be potentially the flower, or the sapling the tree, only because, to begin with, the seed and the flower, the sapling and the tree, are objects of the same kind, i. e., sensible objects; even leaving aside the special kind of relation between them which does not seem to be present in the case of thought and its objects.[28] If so, supposing the ideally coherent system to "agree" with reality, this relation would not be a relation of coherence but of some kind of correspondence; though it would be between the system as a whole rather than of its component propositions in isolation, and the whole of reality. That is, it will not be what any of the ordinary correspondence theories means by 'correspondence,' since these theories regard the relation between true propositions and the matters of fact they assert as obtaining between individual propositions independently of their logical relations to other propositions.

But the advocate of coherence will remind us that if the sensible world is a network of universals, the only kind of relation possible between it and the (perfect) system of thought, even if qualitatively the two are irreducibly distinct, must be one of coherence. This, it will be added, is precisely what is meant by the "identification" of thought and reality.

That the sensible world is not an internally-related system—in the crucial seventh sense—whether of universals or of particulars, we have already emphasized. But even if it were an internally-related system of universals, as thought is supposed to be, the problem remains as to how it and the system of thought can be related by a relation of coherence; since the two systems are different in character. The related terms in the one case are sensible

---

28 Cf. Ewing: "... I find it extraordinarily difficult to take seriously the notion of identity between the idea and its object...." Ewing adds: "... I am aware that the only alternative is to take the cognitive relation as indefinable...." (Review of Blanshard *The Nature Of Thought. Mind*, vol. LIII, No. 209 (January, 1944), pp. 78-79) I do not see how this conclusion follows, and, to begin with, what type of definition Ewing has in mind. Also, what exactly is *"the* cognitive relation"? Further, even if repeated attempts to define the (alleged) cognitive relation, on other grounds than Blanshard's, have failed, this failure is not a sufficient ground for declaring the relation indefinable. I do not see that there is any logical reason why *the* relation should be definable only if we think of it the way Blanshard does. Also Cf. L.A. Reid, *Knowledge And Truth*, London, 1923, pp. 23-24.

qualities, and some of their relations are empirical (the causal relations, spatial and temporal relations); in the other case the terms are conceptual and their relations are purely logical. The logical element of necessity allegedly involved in the case of the causal relations does not diminish the problem; since it is still a fact that the causal relations, as relations, are not logical but empirical, matter of fact, in the sense that they obtain between things and events and not propositions. As for the two systems being systems of universals, their being so would not prevent the relation between them from being a form of correspondence, taking them as a whole and in their parts.

As for the view that judgments are not self-subsistent entities, that in itself does not prevent correspondence from constituting the nature of truth. Correspondence can very well be construed as a relation between what statements mean and facts, even if the meanings of statements are only psychic entities. Or, alternatively, truth can be construed as a relation between the beliefs of the utterer of a statement in making the statement, and facts. And so on.[29]

Let us again consider the notion that an idea is its object partially realized. Obviously, the 'is' here purports to be the 'is' of identity: a completely realized idea would become numerically and not only qualitatively identical with its object. But does this have any meaning? For a thing which is said to be potentially identical with another thing, or is its partial realization, will literally be the other thing when it is actualized. A particular seed *becomes* a particular flower. The particular flower which the seed becomes comes into existence as a result of the process of the seed's growth and change ("actualization"). But this cannot be the kind of relation obtaining between an idea and its object. The object of a given idea either coexists with the idea or does not: if it coexists with it the idea cannot become it; it if does not, it is still difficult to see how it would come into existence *as a result* of a process of "actualization" on the part of the idea; since this and the process of actualization are not a causal or any other

---

29 I am not saying that any of these gives us an adequate account of truth. What I am saying is merely that, logically speaking, correspondence may be construed in these different ways if not in others as well.

temporal and empirical process as in the case of the seed, but merely the continual modification of the idea (judgment) resulting in greater and greater coherence with the system of knowledge.

But there is another point. Since every idea is alleged to cohere in some degree with the system of knowledge, and so has some "reality," it is identical with its object in some degree according to the view discussed. But how can anything be something else *in a degree*: any idea is either identical with its object or it is not. The seed is not a tree when it is a seed; and we may add, it is not a seed when it is a tree. The seed cannot be more or less of a tree. We might say (a) that a germinating seed is *closer to being* a tree than the non-germinating seed. But what we would mean in saying this is that the germinating seed requires a shorter *time* than the non-germinating one to become a tree. Or, (b) if we are comparing a sapling to a seed, in relation to a tree, then in saying that the sapling is closer to being a tree than the seed we would mean (in addition to (a)) that it *resembles* a tree more than the seed. In the case of judgments, when a given judgment is progressively "modified" in the "process" of greater and greater "actualization," what really happens is that the judgment is *replaced* by another which, to use the language of the coherence theory, has a higher degree of truth than the first. This in turn is replaced by another judgment; and so on. The judgment expressed by "This table is green" does not itself become the judgment expressed by "This table is greenish-blue," which we may suppose for illustration to have a higher degree of truth than the former judgment. A thought does not literally become another thought, as a seed literally becomes a tree. There is no temporal process of change involved. So notion (a) above cannot apply to judgments. The only way in which we might meaningfully speak, if at all, of the judgments expressed in "This table is greenish-blue" as closer to being its object than the judgment expressed by "This table is green," is as in (b) above; i. e., that the latter judgment resembles its object more than the former judgment. But this again does not make sense. If as we have tried to show, judgments are by nature qualitatively different from their objects, they cannot resemble them in any literal sense. The only way in which the notion of resemblance can be applicable here is in the sense that the latter judgment corresponds with its object, or reflects it, more faithfully than the former judgment. This is precisely what the coherence theory denies. And even if we take the notion of resemblance in a metaphorical sense, we land into a crude, copy theory of truth. These points and others are well brought out by Ewing—

> As the author [Blanshard] admits, the identity [between idea and object] is never completely attained, so that the only way of distinguishing knowledge from error would have to be by saying that the purpose towards identity was less completely attained in the latter case than in the former. But is this not to define knowledge in terms of resemblance? I do not see how greater or less attainment of a purpose towards identity which will never be completely fulfilled could be measured except in terms of resemblance. The purpose must be to approximate to identity, *i.e.*, to resemble, and does not this bring one back to the copy theory of knowledge which is rightly repudiated by Prof. Blanshard? He admits likeness between ideas and their object, but claims that his theory gives the only intelligible account of this likeness as being "the likeness of what exists in potency to the same thing actualized" (p. 495), and this might be all right if the idea ever were completely actualized as its object so that it was numerically the same, but since this does not happen we cannot define the likeness of the one to the other in terms of becoming the other since the one never becomes the other but only becomes more like the other.[30]

But Ewing errs in locating the ground of his criticism. It is not primarily because no actual idea ever becomes actualized as its object that the relation between an idea and its object is reduced to one of qualitative resemblance. If it were so, this criticism would apply only to ideas which are not a part of the ideal system of thought. The ideal system would still be said to be qualitatively (and for Ewing,[31] numerically) identical with its object. But our point is that the criticism applies equally to the ideal system of thought. The only way in which ideas could, if at all, become identical with their objects, whether these ideas are actual or imperfect, or perfect and ideal, is by becoming qualitatively like and

---

30 Review of Blanshard *The Nature Of Thought*, Mind, vol. LIII, No. 209 (January, 1944), p. 79.

31 This is another point in which Ewing errs. For he does not here distinguish between qualitative and numerical identity. Even if an idea could become qualitatively identical with its object, that does not mean that it could become numerically identical with it.

ultimately, qualitatively identical with their objects. They cannot in principle become numerically identical with them. Hence the inevitable reduction of the relation of ideas (including the ideal system) to objects, to a form of copying.

Taking Bradley's distinction between Appearance and Reality, it is easy to see why and how Bradley thinks of ideas as acquiring greater and greater (degrees of) reality as they become more and more coherent or more and more true; or to put it otherwise, as the "what" or ideal content of a judgment approximates more and more to the "that" of the judgment: the entire Reality. Ideas are real or a part of Reality and not mere Appearance, in so far as and to the extent to which they approach perfect coherence; although for him the perfectly coherent system is not identical with reality but only one aspect of it, and in so far as it is so it is no longer a system of ideas, but something which transcends system. (For, as we know, Reality or the Absolute is not considered by Bradley to be a system of terms in relation.) But to proceed, to say that ideas or judgments become more and more real is not the same as saying that in this way they become numerically identical with the world of Appearance, viz. the sensible world, even *qua* real and not Appearance. For even as an aspect of Reality, the sensible world is a different aspect from the system of thought or truth. It is true that for Bradley Reality is experience; and this includes both thought and the sensible world, its object. But even then the qualitative difference between thought and its object does not vanish. The relation between them cannot be one of coherence, since coherence involves relations and terms in relation; which do not and cannot exist in the Absolute according to Bradley. Bradley holds that the Absolute contains diversity; but such diversity within it cannot be relational if the Absolute is supra-relational. What the nature of this diversity is, and how it can exist if it is not relational, Bradley does not tell us.

The essential point we are making here can be approached from a somewhat different angle. Coherence, to be possible at all, requires discrete terms which are related. So long as there is a relation of coherence, the terms in the relation cannot be numerically identical. And if the terms do become identical, the relation of coherence between them vanishes. So long as the "what" is different from the "that" in a judgment, there is a logical relation between them and there is thought or judgment. When the "what" coincides with the "that," thought or judgment ceases to exist, and there is no logical *relation* between them. The predicate, ideal content or thought sinks into the subject, the Absolute, and thereby "commits suicide."

Hence it is that for Bradley, where we have coherence we have no perfect truth; and where we have perfect truth we have no coherence (or an ideal *system*): perfect truth becomes perfect by passing into something other and more than truth (the Absolute), and thereby ceasing to be truth. This means that coherence cannot be considered to constitute perfect truth while holding at the same time that in perfect truth idea and object become (numerically) identical. So long as there is coherence, there is a *relation*, and so no identity between idea and object; but according to the view under consideration, to have perfect truth we have to have identity between idea and object; hence in perfect truth there cannot be a relation of coherence.

In other words, Bradley and the other Idealists who hold the underlying-reality theory are perfectly consistent. Or, to put it in the opposite way, the notion that ideal truth consists in an identification of idea and object requires the underlying-reality theory. The view that reality, and perfect truth, are systems of internally-related parts and reciprocally implicating terms, respectively, or the view that reality is (and is only) an organic whole (the Organic or Coherence Theory of Reality) is inconsistent with the view that perfect truth consists in the identity of thought and reality. But we have already attempted to show that the underlying-reality theory is untenable.

Apart from this, and even assuming that the theory is true, individual judgments and systems of judgments would *not* be true in the degree in which they cohere with any system of judgments, even the ideally coherent system, since the latter itself would not be perfectly true. They will have a certain degree of truth only in so far as the ideal system of truth they cohere with is the nearest approximation to perfect truth. The degree of their approximation to the ideal system will indicate their degree of truth in so far as the latter is itself the closest to being perfect truth. But then, the approximation of actual systems to the ideal system determines (and also indicates and tests) their (degree of) truth and *makes* them true only if the ideal system itself is true in so far as it approximates to perfect truth. But how can a system, even the ideally coherent system, be true by virtue of approximating to perfect truth if perfect truth is not a system at all? In what sense can we speak of the ideally consistent system as being *closest*, or the greatest approximation, to perfect truth? Someting which is not a system cannot determine a characteristic of something else which possesses that characteristic by virtue of being a system.[32] What are the *stages* between the ideal system and perfect truth? Unless we assume that the ideal system is the nearest approximation, the extent of approximation to *it* cannot serve as the test of (degrees of) truth.

On the other hand, if the notion that perfect truth consists in an identity between idea and object is abandoned, while it is held that perfect truth consists in ideal coherence, then our question as to the evidence that a perfectly coherent system does "agree" (and "agree" perfectly) with reality, remains unanswered.

Bradley's conception of the relation between the predicate and the subject of a judgment can be taken to illustrate our points. When we make a statement, say "The sky is overcast," we affirm a predicate *being overcast* of the logical subject, *the sky*. The judgment is not *being overcast*, but the whole affirmed thought of the sky's being overcast; and neither the entire judgment nor the concept *being overcast* is itself "attached" to or made a property or a qualification of the entity called "the sky." As L. A. Reid points out, when one says that the horse is a mammal, he is not "harnessing his mental state to the beast between the shafts."[33] What (supposedly) qualifies or is a property of the sky now is the physical characteristics we call "being overcast," i. e., the cloudiness of the sky. Hence, to begin with, there is no tearing away or

---

[32] We have already drawn attention to the related difficulty of how a system can pass into or become, in some sense of 'pass into' and 'become,' something which is not and cannot be a system. The above difficulty also entails that approximation to the ideal system cannot be the test of the (degree of) truth of a system; while no other test is forthcoming or possible without abandoning the coherence theory.

[33] *Knowledge And Truth*, p. 24.

"loosening," as Bradley puts it, of the content of an object—its "what," in the form of thought or idea—from its "that" or existence, that it may be partly and imperfectly restored to the object in the judgment made about it. Whether or not the object—in this case the sky—itself is of the nature of thought or experience, the thought we call the judgment expressed by "The sky is overcast" is not, ontologically speaking, a modification or a qualification or an attribute of it, and so cannot be said to have the capacity to become "detached" from it.

In speaking about the relation between truth and reality, Bradley says—

There is... in all truth the separation of idea and being, the loosening of that which an idea itself is from that which it means and stands for. And in my opinion this breach is at once essential and fatal to truth. For truth is not perfect until this sundering of aspects is somehow made good, until that which in fact is, forms a consistent whole with that which it stands for and means. In other words truth demands at once the essential difference and identity of ideas and reality. It demands (we may say) that the idea should in the end be reconstituted by the subject of the judgment and should in no sense whatever fall outside. But the possibility of such an implication involves, in my view, a passage beyond mere truth to actual reality, a passage in which truth would have completed itself beyond itself. Truth, in other words, content with nothing short of reality, has, in order to remain truth, to come short for ever of its own ideal and to remain imperfect.[34]

In another place, arguing for the identity of truth and reality, he writes:

The last thing to which truth pretends, I shall hear, is actually to be, or even bodily to possess, the real.... Truth, it is contended, is not to be the same as reality. Well, if so, I presume that there is a difference between them. And this difference, I understand, is not to be contained in the truth. But, if this is so, then clearly to my mind the truth must so far be defective. How, I ask, is the truth about reality to be less or more than reality without so far ceasing to be the truth? The only answer, so far as I see, is this, that reality has something which is not a possible content of truth.... If such an outstanding element is known, then so far we have knowledge and truth. While, if it is not known, then I do not know of it, and to me it is nothing. On the one hand to divide truth from knowledge seems impossible, and on the other hand to go beyond knowledge seems meaningless.[35]

---

34 E. T. R., p. 251.
35 *Ibid.*, p. 113.

To this argument Ewing, to my mind, gives the appropriate reply. If Bradley means by truth what is known, or that which is known, then truth and reality would be identical. "In so far as we know, what we know is identical with reality or it would not be knowledge."[36] But we might add that this identity of "truth" and reality which Ewing concedes would be valid only in the case of perfect knowledge or "truth." In the case of any actual knowledge of "truth" the two cannot be identical: "truth" will only form *part* of reality. This Bradley himself holds, since for him the foregoing identity holds only in the case of perfect truth. Ewing goes on to point out that what is *true* is not knowledge in the sense of *that which is known*, but judgments about it.[37] And judgments about reality are not identical with reality itself.[38] But something further may be added about Bradley's view. The perfect system of truth (i. e., the system of perfectly true judgments), in so far as it is constituted by judgments, whether we think of them as merely contents of consciousness, or as subsistent entities, or what not, is real : or, if everything that exists forms part of a system, it coheres with the system of "reality." (Cf. "For truth is not perfect until this sundering of aspects is somehow made good, *until that which in fact is, forms a consistent whole with that which it stands for and means.*" My italics.) If this is all that Bradley means by the "identity" of truth and reality, what he says would be true if "truth" and "reality" form a system. But now, when we are speaking of judgments as true, or of a system as a system of truth (of *true propositions*), we do not (nor does Bradley) mean merely judgments *qua* existents or entities, but as entities which have a peculiar property (or relation or what not) called truth. For judgments *qua* entities are real whether they are

---

36 I. C. S., p. 199.

37 The word 'true,' besides being used in the sense in which we are talking about truth throughout the present work, i, e., as something which is applied and applicable to statements or propositions and not to things, is ordinaly also used to refer to things; e. g. in the sentence "The truth is hard to find" (The nature of things is hard to discover). But the two senses of 'truth' should not be confused; while it seems to me that the Idealistic advocates of the coherence view, and specifically in the notion of identity of truth and reality, confuse or identify the two senses.

38 I. C. S., p. 199.

true or *false*; while true judgments are different from false judgments *qua* true (and vice versa); and any judgment, whether true or false, is distinguished from every other possible judgment by its logical content, by what it asserts. If truth lies in coherence, which is a relation between judgments, coherence would itself be real, and in that sense it would form "part" of reality. But note that the relation of coherence which we are here talking about, i. e., truth, is not the same as the relation of coherence between the system of judgments which are true, as a whole, and the rest of reality. *That* relation does not constitute truth, but is a purely ontological (logical) relation. If therefore truth is more than just an ontological (logical) relation between judgments—and it has to be for Bradley and the other advocates of coherence if it has to conform to the ordinary meaning of 'truth' and 'true' in the sense in which these words are applied to judgments; i. e., if (a) it is to involve some relation of "agreement" with or "conformity" to reality, and (b) if it is to involve an element of assertion by a mind[39]—then *qua* truth, or *qua* possessing this element over and above its sheer existence, it is not an aspect of "reality" or "identical" with it. The source of confusion is the word 'reality.' The "conformity" of a judgment to reality, and the element of asserting a judgment are real, like the relation of coherence. But these things, as well as all other real things, possess certain determinate characteristics beyond and above the sheer fact of their being real. Of course, nothing can be real without possessing certain characteristics; but the nature of a thing and its existence are not the same. In so far as things exist, i. e., in so far as they have a certain nature, they are real. Still, in this sense they cannot be said to form "part" or be "parts" of reality, except if we use 'reality' as a collective name for everything that exists taken as a collection. In the latter sense they will form "part" of "reality" in so far as they exist, or have existent characteristics, and not in so far as they have a specific nature or a set of specific characteristics. Existentially, all things form "part" of "reality," using

---

39 For a judgment is not say, "The table's being hard," which is neither true nor false, but "The table *is* hard" asserted by somebody with reference to a supposed existent, at some particular time.

'reality' as a collective name; but each existent thing is discrete, qualitatively speaking.

Now if all existent things are internally related or form one whole, they will form part of reality, taken in the sense of a whole, in a more stringent and significant sense than the above. But even here, they do not form a whole *qua* possessing specific natures or characteristics. I am of course excluding from their characteristics their relations to each other. They remain distinct as far as they go. The situation is not affected if these characteristics belong to common kinds. We may say that, over and above their other qualifications for being said to form part of "reality," they form part of reality in their possession of common characteristics. But the specificity of the characteristics each of them possesses still remains; and *qua* possessing specific characteristics they are not ordinarily said to form part of "reality." We may say, if you like, that the specific greenness of a tree qualifies a real thing, the tree, and therefore qualifies "reality" of which the tree is a part in so far as it is real. But the tree, *qua* being a particular green, is distinct from other entities which also exist or are real.

It is true that to say that truth is not identical with reality is to say, in a sense, that "there is a difference between them." But on the basis of what we said above, this merely means that truth (assuming for the moment that it lies in coherence) is a specific kind of relation between judgments different from other existent or possible kinds of relations and from real things which are not relations, such as chairs and mountains. And since the relation of truth is different from the things we mentioned, the characteristics of the latter are not "contained in the truth." But from this Bradley's conclusion that the truth will then be defective will not follow at all, unless it is a defect on the part of anything that it is not at the same time what it is and everything else besides. There is no question of truth being "less or more than reality" and therefore "ceasing to be truth"; and we are not driven to say that "reality has something which is not a possible content of truth" in the sense in which Bradley here uses the term 'content.' The characteristics of things other than truth will not be part of the content of truth, in the sense that truth (a true judgment or a set of these) lacks these characteristics. But this is different from saying that these characteristics cannot be the *logical content* of true *judgments*, the referent of judgments or what the judgments are about. This last does not at all follow from our position. Hence also, our view is not open to Bradley's criticism that—

> If such an outstanding element is known, then so far we have knowledge and truth, while, if it is not known, then I do not know of it, and to me it is nothing. On the one hand to divide truth from knowledge seems impossible, and on the other hand to go beyond knowledge seems meaningless.

That no proposition can be true or false in isolation, that it can be true or false only in so far as it coheres or does not cohere with a system of propositions, ultimately the ideal system, is the view of the coherence theory. But this does not seem to me to be true and can be seen, I think, from the following considerations. We have attempted in Chapter IV to show that language does not form a coherent or a relatively coherent system, in the sense in which the coherence theory understands the term 'coherence.' But let us suppose here for the sake of argument that language does form such a system. That means that *statements* (sentences in use) are meaningful only within a system of language. Even then the *propositions* expressed by them in specific contexts will not form part of this system. A proposition, according to the coherence theory itself, forms part of a system of propositions; while a linguistic system is not a system of propositions. (We may of course make *statements* about a given language or about some particular aspect of it; and these statements may be expressed in the same language (say English) in which statements about extra-linguistic matters are made). The distinctness of the linguistic system in which statements expressing propositions exist and the supposed system (of propositions) within which the propositions are true or false, fits in with the fact that in order that a proposition may cohere with a system of propositions at all, it must *already* be a proposition; that is, that it should be expressed or expressible by a statement (which, as a statement, has meaning).

Now if statements derive their meaning through forming a part of a linguistic system, the specific character (logical content) of the propositions they express would be determined by the logical place of the statements which express them in the linguistic system. Since the truth or falsity of a proposition depends (in part)[40] on its specific character (its logical content), the truth or falsity of a proposition (its relation of coherence to other propositions, according to the coherence theory) will depend on and be determined by the linguistic system. However, this system is not itself a system of propositions, and therefore not a system of true (or false) propositions. And unless it is shown that (any and all) linguistic systems form a part of the ideal system of truth—something which, so far as I know, the advocates of coherence have not done or attempted to do—it would remain that propositions are not true or false by virtue of cohering within a system of propositions, ultimately the ideal system. Rather, their cohering with one another (if they do cohere) within a system, and therefore according to the coherence theory itself, their truth, will depend in part on a linguistic system which is not a system of truth; even if the matters of fact on which their truth also depends in part form a part of an internally-related system.

We may approach the problems of meaning and truth from another angle. On the grounds of the coherence theory itself, propositions will be propositions—will have logical content or will have a reference to something else—if and so long as they are numerically distinct (at least partially) from their object, reality. That is why Bradley for instance holds that thought "commits suicide" and ceases to be thought (i. e., propositions cease to be propositions *qua* logical entities) in passing into its object and becoming a part of it; this object being conceived as Reality or the Absolute. On the other hand, the advocates of coherence hold that no proposition can be a proposition outside of a system of propositions which coheres in some degree or other with the ideal system. A proposition is *real* in the degree in which it coheres with the ideal system, which itself is an aspect of Reality; but it is a proposition (has a reference to something other than itself) only in so far as it is distinct from its object. At the same time a proposition is *true* to the extent or the degree in which it coheres

---

40 It also depends in part on matters of fact, on the existence and character of what it asserts in the case of a true proposition, and on the non-existence of what it asserts in the case of a false proposition.

with the ideal system and therefore to the extent in which it is identical with its object. Now for the coherence theory degrees of meaning vary directly with degrees of truth, and conversely. The more a proposition coheres with the ideal system, the greater meaning it has, since its meaning is derived from the ideal system; and the greater its degree of coherence with the ideal system, the greater is its degree of truth. That means that the ideal system itself has the highest degree of meaning possible (as well as the highest degree of truth possible). But how can this be so if the ideal system is identical with its object, Reality, especially as Bradley himself states that thought ceases to be thought (and therefore ceases to involve meaning and truth) when it passes into the Absolute? The solution seems to me to lie in the meaning of 'meaning' as used by the advocate of coherence. A proposition has meaning depending on the extent or comprehensiveness of its implications. So a perfectly meaningful proposition is one which implies the whole of Reality and hence is perfectly coherent or perfectly true. However, when we said that a proposition, to be a proposition (to assert something), has to be distinct from its object, we had in mind "meaning" in the ordinary sense in which we speak of the meaning of a statement (of a sentence in use). The question now is whether or not in this sense of 'meaning'—and not in the peculiar sense in which the advocate of coherence uses this term[41]—the meaning of a proposition is derived from the system of propositions with which it coheres: ultimately, the ideal system. Here two alternatives arise: the advocate of coherence may say that the question is meaningless, since propositions cannot be said to have a meaning; that it is statements rather than they that have or can have a meaning. If so, our remarks in the previous section will be pertinent here. Alternatively, the advocate of coherence may say that propositions do or can have a meaning. If so the ideal system cannot give individual propositions, and systems of propositions, a meaning in the present, ordinary sense. As we have already said, a proposition can have a meaning only if, to begin with, it is or can be regarded as distinct from its object.[42] But the ideal system is

---

41 See Chapter VI.
42 A proposition can perhaps be self-referential. But even in that case we

identical with its object; hence it cannot be properly said to have a meaning, to mean anything. That is, it cannot be a system of propositions. This last is what Bradley himself holds. But then how can the ideal system give any proposition the meaning it has? If a proposition can have a meaning—which seems to be the case— it will have it independently of the ideal system. From this it seems to follow that it can also be true or false independently of the ideal system. For one of the chief grounds for the view that propositions cannot be true or false in isolation is that they cannot have any meaning (and I think in the present, ordinary sense of 'meaning') in isolation.[43] If they can have meaning in isolation from the ideal system of propositions, there does not seem to be any reason why they should not be true or false in isolation from it; that is, why they should not be true or false individually by reference to the specific matters which they assert. This does not seem to me to be precluded even if all matters of fact in the universe are internally related.

It may be objected that we cannot know or understand the *full* meaning of any true propositions (and since all propositions for the advocate of coherence have some degree of truth, of any proposition) unless we understand the meaning of everything it implies. Further since for the advocate of coherence any proposition implies and is implied in some degree by a system of propositions, ultimately the ideal system, we fully know the meaning of any proposition only if we know the meaning of the system. In this sense, it will be said, the meaning of a proposition depends on the ideal system.

Leaving aside for later discussion the problems which this notion of meaning raises, it seems clear that even if this notion of meaning is justified, it rests on the view that reality is an internally-related system, which we have rejected. Apart from this, the criticism we have made at the beginning of the present discussion

---

distinguish logically between the proposition as designating and the proposition as designatum. Also, many propositions are not self-referential; as a matter of fact, most if not all propositions expressed in the object language are not self-referential. So even if the above does not apply to self-referential propositions, it still seems to apply to propositions that are not self-referential.

43 See Chapter VI.

still hold, and apply equally to this interpretation of the dependence of the meaning of a proposition on system. For unless some (at least one) proposition does not derive its meaning from coherence with other propositions but from a relation of designation with matters of fact, such as the use by social convention of certain marks to designate certain objects, events, etc., or to signify certain properties, or both, there can be no system of propositions to begin with; hence no meaning to be derived from or to depend on it. You cannot have a system of meanings, like a system of propositions considered to be true, which is hanging in the air so to speak; which does not derive its meaning in some place in the system from a relation of designation and/or signification with something outside *that* system; namely, matters of fact (irrespective of whether or not matters of fact are considered as forming a system).

There is another point. Suppose we concede the view of meaning we are criticizing. Suppose that to understand the "full" meaning of any proposition we have to know the nature of everything in the universe; that is, suppose that any and every proposition implies (though only in some degree) the entire ideal system of truth or knowledge. It still remains that a given proposition purports to assert something about something finite and limited. "The snow is falling fast" asserts something about the snow now. This something is not being isolated either actually or conceptually from everything else in existence in or by our making an assertion about it. The relation of the rate of the snowfall to the temperature, pressure, wind speed, etc. at that moment is neither actually eliminated nor denied when one asserts something about the rate of the snow's fall. Similarly, the proposition "The snow is falling fast" is not being torn away or isolated from the system of knowledge; it still implies and is implied by the rest of the system (supposing that it could do so to begin with). No violence is done or any falsification made of either the referent of the assertion (the matters of fact involved), or the meaning (signification as well as denotation) of the assertion. The proposition "The snow is falling fast" has, or lacks, some kind of relation (which the correspondence theories crudely designate by 'correspondence') to the matters of fact it asserts, *no matter what else* the "full" meaning—the meaning of everything which the proposition implies, or affirms—may include or involve. If snow is falling fast when somebody points to the snow and says: "The snow is falling fast" (assuming that 'falling fast' is given a relatively precise meaning) the proposition will have that specific kind of relation to facts ("correspondence"), no matter what else may be the case and what other propositions implied by "The snow is falling fast" may be true.

Thus our main point still seems to hold even if we admit the Idealist's view of meaning.

Further, let us suppose that if the organic theory of reality is true, we cannot know the "full" meaning of any proposition unless and until we know all the propositions which it entails and is entailed by. From this it would not follow that the propositions which we have to know in order to understand the "full" meaning of a given proposition are necessarily all *entailed by* and *entail* it. If, in order to know fully the meaning of a single proposition we have to know the ideal system, and if knowledge of the ideal system is a *sufficient* as well as a necessary condition, we can logically infer and therefore know fully all the component propositions in the latter if we know the system as a whole. But this is a truism. For to know the ideal system is already to know every one of its components and their relationships, and hence it is to be able to infer any particular propsition in it from the rest of the system. Suppose in a system ABCD composed of propositions A, B, C and D we cannot know the "full" meaning of A unless we know B, C and D. Since the same is true of B, C and D themselves, if we know B, C and D fully (or know their "full" meaning), we will also know the "full" meaning of A. But these conclusions will be true not because B, C and D together logically entail A; or A, B and C together entail D; and so on. Rather, these conclusions will be true because by definition the "full" knowledge of D *presupposes* knowledge of A, B and C; and so on. In other words, the expression 'the full meaning of A' itself, by definition, here *means* the knowledge of B, C and D as well as of A. A cannot be fully known unless B, C and D are also known because this is the way 'the full meaning of a proposition' has been defined. And this logically follows from the organic view of reality. We can know A fully from a full knowledge of B, C and D together only because a full knowledge of B, C and D presupposes, according to the theory in hand, a knowledge of A. We might know B, C and D partially, in which case we may not know A. And we may know A partially, from which we may know only B (or C and D) partially, or B, C and D partially. Actually the situation remains the same if we admit degrees of partial knowledge of propositions; and even if the most fragmentary and partial knowledge of one proposition requires and involves a partial knowledge (however meager) of every and all other propositions in the system. Thus suppose to know A, even partially, we have to know B, C and D, even if only partially; similarly with B, C and D. Still, from this it does not follow that A logically entails B, C and D, and that B, C and D entail A. We cannot know A even partially unless we also know B, C and D. I. e., if we know A partially, we also know B, C and D partially. The *knowledge* of A entails, in the sense of presupposes, a knowledge of B, C and D; and a partial knowledge of B, C and D (or each one of them alone) entails (presupposes) a partial knowledge of A. But unless we identify the knowledge of a proposition's meaning (or entertained meaning) with the proposition's meaning itself,[44] the proposition A will not logically entail B, C and D; and B, C and D will not entail A.

We may approach our point from another angle. If we have (1) a system of internally-related entities *abcd*, such that some of *a*'s characteristics are determined by *a*'s relations to *b*, *c* and *d*, and if (2) a proposition A corresponds to *a*, then the propositions B, C and D, which correspond to *b*, *c* and *d* respectively, would be logically entailed by A and would entail A and each other, in the sense that A would presuppose them and each of these would in turn presuppose every other proposition in the group. But A, B, C and D would not entail and be entailed by each other if A does not correspond to *a* in the first place.

We have seen that Blanshard holds that in the perfectly coherent system *every* proposition would entail all others. The reason he gives for this is that the meaning of a proposition "... could never

---

[44] See Chapter VI.

be fully understood without apprehension of the system in its entirety."[45] Now if any and every proposition *entails* every other proposition in the perfect system, and if we define the "full" meaning of a proposition as constituted by the meaning of each and every proposition which the former entails, as well as by the meaning of the proposition itself, it would obviously follow that we cannot understand the full meaning of a proposition without knowing the rest of the system. But can we derive the first premise, namely that any and every proposition entails every other proposition in the perfect system (i.e., the rest of the system), from the second premise and the conclusion? Let us try:

The "full" meaning of a proposition is constituted by the meaning of every proposition it implies as well as by its own meaning; and we cannot know the full meaning of a proposition without knowing every proposition in a certain perfect system. Does it follow from these together that any and every proposition implies the rest of the system? Yes, if a proposition implies any propositions at all: which we grant. But first, the conclusion does not mean that the implying proposition itself is *implied by these same propositions*, either singly or even as a group. Any of these propositions, like our proposition, implies a group of other propositions from which it (allegedly) derives its meaning. But that does not mean that the propositions implied by a given proposition also imply it, jointly or singly. It may well be that a proposition A implies propositions B, C and D, B, C and D, either singly or together, imply propositions N, M and O *but not A*. Whereas, what Blanshard holds is that a proposition A,

---

45 N. T., vol. II, p. 266, footnote. Blanshard, in arguing for this view, says immediately before the above passage: "In no mathematical system... would anyone dream of trying to deduce all the other propositions from any proposition taken singly. But when we are describing an ideal, such a fact is not decisive...." That all the other propositions in such a system cannot be deduced from any proposition taken singly is indeed not decisive evidence against the possibility of its opposite. But rather than the critic's proving that the state of affairs envisioned by Blanshard is impossible, Blanshard should prove that it *is* possible despite the plain fact that in no actual system this is the case. The only reason he gives in its support is one which follows from his general position and hence is acceptable only to a person already committed to the latter. He does not give independent grounds based on a consideration of logical or mathematical systems as systems.

say, implies and is implied by all the propositions in a perfect system. This would be true either if (a) A, B, C and D are the only members of the perfect system; or if (b) A, B, C and D, and N, M and O are members of one system composed of only these propositions. In order that (b) may be the case, the "full" meaning of B, C and D should depend on A as well as on, say, N, M and O. But to assume that this is so is to assume that N, M and O as well as A, B, C and D constitute the ideal system: which seems to beg the question. To show that the apprehension of the "full" meaning of any proposition presupposes the apprehension of a system we have to show that there is a system in which every proposition implies and is implied by the rest of the system, and that any proposition we may be talking about is a member of this system. Hence the former cannot be proved from the second or derived from it.

If the universe is an internally-related system, the apprehension of the "full" meaning of any and every proposition involves the apprehension of the meaning of all other possible propositions about the universe if these propositions correspond with reality. From this it does not follow that every proposition logically entails and is entailed by every other possible proposition about the universe. Only a proposition which corresponds with reality will entail every other proposition which likewise corresponds with reality. Since what any such proposition corresponds with would be what it is by virtue of its relation to everything else which exists, the "full" meaning of such a proposition would involve the meaning of all other propositions which correspond with the rest of reality.

However, this will not do for Blanshard and the other advocates of the coherence theory, for obvious reasons. Hence their position seems to be untenable.

As we shall see in detail in Chapter VI, the advocates of the coherence theory hold that any and every possible proposition has some degree of truth. Hence it might be thought that if this view is admitted, the above argument *would* show that any and every possible proposition in some degree entails and is entailed by every other possible proposition. Unfortunately this is not true. What the advocate of the theory means by 'having a degree of truth' is "entailing and being entailed in some degree" by all other possible propositions. Accordingly, to say that any and every possible proposition entails and is entailed by any and every other possible proposition is merely to repeat the definition of 'proposition.' It is not to prove, from the assumption that reality is an internally-related system, that every possible proposition entails and is entailed by every other possible proposition.

The view that in the ideal system every proposition entails and is entailed by every other proposition might be thought to follow from (1) the doctrine of internal relations together with (2) the view that the system of internally-related entities in existence is determined by the nature of the Absolute; assuming that the latter is a *necessary* as well as a sufficient condition for the former. For if the Absolute is a necessary as well as a sufficient condition for the system of internally-related entities, every true proposition about the former will be entailed by every true proposition about the latter as well as the other way round. This would ensure that *a number* of true propositions about the Absolute would together entail and be entailed by all true propositions about the system of internally-related entities in the universe. But there is no evidence—at least the advocate of the coherence theory offers no evidence—that every single true proposition about the Absolute would entail all true propositions about the system of the universe; that every single true proposition about the latter would entail every single true proposition about the Absolute. Apart from this, the advocate of the coherence theory offers no evidence that the Absolute is a necessary as well as a sufficient condition for the existence of the system of the universe. And I do not see how evidence for it can be found.

Another point is pertinent here. If the Absolute as Bradley conceives it is itself not a system of related terms—not even of terms related internally—I do not see how different true propositions about it can form a coherent system in which every proposition entails and is entailed by all other true propositions. For though, as we emphasized, the doctrine of internal relations does not entail this view, this view logically presupposes the doctrine of internal relations. But if true propositions about the Absolute do not form a coherent system, then (1) coherence cannot constitute the truth of these propositions. The only alternative to accepting this conclusion is to hold that there are not and cannot be any true propositions about the Absolute. That we *do not have perfectly true* propositions about the Absolute is one of the things which the advocates of coherence, especially Bradley, emphasize. But that there *cannot be* any perfectly true propositions about it the advocate of coherence would flatly deny; since for him the ideal system of truth includes all (perfectly) true propositions about Reality and not least (perfectly) true propositions about the Absolute. Also, it follows, (2) that (perfectly) true propositions about the Absolute cannot form a part of the ideal system of truth, since they do not cohere with one another in the technical sense of 'cohere' we are talking about; whereas the ideal system, by definition, is a system in which every proposition entails and is entailed by every other proposition.[46]

In arguing that the all-inclusive system of truth must be one in which every proposition necessitates every other proposition, Blanshard finds supporting evidence in what seems to him to be the system of truth we actually possess. I quote:

We can show that in the system of truth, *so far as reflected in our knowledge,* such interconnection holds, and that the denial of an apparently isolated judgement does in fact have implications for every other.... I never simply discharge judgements into the air with no ground or warrant at all. And by the rules of hypothetical argument, to admit the falsity of a judgement is to throw doubt upon its ground.... It is to throw doubt, if I am consistent, upon *all* evidence of this kind and degree.[47]

This is the case, for instance, if I say that Bishop Stubbs died in his bed:

Now the evidence on which it is believed that Bishop Stubbs died a natural death is of the kind and degree that would be accepted without hesitation by any historian or scientist. It is the sort of evidence on which science and

---

46 These criticisms also apply in the case of a less stringent definition of the ideal system than the one made use of above (Joachim's and Blanshard's definition); namely if we define the ideal system as a system in which a part of the system (a group of propositions taken together) entails and is entailed by the rest of the system.
47 N. T., vol. II, p. 292. Italics in original.

history generally rest. Hence if I deny this proppsition, and thus call in question the value of this sort of evidence, I must in consistency call in question most science and history also. And that would shatter my world of knowledge.[48]

This argument is invalid because it ignores the following points: (1) that if we deny a given proposition, such as "Bishop Stubbs died in his bed," which is assumed to have historical evidence in its support, its denial would entail denying other well-accepted historical propositions only if it *validly* follows from them. For a certain group of propositions may be falsely *thought* to constitute logical grounds for a given proposition. In such a case, if the supposed evidence is of the "kind and degree that would be accepted without hesitation by any historian or scientist," "the sort of evidence on which science and history generally rest" would not be shattered or even affected in any way by denying the proposition. On the contrary, in rejecting the proposition on the ground that it does not really follow logically from them, we will be upholding the laws of valid reasoning; which are fundamental in all knowledge-seeking, including the knowledge which was supposed to be the logical ground of any proposition. Also, of course, we may have first affirmed the proposition on authority, and then discovered that it was false. (2) Even if the given proposition logically follows from historical evidence, the denial of the proposition would not necessarily throw doubt on the *type* or *kind* of evidence involved, or on the empirical *methods* used in arriving at the particular evidence. On the contrary, our rejection of the given proposition may be a result of our discovering that the supposed "evidence" is not evidence at all, being false, precisely because it was not arrived at by a correct application of empirical methods; that it is not the kind or type of evidence which would be arrived at if the methods were properly applied. Hence again, our rejection of the proposition and the particular propositions on which it rests, instead of destroying empirical methods and the kind of evidence used in knowledge, will be a result of upholding these methods and the kind of evidence which can be arrived at through their correct application.

---

48 *Ibid.*, pp. 292-293.

Blanshard is confusing the type of evidence or ground for a given proposition, and the specific propositions which are instances of that type of evidence, these specific propositions forming the actual evidence in the specific case. For instance, the specific evidence for a given proposition may be empirical in nature; the denial of the proposition would then entail denying this specific evidence. But this does not entail the rejection of the empiricistic or scientific reliance on fact as a (kind of) ground for belief, the method or methods employed in arriving at empirical fact in general, or the specific methods employed in arriving at the particular evidence in hand. (3) Blanshard will probably reply that what we are saying misses the point, since the assumption he is starting with is that the proposition rejected is *true*, while we have been actually assuming that it is false. Of course the rejection of a *false* proposition, it will be said, does not entail rejecting any true propositions, or any correct kind of evidence or correct methods of arriving at such evidence. But in the case of a true proposition the situation is different. The proposition "Bishop Stubbs died in his bed" is true; hence its rejection wrecks all our knowledge.

But is Blanshard entitled to affirm unconditionally that any proposition is true? For even assuming that an allegedly true proposition is entailed by the entire system of "knowledge" (which is what is to be proved here), Blanshard cannot affirm that the proposition is consequently true, since this would be so only if the entire system of "knowledge" itself is true, i. e., *is* knowledge, or coheres with the ideal system. And that, he or anybody else cannot know. The only thing which Blanshard can actually assert is that so far as the evidence goes the proposition appears to be, or is probably, true; which makes it logically possible that the proposition may after all be false—and this is what we are assuming. In that case the question still remains: what evidence is there that a given proposition, which is supposed to be true on empirical grounds, is entailed by the entire system of what is called present knowledge; i. e., that if we reject such a proposition we will be rejecting the entire system of "knowledge"? We have seen that Blanshard's evidence that the answer is in the affirmative, is not conclusive. Even if the rejection of such a proposition does entail the rejection of all propositions about matters of fact in the system of "knowledge," the methods of arriving at such propositions are not necessarily affected.

The phrase 'propositions about matters of fact in the system' needs clarification. By it I mean all the propositions which constitute the system, excluding from this description the logical principles and the empirical methods used in arriving at the constituents of the system and therefore at the system as a whole. For these principles and methods are not themselves propositions, but tools employed in arriving at propositions. We can form true or false propositions about them, and about the system of propositions about "matters of fact"; and these propositions, if true, would, according to the coherence theory, ultimately cohere with or form part of the ideal system of truth. Still, they would not form part of the system of propositions about "matters of fact." To illustrate, the system of scientific knowledge is ordinarily understood to comprise propositions about particular events, objects, characteristics, and about the laws governing these events, objects, and characteristics. Propositions about logical principles and the scientific methods (such as induction) used in arriving at these propositions form part of logic and of philosophy—the philosophy of logic and the philosophy of science. Of course, to repeat, the latter as well as the former is part of human knowledge; and if this knowledge forms a system, it will be part of a wider and more inclusive system which includes the system of scientific knowledge as well. Notwithstanding this, and as we have said, the rejection af any particular proposition or even of all the propositions in the system of scientific knowledge need not affect the propositions comprising logic, the philosophy of logic, and the philosophy of science. For once more, the scientific propositions may not have been arrived at by a correct application of the principles about which we now frame propositions. The validity of these principles entails that propositions correctly arrived at with their help are true—or rather, are probably true. But we are never certain either that they have been correctly used, or that the supposed facts from which they have been arrived at with their help are really the facts. So they are not abandoned when empirical propositions supposed to be true turn out to be false or improbable. This is not to say that some empirical methods are never modified, even abandoned; but that is not because some empirical propositions thought to be true are found to be false. On the contrary, it is with the help of these principles that such errors are discovered. Some may be modified or abandoned, but not all; and even if all are modified or abandoned, at least the attitude that a valid method must be either an empirical method—that is, one which looks to what exists and occurs in the world—or a logical method, or both, is never abandoned. With that, propositions affirming that all knowledge is based on experience or facts, are not abandoned. For knowledge, by definition, is the apprehension of what is (or was or will be), and unless we change the meaning of the term 'knowledge' this attitude or view cannot be legitimately attacked or abandoned.

One final word about the ideal system. Blanshard, as well as the other advocates of coherence, speak of *a* or *the* ideal system of truth or knowledge; and for the sake of argument, we ourselves have spoken in this way throughout the present work. In reality, actual and possible propositions form an infinite hierarchy of orders of propositions, one order in the object-language and the rest in the metalanguage. And though we may suppose that at any given moment the number of possible propositions in the object-language is finite—since we can assume I think that at any given moment the number of entities in the universe is finite in number and therefore that the number of possible propositions in each and every higher order is also finite, it remains to be shown that all *true* propositions in one order would entail and be entailed by every other true proposition in each and every other order. (This, of course, in addition to showing that within one and same order every true proposition would entail and be entailed by every other true proposition. See footnote 45 page 176.) This is especially important since it is possible to mention any number of propositions in one order which would ordinarily be regarded as true, but which do *not* entail other true propositions in another or other orders. For example, "This table (the one I am writing on now) is white," is true, since the table *is* white. But this proposition does not entail and is not entailed by the true proposition " 'This table is white' is an English sentence"; similarly in the case of "This table is white," " 'White' is used in the sentence 'This table is white,'" and "'White' is mentioned in the sentence '"White" is used in the sentence "This table is white"'." (However, propositions like "This table is white," which in the particular case is true, does entail and is entailed by "'This table is white' is true," "'"This table is white" is true' is true," and so on with higher-order propositions.) The advocate of coherence would of course reply that no actual proposition we may cite is perfectly true; hence the fact that some imperfectly true propositions do not entail other imperfectly true propositions is no evidence that they would not entail them if they were perfectly true. We have already met this reply by Blanshard (footnote 45 page 176). Whether or not this reply can stand depends on whether or not the doctrine of degrees of truth is true. To this doctrine we shall turn in the following chapter.

To sum up what we have said in this chapter. In our discussion of the doctrine that coherence constitutes the nature of truth, we have attempted to point out certain difficulties in the doctrine; especially with regard to its conception of the relation between thought and its object in the case of (a) actual and (b) ideal truth or knowledge. We have also offered some criticism of the coherence theory's conception (c) of the relation between (i) the meaning and (ii) the truth of individual propositions, on the one hand, and the ideal system on the other hand. Finally, (d) we have criticized the coherence theory's conception of the ideal system itself. In Chapter VI we shall offer further criticism of the coherence view of truth by criticizing the crucial doctrine of degrees of truth and falsity.

CHAPTER VI

THE DOCTRINE OF DEGREES OF TRUTH AND FALSITY

There is a sense in which this chapter is the most important and crucial in our entire analysis and critique of the coherence theory. The reason is simple: in chapters two through five we discussed and criticized the doctrine of internal relations, and then the coherence theory as an account of the test of truth as well as of the nature of truth; but without taking into consideration the doctrine of degrees of truth. We criticized the doctrine that all relations are internal, and also that the test and the nature of truth lie in coherence, implicitly assuming that the distinction between internal and external relations, and the distinction between truth and falsity, is one of kind and not of degree. This is indeed what we do hold to be the case. But it is not what the Idealist advocates of the doctrine of internal relations and of the coherence theory of truth themselves hold. As the advocates of these views would say, we have implicitly assumed that (a) relations are either absolutely internal or absolutely external; and that (b) a proposition or a set of propositions is either true absolutely or false absolutely: that truth and falsity do not admit of degrees; although we did implicitly assume that in a sense propositions could be *partly* true and partly false. It is now incumbent upon us to show that the doctrines of degrees of internal relations and degrees of truth are mistaken. These doctrines are of special importance; for unless they are true the view that coherence constitutes the nature of truth cannot be true, as Blanshard himself recognizes.[1]

But it is important to make clear, first, that our criticism of the doctrine of internal relations and of the coherence theory of truth is not invalidated by the supposed fact that the internality of relations, and truth and falsity, are a matter of degree. One reason is that in none of our arguments against the doctrine of

---

[1] N. T., vol. II, p. 301.

internal relations did we use as a premise the unproved assumption that relations must be either internal or external absolutely speaking. Similarly in our criticism of coherence as an account of the test and of the nature of truth. Our attempt to show that at least some relations are external in the crucial senses of 'external,' if successful, shows without begging the question that relations cannot be *both* internal *and* external in some degree or other. If some relations are not internal, then they are not internal whether or not internality admits of degrees. And if truth does not lie in coherence, truth and falsity cannot admit of degrees in the sense in which the coherence theory envisions this; though it is possible that they admit of degrees in a different sense. Thus the (specific) doctrine of degrees of truth and falsity we are concerned with cannot be true unless the view that truth lies in coherence is true to begin with, as much as the latter cannot be true without the former. Concerning relations, it is of course true that the relations which we did find to be internal, or which we did not expressly show to be external, can, logically speaking, still be held to admit of degrees of internality (and hence degrees of externality). But the relations which we attempted to show are *not* internal could not be consistently held to be *internal* in some degree and therefore also external in some degree.

In this chapter we shall attempt to show (a) that relations, even if they are all held to be internal, and (b) that truth, even if it is considered to lie in coherence, cannot admit of degrees; that to think of relations and of truth as admitting of degrees raises insurmountable difficulties over and above those which led us to reject the view that all relations are internal (absolutely), and that truth lies in coherence.

Our main task in this chapter is to criticize the doctrine of degrees of truth. But in order to deal with it adequately, we also have to examine and criticize (a) the doctrine of degrees of meaning, and (b) the doctrine of degrees of necessity or implication. Both of these doctrines constitute logical grounds from which the doctrine of degrees of truth can be inferred. Each is a sufficient though not a necessary ground for it. But further, the doctrine of degrees of necessity or implication can itself be inferred from (c) the doctrine of degrees of internality and externality of relations. Hence this doctrine is also a logical ground for the doctrine of degrees of truth.

Starting from the doctrine of degrees of internality and externality of relations, the doctrine of degrees of truth can be arrived at in this manner: If relatedness is a matter of degree it follows that logical necessity or implication is also a matter of degree. For according to the advocate of coherence to say, for instance, that two or more terms are internally related in the seventh sense of 'internal relations,' is to say that they could not and not merely would not be the same if the relation were absent or were different.[2] In other words, for the advocate of coherence, internality of relations involves an element of logical necessity or logical implication between the relations and the terms they relate. We have seen this explicitly in the case of "the causal relation" as it is understood by the defenders of coherence. Consequently, if internality of relations is a matter of degree, the necessity or logical implication it involves would also be a matter of degree. But then the relation of coherence between individual propositions in a system, and the relation between one system and other systems, ultimately the ideal system, would also be a matter of degree. For the relation of coherence, as will be remembered, is a relation of reciprocal implication. Consequently, truth and falsity, which lie in coherence and in the absence of coherence, respectively, are matters of degree. That is to say, no proposition (short of the ideal *system*) will be perfectly true, and no proposition will be completely false (there being no external relations absolutely speaking); but all actual propositions will be true in some degree, and false in some degree, short of perfect truth and perfect falsity.

A. *The Doctrine of Degrees of Internality and Externality of Relations.*

This doctrine can be stated as holding that relations admit of degrees of internality and externality and so that all actual relations are both internal and external, and not one to the exclusion of the other. For it, the view that all relations are internal

---

[2] The same applies, *mutatis mutandis*, to senses eight and ten of 'internal relations,' though not to sense nine.

absolutely, and the view that they are external absolutely, are defective. As a matter of fact, it holds that it is impossible to have perfectly external relations; for as we have seen (Chapter II) the defenders of coherence hold that to posit perfectly external relations is tantamount to destroying relations or holding that relations do not relate. As for perfectly internal relations, the situation is somewhat different and, as expected, analogous to the situation in the case of perfect or absolute truth. Whereas relations cannot be external absolutely without ceasing to relate, relations cannot be internal absolutely without the disappearance of the very distinction between terms and relations; without the merging of terms into a supra-relational unity or continuum. In that sense an internal relation, absolutely speaking, cannot exist as an absolutely internal relation. The absolutely internal relation would, so to speak, relate too well to be only a relation; whereas the absolutely external relation would, so to speak, relate too little to be a relation at all. So absolutely external and absolutely internal relations are only conceptual or ideal limits, never actually realizable. Reality, conceived as an all-inclusive internally-related system, is the nearest approximation to a "system" of absolutely internal relations. But reality conceived in accordance with the underlying-reality theory transcends relations; hence it does not contain even absolutely internal relations.

But what do the advocates of coherence exactly mean by saying that actual relations are both internal and external in some degree; or waiving the distinction between "external" and "internal," what do they mean in saying that a relation admits of degrees of relatedness, that one relation relates more or less (or more or less closely) than another relation? For this seems to be one simple though perhaps crude way of putting the view.

The notion of degrees of necessity for Blanshard and the other advocates of the coherence view applies to (a) matters of fact, and (b) propositions and systems of propositions. In the case of (a), (i) a *characteristic* or a set of characteristics may be said to be more necessary (or more essential) than another characteristic or set of characteristics to a given object to which they belong. For instance, to use Blanshard's example, a heart (or the possession of a heart) is more necessary to a man than a little finger (or the possession of a little inger).³ Blanshard's thesis is that *all* the characteristics of a thing are necessary or essential to it in some degree, though some may be more necessary than others; that is, that the traditional distinction between essence, property and accident is one of degree, not of kind.⁴ (ii) Blanshard also speaks of degrees of causal relevance. Thus to use essentially his own example, suppose a given bacterium can cause a disease in the person it attacks under a certain range of atmospheric temperatures, say 60°-85° F. The disease would not occur in the absence of the bacterium; but it would occur if the bacterium is present, whether the temperature is 60° or 65° or 75° F, and so on—so long as the temperature is somewhere between 60° and 85° F. This means that a temperature of 60° (or 70° or 75°, etc.) is causally less relevant or necessary for the occurrence of the disease than the (action of the) bacterium. Put schematically and generally, if event X is caused either by A and B together, or A and C together, or A and D together, and the like, A can be said to be more relevant or more necessary for X than either B, C, or D, though *either* B, *or* C, *or* D must be present with A in order that X may occur.

In the case of systems of things, we can see how the notion of degrees of necessity operates for Blanshard by considering such things as a plant or a machine.⁵ Thus we ordinarily say that the parts of a plant or a machine are more closely or intimately related than, say, the parts of a heap of stones. The difference here seems to lie in one or both of the following factors: (1) the number of parts affected by a change in one part of the system, and (2) the extent of the effect on the parts affected. The removal of a stone from the heap has a very slight effect on the rest of the heap (it changes the gravitational forces acting upon it). It affects all the parts, but only very slightly. In the case of a plant, the destruction of the roots, say, destroys the whole plant. The effect is both all-pervasive and very profound: vastly more than in the case of the heap of stones. Hence according to this account we can say that the relation between the roots of the plant and the whole plant is

---

3 N. T., vol. II, p. 298.
4 For Blanshard, this also applies in the case of mathematical objects, where the relations involved are purely logical. But for our present purposes we shall discord pure mathematical systems, which we regard as analytic and not synthetic
5 N. T., vol. II, p. 447.

more necessary (or has a higher degree of necessity) than the relation between the stone and the heap.

Now it will be remembered that the causal relation is regarded as internal by the advocates of coherence. Hence if the causal relation admits of degrees of necessity, internality of relations, at least in the case of the causal relation, also admits of degrees. Further, since the causal relation is held to involve an element of logical necessity, the existence of degrees of causal necessity would entail that logical necessity or implication admits of degrees of necessity. This brings us to (b), that is, to the notion of degrees of necessity as it applies to propositions, the notion of degrees of logical implication in the purely logical sense. But before we pass to this we should note the following points:

(1) It is plain, I think, that in the various cases of "degrees of causal relevance or necessity" which we have mentioned, it is not really the causal *relations* involved which are more or less relevant or necessary. In the example of the disease, it is the *bacterium* (or its action) which is more necessary for the occurrence of the effect (the disease) than a given *temperature*. As a matter of fact, here we can say that the bacterium is more necessary for the causal relation itself than a given temperature, since this relation obtains only as a result of the action of the bacterium (at one temperature or other) on the patient. Similarly in the case of the heap and the plant it is the roots (or their action) which are causally more necessary for the plant than is a stone for a heap of stones (and we may also add, the roots are also more necessary for the plant than its leaves, say. And this brings us to the example of the heart and the little finger. The heart is causally more necessary for a person's life, or for his existence as a man, than a little finger). Thus Blanshard seems to me to be mistaken in regarding the causal relation itself as admitting of degrees of necessity and therefore of degrees of internality.

We can look at the matter from another angle. We have attempted to show in Chapter III that the cause-effect relation (and its converse) is external in sense seven of 'internal relations' as we have construed this, except in a trivial sense. Hence even if we derivatively speak[6] of a cause-effect relation (or its converse)

---

6 I say this because we do not ordinarily speak of a relation as more necessary

as more or less necessary than another in the sense, for instance that the agent in the former case is more necessary for a given effect than is the agent in the latter case for the same (kind of) effect, we cannot infer from this that the causal relation admits of degrees of internality (in the seventh sense).

(2) The advocates of coherence do not attempt to show that relations other than the causal relation can admit of degrees of necessity and so degrees of internality. But it is clear, I think, that the notion of degrees of necessity does not apply at least in the case of the relations of similarity and difference. For intance, a relation of similarity s_1 between objects A and B cannot be meaningfully said to be more necessary to them *qua* A and B than another relation of similarity s_2 between them; though the *characteristics* by virtue of which A and B are related by similarity in the case of s_1 may be said to be more essential or more necessary to A and B than in the case of s_2. Similarly a relation of similarity cannot be said to be more necessary than a relation of difference, or a relation of difference as more necessary than another relation of difference. Yet even if the opposite were true, it would not follow that there can be degrees of internality in the seventh sense in the case of these relations, since we have already attempted to show that they are external in that sense.

The view of degrees of logical implication we are concerned with is expressed by Blanshard as follows :

> We hold that one cannot define implication in terms of *p* and *q*, because more is always involved. If one is said to imply the other, it is because both belong to a wider system and to grasp the implication between them *is* to grasp them as members of that system. Implication is systematic interdependence. It is a relation between parts of a whole imposed on them by the nature of the whole itself. Since there are many kinds of whole, there are many varieties of implication. Since wholes, again, have many degrees of

---

than another relation. A relation r_1 between A and B may be said to be more necessary for A, say, than a relation r_2 between A and C. But in these cases, r_1 is derivatively said to be more necessary than r_2 because (a) B is regarded as more necessary to A than C, and (b) B *determines* r_1's nature in part, while C *determines* r_2's nature in part. A relation r_1, determined (in part) by a term (B) more necessary to another term (A) than a third term (C), is thus said to be more necessary than another relation r_2 determined (in part) by the term less necessary to the same term (A).

unity, there are many degrees of necessity with which one proposition may imply another. The points of most conspicuous challenge in such a view of implication would appear to be three: (1) it maintains that implication is never a function of one proposition alone, or of two propositions alone, but always of a system partially revealed in the terms as related. It holds that implication is (2) various in kind and (3) various in degree.[7]

But what is the degree of necessity or implication of a system as a whole? What is the standard in terms of which a given system has a given degree of necessity and another system another? The answer given by Blanshard is: the ideally coherent or necessary (and ideally comprehensive) system. Blanshard writes: "Any partial system, just because partial, must be rejected and transcended; the impulse to expansion will tolerate no arbitrary arrests; its goal is nothing short of a system perfect and all-embracing."[8] Thus we can think of a hierarchy of systems of increasing coherence and comprehensiveness,[9] and therefore of increasing degree of necessity, each system approximating to the ideal system in a different degree.

The necessity and unity of a system depend on the necessity of its parts. But different parts may have different degrees of necessity. To take systems or objects, the heart is more necessary for a person's life than a little finger, the roots more necessary for a plant's life than its flowers or even its leaves. And the same, at least *prima facie*, seems to be possible in the case of systems of propositions. How then can the advocates of coherence speak of *the* unity, coherence and necessity (or of *the* degree of unity, coherence, and necessity) of a system? What part or parts of a system—in the case of systems whose parts have different degrees of necessity—determine the degree of necessity of the whole? The advocates of coherence do not give an answer to this question.

---

[7] N. T., vol. II. p. 430. Italics in original.

[8] *Ibid.*, p. 438.

[9] In the ideal system, perfect coherence or system and comprehensiveness or all-inclusiveness coincide. But in actual systems the two may diverge: a system may be coherent and comprehensive in different degrees relatively to the ideal system, and therefore also relatively to other actual systems. (Cf. P. L., vol. II, Terminal Essay VIII, pp. 685-686)

But taking different systems in relation to one another, the advocates of coherence would probably say that a given system A is more necessary than another system B if a greater number of its parts affect a greater number of other parts,[10] and/or a greater number of its parts have a more pronounced effect on a greater number of other parts, than in the case of B.[11] However, even if on this basis it is possible to give a precise measure of *the* degree of necessity of a given (actual) system, it would remain that at least in the case of some actual systems different parts may have different degrees of necessity. If this is also true in the case of propositions, then it would mean that propositions in one and the same (actual) system may have different degrees of *truth*, insofar as degrees of truth are determined by degrees of necessity.

The doctrine of degrees of necessity (and we might add, of implication, in the case of propositions and systems of propositions) and of degrees of truth cannot be fully understood without a consideration of its metaphysical grounds: the view of the Idealist advocates of coherence that reality is of the nature of experience, and their consequent identification of (perfect) truth and (perfect) knowledge. We shall therefore give a brief sketch of these metaphysical grounds. If Reality is a systematic whole, then truth is also a systematic whole. But Reality, of which truth is an aspect, is experience. It has no existence outside and apart from the experience or consciousness of some self; or rather it is itself the content of experience or consciousness of some self. But the Whole which is Reality, and consequently ideal truth, is not the experience of any finite self but of the Absolute. Our knowledge is always part of, but at the same time a fragment torn out of, the total truth. Our knowledge always falls short of and falsifies ideal truth. In so far forth, it is not and cannot be identical with ideal truth. Only in the Absolute do perfect truth and perfect knowledge coincide and become identical. No actual proposition or actual system is perfectly necessary (and perfectly true), since

---

[10] In the case of systems of propositions, 'implies' has to be substituted for 'affects.'

[11] This factor does not seem to be involved in the case of systems of propositions.

it is torn out from its total context, the ideal system. Seem in the light of the ideal system, "it" is perfectly necessary and true. But the propositions we actually know have only a finite degree of necessity and truth (are false in some degree) because we never can and do see them in their entire context. Our knowledge is always an abstraction from the whole. However numerous may be the conditions of a given proposition or system we may know or discover (i. e., however comprehensive may be the system which they imply) there always remain further, and to us unknown, conditions.[12] That is why no finite number of conditions or premises, short of the ideal system, *necessitates* a logical conclusion. The greater the number of conditions which are known and stated, the closer to perfect necessity the implication of the conclusion by the premises or the higher its degree of necessity.[13]

The crucial point is this: propositions or systems seen in a finite setting, in abstraction from the ideal system: viz., all the actual propositions and systems we have, are not the same when seen in their total context. Abstraction is a process of falsification, distortion. Propositions, as they exist in the matrix of the ideal system, form an integral part of it; they are intrinsically and essentially related to every other part of the system. Hence when they are torn out of this context, their relations are destroyed and they themselves are distorted. The extent to which they become distorted depends on the number and importance of the relations which are destroyed, on how many of their total conditions are left out or ignored. The fewer the conditions left out, the wider and the more coherent the system in which they are apprehended, the less they are distorted and the higher their degree of necessity and truth.

But—and this is the crux of the matter—suppose we take any actual proposition, say "$2 + 2 = 4$." Suppose we know only a few of the conditions which it implies. In that case, "$2 + 2 = 4$" will have a low degree of necessity and truth. Suppose we now discover more and more of these implied conditions, and hence "$2 + 2 = 4$" is progressively modified and becomes more necessary and more

---

12 Cf. P. L., vol. II, Terminal Essay I, p. 601.
13 Cf. N. T., vol. II, pp. 442-443.

true. What about the original "2 + 2 = 4"? What has become of it? Does it not still exist alongside the new, modified propositions which have higher degrees of necessity and truth than it? Does it not exist alongside "2 + 2 = 4" as seen in the light of, as forming part of, the ideal system—that is, alongside the proposition as purged of all falsity? If it does, then there is no reason why all the other possible finitely necessary propositions "2 + 2 = 4" should not continue to exist alongside one another and alongside the ideally necessary and true "2 + 2 = 4"! This would give us the odd situation of an indefinite number of co-existent propositions all having the form "2 + 2 = 4," ranging from almost zero necessity and zero truth all the way to perfect necessity and truth. Similarly with the finite systems which the different finite propositions having the form "2 + 2 = 4" would then imply. But this is incredible. The premise on which all this depends is of course the assumption that "2 + 2 = 4"—and any other proposition— is necessary or true independently of its being entertained or known; that knowledge of the truth does not affect the truth (the propositions known) in any way. This is rejected by the Idealist advocates of coherence. A proposition seen in the light of a given finite system *is* different in some degree (to some extent) from the proposition as seen in the light of a wider and more coherent system. But this does not mean that we now have a second proposition alongside the old one; the old proposition is no longer what it was, since it itself has developed, or changed, into the new proposition. This development is self-development; as the old grows into the new it becomes more and more itself until it reaches, ideally speaking, its complete self-realization in the perfect system. A proposition is a thought entertained, a content of consciousness; it is at once the object thought about and the consciousness or knowledge of that object. The transformation or development of the less necessary and less true proposition into the more necessary and more true proposition is the growth of thought or knowledge in the mind of the person entertaining the proposition. As a matter of fact it is the growth of that person's mind as a system within the wider system of Reality. But if a proposition is a thought, it ceases to exist as that thought once it ceases to be entertained as it was originally entertained and is entertained in a new light; in the same way as the seed is no longer there as a seed, but is a sapling, once it has grown into one. Hence there are not and cannot be an indefinite number of independently existing propositions with all possible degrees of necessity and truth, waiting to be known as they independently exist; some of which do come to be known and others not. Further, and in the same way as in the case of finite minds, the finite and imperfect propositions we entertain exist in the Absolute not as finite and imperfect, not as we entertain them, but as they would be if they are purged of all distortion. As such they would be perfectly necessary and true. But then no question at all would arise as to the coherence or incoherence, with the ideal system, of the *finite* and imperfect propositions. To raise that question or other questions based on the same premises is to misunderstand completely the doctrine of degrees of necessity and truth.

We have here described the self-development of propositions or thought in metaphysical terms. But the same can be done from the standpoint of the meaning of propositions or the content of a thought. The self-development of thought or the progressive modification and correction of actual propositions is, from that standpoint, the progressive deepening and enriching of the content of the thought or the meaning of the propositions. To see a proposition in the light of a wider system is to see it as more meaningful (as possessing a higher degree of meaning) than before. So "$2 + 2 = 4$" as entertained by a schoolboy and as entertained by a mathematician is not the same but different propositions with different degrees of meaning, and so with different degrees of necessity and truth.

These considerations put our problem in a new light, and clearly make it imperative for us to show, at least, that the immediate metaphysical premises on which the doctrine of degrees of necessity and truth rests are false or dubious. Without this, some if not all of our earlier criticisms in this chapter will not stand.

It is my view that the Idealistic metaphysics as a whole is untenable. But to show this adequately requires a separate work— a luxury we cannot afford. Criticism of the foregoing position on these grounds is therefore not available here. Nevertheless, there are certain points which we can make without going into a full-scale critique of Idealistic metaphysics.

(1) First, it is to be noted that in ordinary language we distinguish between truth and knowledge or awareness of the truth. We say for example that the truth of the proposition "$2 + 2 = 4$" is independent of our knowledge that the proposition is true; that our knowledge that 2 plus 2 is equal to 4 does not affect the truth of the proposition or make it true in the first place. Now as we mentioned, the coherence theory only identifies perfect truth and perfect knowlege, or truth and knowledge as they exist in the ideal system or the Absolute (we may disregard here Bradley's view that the Absolute itself is not a system). Thus the coherence view agrees with the ordinary view and with ordinary usage so far as our finite knowledge and relative truth are concerned; namely with the view that we discover the truth and do not make it. Obviously, the independent existence of truth is a prerequisite for our knowledge of the truth. This also means that for the view we are concerned with, truth is objective and not private or subjective. Hence our question really is whether or not knowledge is ever, even ideally speaking, identical with truth. That it is not follows, for one thing, from our attempts in Chapter V to show that there cannot be such a thing as the ultimate identification of truth and its object. For if the Absolute or Reality is conscious experience, as the Idealist holds, and if perfect knowledge and truth are identical, it follows that if truth is not identical with Reality (as one aspect of it), knowledge is likewise not identical with it. But then, what becomes of perfect knowledge? Truth, as far as we are concerned, can (and must) be different from its object. But in the case of knowledge the situation is different. Knowledge cannot exist, or cannot be knowledge, if it is not a self's consciousness of what we call the truth. And if perfect knowledge cannot be the consciousness or experience of the Absolute, it either is not and cannot be real, or it must be the knowledge of finite selves. But no finite self has or can have perfect knowledge. On both scores perfect knowledge would not exist (would not be real), and we would be left with finite knowledge. But finite knowledge is identical with truth. Hence our point seems to be confirmed.

But an objection looms on the horizon. Finite knowledge, it will be said, is not identical with truth; but only as far as perfect identification is concerned. Even finite knowledge—and the humblest knowledge at that—is identical in some degree with truth, in the same way as finite truth and its object are identical in some degree. But now, in what sense can we speak of degrees of knowledge? Blanshard (who makes use of this notion) does not give us a precise answer. However, I think we can safely say that as in the case of truth, degrees of knowledge are determined by degrees of coherence and comprehensiveness. The more systematic or coherent and the more extensive or comprehensive is our knowledge, the more perfect it is as knowledge, the higher the degree of knowledge we have.

Now if knowledge or awareness of true propositions is distinguishable from the logical content of the propositions and of their truth—and it must be so if there is to be knowledge *of* something—this distinction remains even if propositions exist only as thought. But if so, the truth of a proposition is logically prior to its being known and depends on its coherence (according to the coherence view) with a system of other propositions, whether or not this system is known by the mind which entertains the implying proposition. Otherwise our knowledge would be the ground for or what makes a proposition cohere with a given system; which is absurd. A proposition implies or is implied by other propositions or sets of propositions independently of our knowledge of these relations. On the other hand, if a proposition does not imply the conditions which we are supposed to discover in pursuing the activity we call knowledge, because these conditions, being unknown, do not exist, then in what sense can we say that the degree of truth of a proposition changes with the increase of our knowledge of the conditions it implies? It is conceded that to know any proposition at all implies knowing something besides what the proposition itself asserts; but this additional knowledge may be very little. A child may know that $2 + 2 = 4$ without knowing all that a mathematician knows about the science of arithmetic. What then about the conditions which I do *not* know, but which "$2 + 2 = 4$" implies (the whole system of arithmetic)? Do they exist or not when I do not know them? You may answer that they exist in the Absolute consciousness, and hence that they certainly exist. But in what form do they exist in the Absolute consciousness? They do not exist in the form in which the *imperfect* proposition "$2 + 2 = 4$"

which I entertain implies them. They exist there in the form in which the proposition "$2 + 2 = 4$" itself exists in the Absolute, viz., as a perfectly true proposition: It is *there* and in *that* form that it implies them. The question is whether they exist in the form in which my imperfect proposition implies them. If you reply that "$2+2=4$" as I entertain it implies only a part of these conditions —a part of the conditions it would imply if it were perfectly true—the question would again be whether (a) this part is only the conditions which I know, or whether (b) it is the conditions which I know plus others which I do not know. If it is the former, (a), our reply will be that this entails that "$2 + 2 = 4$" does *not* imply the conditions which I do not know: conditions which, at the same time, are *supposed to be implied by it*. For if the latter, (b), is rejected (which would be the case if (a) is accepted), a proposition would imply only those conditions which it is known to imply, and we are led back to the difficulty from which our objector is trying to escape: the conclusion that our knowledge makes the truth what it is rather than merely being its discovery and possession. But if (b) is accepted, then the conditions which I do not know but which are implied by "$2 + 2 = 4$" as I hold it, will not be the *same* as these conditions as they would exist in the Absolute consciousness. For in the form in which they would exist in the Absolute consciousness they would not be conditions of, or be implied by, my imperfect proposition. Hence they would exist outside and independently of both the Absolute consciousness and my consciousness; i. e., they would not be a content of experience or thought; for, *ex hypothesi*, they would exist, they would not be nothing.

But this assumes that they do not or cannot exist in some other finite mind. Well, can they? Would they be the same, not merely in logical content but also numerically, on the grounds of the coherence view itself, if they are thought by some other finite mind? And would "$2 + 2 = 4$" which implies them be logically identical with the proposition having the same form of expression, which I entertain? If it is, and yet at the same time the conditions which I entertain are logically identical with the ones the other mind entertains, though the other mind also entertains conditions which I do not entertain, then either of two consequences would follow. The first is that two propositions having the same form of expression can be logically the same and hence have the same degree of truth, even though they do not imply the same number of conditions. If this is accepted, it would completely wreck the interpretation of degrees of truth we are considering, and which is held by the advocates of coherence. The alternative consequence is that the two propositions are logically different; that is, that they must have different degrees of truth.[14] On the doctrine of degrees of truth this means that the conditions which they imply—including those which *prima facie* both minds entertain—are *logically different* though some of them have the same form of expression as those entertained by me. But this amounts to saying that the conditions which "$2 + 2 = 4$" as entertained by me implies, but which I do not know, cannot exist in the other finite mind. And this would be true in the case of *any* other finite mind. Consequently our earlier criticism would still seem to stand.[15]

The defender of the view will reply that "$2 + 2 = 4$" as I entertain it has a degree of truth by virtue of the extent (and coherence) of the conditions it implies. But these conditions are at the same time conditions which I know. For it is my abstraction in knowledge of some of the conditions of "$2 + 2 = 4$" which it implies in the

---

[14] Not merely that they are numerically distinct. For *that* would be true in any case if the propositions exist only in relation to some consciousness or other.

[15] The difficulties encountered in the entire foregoing section can be focussed by considering a passage by Bosanquet. Speaking of his contention that ideas must be expressive of reality, and that any and all reality must have an expression in ideal form, he says: "This is the only way of understanding the paradox about the making of truth and its discovery. You can hammer upon either side of this antithesis for ever; but you cannot possibly make sense without both. Certainly truth comes to be when we find it out; the very determinations in which it consists, the selection and connection of things and relations, had for all we know no emphasis, no distinguished place in the scheme of the universe before or apart from our mental operations. But no less certainly it was true before it was found out; if it was not true before it could not be true when it was found out. It is of no use to deny either of these paradoxes; they naturally affirm themselves if we insist on dismembering an essential unity." (*Implication and Linear Inference*, pp. 148-149) What Bosanquet calls a paradox seems to me to be a genuine contradiction. If truth exists before it is found out, then it cannot come to be when we find it out; and if it comes to be when we find it out, it cannot exist before we do so. (But see the reply to our criticisms in the text above.)

ideal system, that distorts and falsifies the perfectly true "2+2=4" and gives it its relative truth or finite degree of truth. Thus, by definition, "2 + 2 = 4" as I entertain it does not imply conditions other than those I know. Consequently there are no difficulties at all. The ideal conditions, which the absolutely true "2 + 2 = 4" implies, exist in the Absolute; while the limited conditions which the relatively true "2 + 2 = 4" implies exist in my consciousness. So there are no conditions, implied by the relatively true "2+2=4," which exist neither in my consciousness nor in the Absolute. The alleged difficulties are generated by assuming that "2 + 2 = 4" whenever entertained, and irrespective of the extent of the knowledge which the person entertaining it has, implies a certain fixed set of propositions (here the system of arithmetic). And this error stems from the rejection or ignoring of the view that "2 + 2 = 4" does not always have the same logical content or meaning; i. e., it stems from the rejection of the doctrine of degrees of meaning. If this doctrine is admitted, the apparent difficulties vanish.

This is perfectly true; and it is imperative for us, if our previous criticisms are to stand, to refute the doctrine of degrees of meaning. To this we now address ourselves.

(3) Blanshard distinguishes three things in any assertion: (a) the metaphysical subject, (b) the judgment or proposition asserted, and (c) the words in which the judgment is expressed. The metaphysical subject "... is reality, or more immediately the region or point of reality of which assertion is made...."[16] And Blanshard's contention is that "... the metaphysical subject may be the same, and the form of expression may be the same, while the judgment differs."[17] Two persons may be talking about the same metaphysical subject and using the same form of expression, and yet the judgments they thus express may be different. The proposition asserted by a person in making a statement depends on the extent of his knowledge. As his knowledge increases the proposition asserted by the statement changes. Suppose we take the statement "Napoleon lost Waterloo." This, as made by a school-boy, asserts

---

16 N. T., vol. II, p. 307.
17 Ibid., p. 308.

a different proposition from "Napoleon lost Waterloo" made by a historian. But even in the case of the school-boy:

As the boy's historical grasp advances, he may repeat verbally many times his judgement about Napoleon, but it may be that at no two repetitions of it is he asserting precisely the same thing. His accumulating knowledge penetrates his earlier conceptions through and through. He cannot think of Napoleon in the old way, now that he has explored the Napoleonic character; Waterloo has become a complicated set of military evolutions; the loss of the engagement is no longer a white horse flying, but the dominance of Europe by new political and national ideals.[18]

This change is not one of kind but of degree:

The earlier thought has been not so much annihilated or directly contradicted as dissolved in a new medium. From all this it is clear that meaning, in the sense of what we mean to affirm when a certain form of words is used, is undergoing incesssant and insensible change. And change so organic and continuous is properly to be described only as change in degree.[19]

The change in degree of meaning involves also a change in degree of truth:

If meaning is used in the sense suggested, truth is the adjective of meaning and follows it like a shadow. The school-boy's advancing thought, so far as it is an advance in knowledge, implies also an advance in truth, and it is incredible that the first of these should admit degrees and the others not.[20]

If we leave aside for the present the problems raised by Blanshard's use of 'proposition' or 'judgment' as a synonym for 'meaning,' and if we use the former two terms as he uses them,[21] our contention, on the contrary, will be this: (1) If two statements differ in meaning in Blanshard's sense although they have the same form of expression, then the metaphysical subject will be different in each case. If they have the same form of expression

---

18 *Ibid.*, p. 309.
19 *Ibid.*
20 *Ibid.*
21 But see section (4).

and the same metaphysical subject, they will express the same "proposition." In still other words, if the form of expression is the same but the "proposition" expressed is different, the person making the statement is using at least some of the words in different senses in each case: either in different senses which the words ordinarily have, or in a purely private and peculiar way, different from their ordinary meaning or meanings. And this entails that the metaphysical subject will be different in each case. This is illustrated by Blanshard's own example of the school-boy's assertion that Napoleon lost Waterloo: "When he says that Napoleon lost Waterloo, what he is really thinking is perhaps that a plucky little fighter in a coked hat and riding a big white horse had to gallop off at top speed to get away from pursuing red-coats."[22] Here the metaphysical subject is clearly not the same as that of the historian, say. The school-boy is not really talking about the historical Napoleon, the man of flesh and blood who became French emperor in 1804 and lost Waterloo; i. e., the words 'Napoleon,' 'was defeated,' 'Waterloo' do not have here their ordinary meaning. The "plucky little fighter" is not Napoleon, and "he had to gallop off at full speed..." is not the defeat at Waterloo! (2) We may say, if you like, though misleadingly, that the school-boy did not purport[23] to mean by "Napoleon lost Waterloo" what the statement ordinarily means, since he did not know what are the exact referents of 'Napoleon' and 'Waterloo' as they are ordinarily used. Nor did 'defeated' have its ordinary meaning here; i. e., the boy's judgment was also different. Blanshard himself unwittingly says as much when he writes: "When he [the child] says that Napoleon lost Waterloo, what he is *really thinking* is perhaps that a plucky little fighter in a cocked hat and riding a big white horse had to gallop off at top speed to get away from pursuing red-coats."[24]

(3) A good deal of confusion is avoided if we see that statements are sentences in use, that they exist in a concrete context, and not in a vacuum so to speak. One and the same sentence can

---

22 *Ibid.*, p. 308.
23 It is misleading because it suggests that the boy is conscious, or fully conscious, of what he is thinking of expressing in words, what he wants to say.
24 *Ibid.*, p. 308. Italics mine.

"make" different statements depending on the context.[25] Bradley says that in seeking truth in ideas—

You not only endeavour to say what you mean, but you are once for all and for ever condemned to mean what you say. *Your judgements as to reality are here no less or more than what you have expressed in them, and no appeal to something else which you fail to make explicit is allowed.*[26]

This is a consequence of Bradley's failure to distinguish between sentences and statements. What Bradley says about 'judgments' is not true of statements in our sense. What a statement "expresses" does involve an "appeal to something else" which is not stated but is implicit in the nature of the context in which it is made. It is statements which are true or false, and hence it is statements which have to be shown to admit of degrees of meaning if a case is to be made for the doctrine of degrees of truth. What we have said about the distinction between sentences and statements means, using Blanshard's distinctions, that both the metaphysical subject and the "proposition" involved in the case of a given *sentence* may differ in different contexts, although the form of expression used may be the same. But the main point is that if the metaphysical subject is different, the "proposition" will be different; or rather, if the "proposition" is different, the metaphysical subject will consequently be different.

That the metaphysical subject changes when the "proposition" changes and, consequently, that when the metaphysical subject is different the "proposition" expressed will be different, is also seen in the case of increases in a person's knowledge. Take, again, the example of the school-boy's statement about Napoleon. As the boy's knowledge of the relations between the battle of Waterloo and subsequent historical developments increases, or as he discovers more and more connections between the loss of the battle and

---

25 Here as elsewhere I follow P. F. Strawson in my use of 'statement' and 'sentence' (see Chapter IV, p. 100). Strawson writes: "A particular statement is identified, not only by reference to the words used, but also by reference to the circumstances in which they are used, and, sometimes, to the identity of the person using them." (*Introduction to Logical Theory*, p. 4)

26 E. T. R., p. 234. Italics mine.

subsequent events, he may be thinking of some or all of these connections when he subsequently says "Napoleon lost Waterloo." But again this depends on the particular context, and on what may be before his mind at that moment. He may, with all this increased knowledge, make the statement and yet mean (purport to mean) merely and literally that Napoleon lost a battle at Waterloo. Our knowledge about a given subject is never present before our consciousness in its entirety every time (even at *any* time) we make a statement about it. How much, and what part of it is present depends on all sorts of psychological and physical factors. However, as far as our discussion goes, when at one time a person means more by a statement than he means by it at another time, the metaphysical subject he is speaking about will be more *inclusive* than in the latter case. In saying "Napoleon lost Waterloo," he may be referring not merely to the immediate events called the battle of Waterloo, but to other, connected events as well; or he may be referring to different aspects or temporal parts of the battle itself. In this case the metaphysical subject will be different though the form of expression may be the same; but it will not be entirely different. Part of it will be what the other statement "Napoleon lost Waterloo" has for a metaphysical subject—the battle itself; but now it is the battle in relation to other events, say Napoleon's confinement at Elba. At the same time the proposition expressed is also different, or includes more: it is the thought of the confinement at Elba in addition to that of the battle of Waterloo itself. What is more, however inclusive or its opposite may be the meaning of the statement and hence the metaphysical subject, the statement will either refer or not refer to it, mean it or not mean it; the statement cannot mean one and *the same metaphysical subject more or less.* Thus no degrees of meaning are possible. But as we said, despite his increased knowledge one may still want to refer merely to the battle of Waterloo itself, apart from its connections to other things. In that case increased knowledge will not mean that the metaphysical subject is different. What is more—and here comes our disagreement with Blanshard—the proposition expressed in this case will also not be different; it will be merely the thought of Napoleon's loss of the battle at Waterloo, no more, no less. With regard to this, L. T.

Walker is right when, in talking about a boy's acquisition of arithmetical knowledge, he says that as the boy develops into an arithmetician, he comes to know *more about* "3 × 3 = 9," "... because he knows its relation to other items of knowledge and its place in the general science of Arithmetic"; but "it is still the same item of knowledge that it always was...."[27] The reason he gives is this: "The doctrine that every item of knowledge is related to every other item of knowledge is true; but to suppose that each item is *intrinsically* affected by its relations to other items, and, in consequence, changes as these other items become known, seems to lead to absurdity."[28]

That each item of knowledge "is not intrinsically affected by its relations to other items" we of course endorse. Thus when our new arithmetician asserts "3 × 3 = 9," he can and may merely mean what the statement literally says, without this being in any way affected or falsified by the fact that he is conceptually abstracting it from his total body of arithmetical knowledge. This, we need not say, rests on our view (a) that the universe is not an internally-related system, and (b) that even if it were, conceptual abstraction does not falsify. This means that the extent of our knowledge affects neither (i) the metaphysical subject referred to, nor (consequently) (ii) the "proposition" which is about this metaphysical subject. For the Idealist advocate of coherence the existence and nature of the metaphysical subject does not depend on *our* knowledge of it; but our knowledge of it (its extent and degree of coherence) affects and determines propositions about it; i. e., the more extensive and coherent is our knowledge, the more meaningful and hence the truer are the propositions about the subject.

(4) In the preceding section we said that if two statements have the same form of expression and the same metaphysical subject, they will also express the same "proposition" or "judgment." This was because we used the terms 'proposition' and 'judgment' in the sense of 'meaning' (of statements). But Blanshard's use of 'proposition' or 'judgment' is unfortunate, and blurs the distinction between (a) the meaning (signification) of a sentence, (b) the

---

[27] *Theories of knowledge*, p. 520.
[28] *Ibid*. Italics in original.

knowledge of the person who utters the sentence, about the metaphysical subject, and (c) what the person who utters the sentence may intend to mean or express by it. Blanshard, as a matter of fact, identifies all three by using 'proposition' or 'judgment' to mean now one, now another of these. Once we make these distinctions we see that Blanshard's contention that "the metaphysical subject may be the same, and the form of expression may be the same, while the judgement differs" is false if 'judgment' is used in sense (a); while it may be true if 'judgment' is used in sense (b). And it is in sense (a) of 'judgment' that Blanshard's contention is significant and crucial. The meaning (signification) of ordinary words is implicitly fixed by usage, and the meaning (signification) of technical terms in science, mathematics, etc., is explicitly fixed. In both cases all but certain characteristics (whether identical in all or only having a "family resemblance" or something else is immaterial here) are excluded from the word's meaning (signification).[29] An individual's discovery[30] of new characteristics in the word's referent therefore does not affect or alter the word's meaning (signification). So the meaning of a statement affirming something or other about the word's referent does not change if the person making the statement comes to know more about it. If *all* the characteristics of a referent R were included in the signification of the term 'R' which names it, any increase in knowledge of the latter would change the meaning of statements about it by changing 'R's' signification. But this is not the case. It is clear also that our conclusion is not affected, if, as Blanshard holds, the distinction between essence, property and accident is one of degree and not of kind. Even if this is true, it

---

29 I am ignoring for simplicity's sake the vagueness of some ordinary words and what F. Waismann calls the "open texture" of ordinary concepts. What we said in the text above is not affected by these matters.

30 I say "an individual's discovery" because the signification of a word, in use, *may* be modified and widened to include characteristics originally not included in it, as a result of the acquisition of new knowledge about the referent. This, as a matter of fact, is at least one important basis for the transformation of what are originally synthetic statements, into analytic statements. But this normally occurs, when it does, as a result of the acquisition of new knowledge on the part of a great many of the word's users, not one or a few users.

would still remain that some but not all of R's characteristics are implicitly taken as "essential" (and therefore others as "non-essential") in the ordinary *use* of 'R.'

With regard to 'judgment' in sense (c), a word must be said first about the distinction between the meaning of a sentence and what its utterer may intend to mean by it. Leaving aside questions concerning the role of intention in the genesis of languages, with which we are not here concerned, and second, without assuming that in every instance of the use of language an intention to communicate is present, the distinction and difference between an intention to mean something particular by means of a sentence, and the meaning of the sentence itself, is seen most clearly when the two fail to coincide. By this I mean that we sometimes find, when we utter a sentence, that the hearer construes it in a different way from the way in which we intended it to be construed. Our natural reaction in such a situation is to retort: "But this is not what I meant!" This may be the result of all sorts of things: e. g., of our uttering an ambiguous sentence or our using one or more words in the sentence in peculiar, extended or figurative senses. In such cases we discover that what we have said does not correctly express our thoughts. Also it may be that we intended to express more than what the sentence actually expresses; in which case we may say, on becoming aware of this: "I did not mean merely this!" In any case what a sentence means or expresses is independent of what the maker of the sentence may intend or want to mean. Of course what specific sentence a person makes depends on what he wants to express; but the sentence, once framed, is autonomous, so to speak, so far as its meaning goes; what one intends to express itself has to conform, in the attempt to express it, to the conventions of language. In many cases what one expresses in words coincides with what he intends to express; in some cases, it fails to do so—assuming, in both kinds of case that an intention to express is present.

From these considerations it is seen that Blanshard's contention may sometimes be true if 'judgment' or 'proposition' is taken in sense (c); namely, where the same sentence is used in two different contexts and refers to the same metaphysical subject, but where the sentence in the one context does express what its maker intends to express, while it does not do so in the other context due to one or more of the reasons we mentioned above, or to some other, similar reason. But Blanshard's contention would be false if both sentences express (mean) what their maker or makers intends or intend to express (to mean), if the two sentences, besides having the same metaphysical subject, assert the same logical predicate of this subject (i. e., if the two sentences have the same meaning in the two contexts). We might add that what one may intend to express by means of a given sentence, (c), may be affected by the extent and nature of his knowledge, (b), about the metaphysical subject of the sentence he makes. Hence if 'meaning' is taken as 'what one means to affirm (or deny) when he uses a form of words,' "degrees" of meaning may be dependent on "degrees" of knowledge.

(5) The doctrine of degrees of meaning logically rests on the view that a thing's relations constitute part of its nature[31] (Cf. Chapters II and III); hence that the more of these we know the fuller will be our knowledge of its nature. In terms of statements, this means that a statement about a thing's nature would designate (mean) it in the degree in which the proposition which this statement expresses includes the thought of these relations. That is why "Napoleon lost Waterloo," say, has a higher degree of meaning as made by the historian than by the school-boy. Since we have rejected the view that a thing's nature is determined by all the relations it has or can have (Chapter III), it follows if our position is correct (a) that an increase in our knowledge of a thing's relations does not necessarily mean an increase in the degree of meaning of statements about it; (b) that even if we consider as part of its nature those relations which do determine (some of) its characteristics, the nature of a thing can be completely known without knowing its relations to everything else in the universe. On the theory of degrees of meaning itself this means that we can have statements having the highest possible degree of meaning—and therefore, according to the doctrine of degrees of truth, statements which are perfectly true—but not implying the ideal

---

31 Cf. N. T., vol. II, pp. 318-319.

system of knowledge. That is, that it is false that only statements within the ideal system can be perfectly meaningful and so perfectly true. But even the assumption made in (b) above is unjustified. A thing's relations, which determine some or all of its characteristics, cannot be properly said to constitute a part of its nature (Chapter III). Only relational characteristics generated by them, if such characteristics exist, can be said to form a part of its nature. This is reflected in the meaning of the ordinary term 'nature of a thing,' which does not include the notion of a thing's relations. As for relational characteristics, we have already contended that they do not exist. The doctrine of degrees of meaning, and with it the doctrine of degrees of truth, thus seems to be untenable.

(6) Suppose, in accordance with the doctrine of degrees of meaning, we take two statements having the same form of expression and about the same metaphysical subject; and suppose that the proposition expressed by the first is more inclusive than the proposition expressed by the second. Let us symbolize them by "A_1 is B_1" and "A_2 is B_2," respectively, merely in order to differentiate them. Now to say that the proposition expressed by "A_1 is B_1" is more inclusive than the one expressed by "A_2 is B_2" is to say either (a) that "A_1 is B_1" *asserts* more about the metaphysical subject than "A_2 is B_2" does, or (b) that is asserts what "A_2 is B_2" asserts, but that it *implies* more than "A_2 is B_2" implies.

Now in ordinary discourse, when we speak of 'the meaning of a statement,' we normally mean what it explicitly asserts or states[32]—the meaning it has by virtue of the ordinary or dictionary meaning of its component words and the grouping of these words according to the correct rules of syntax. What it implies by virtue of this meaning is not thought of as part of the ordinary meaning of 'the meaning of a statement.' Unless the term 'meaning' is

---

32 The term 'meaning' has of course all sorts of meanings in ordinary languages; and even the expression 'the meaning of a statement' may have more than one meaning. As a matter of fact, there is at least one other meaning which this expression has in addition to the one considered in the text above: namely, the meaning of a statement in the sense of its significance. This meaning of 'meaning' we shall discuss presently. For the moment, the main thing is that we are not thinking of significance in speaking of 'the meaning of a statement.'

given a special meaning, we cannot properly say that "A_1 is A_1" means more or has a higher degree of meaning than "A_2 is B_2." A view which holds that two statements having the same form of expression and asserting something about the same metaphysical subject may yet have different degrees of meaning, becomes philosophically significant only if 'meaning' (in the sense of the 'meaning of a statement') has the same meaning as in ordinary language.[33] For otherwise, why call this thing which is supposed to have degrees, "meaning" at all? What would it have in common with meaning as ordinarily understood? To call what a statement implies a part of a statement's meaning is merely to lead to the confusion of making one suppose that what we ordinarily mean by 'the meaning of a statement' can have degrees; whereas actually this is *not* what the doctrine in hand would be saying. To put the matter otherwise, if the doctrine of degrees of meaning is interpreted as asserting that what a statement implies is part of its meaning, and that this meaning admits of degrees, 'the meaning of a statement' will not be used in its ordinary meaning. It will therefore not follow, or it will not have been shown, by showing that the implied element can vary, that 'the meaning of a statement' in its ordinary meaning can admit of degrees. Another way of looking at the matter is this: when we say that "A_1 is B_1" implies more than "A_2 is B_2," we mean that "A_1 is B_1" logically implies more statements about the metaphysical subject than "A_2 is B_2." But unless "A_1 is B_1" itself, as such, has a meaning, it cannot imply other statements. Does *this* meaning admit of degrees? The answer is No. For the doctrine of degrees of meaning, *ex hypothesi*, is here supposed to assert that a statement has a degree of meaning by virtue of and as determined by what it implies. Hence it would be absurd to say that the meaning of "A_1 is B_1" by virtue of which it implies what it implies, is itself determined by what it implies.

The doctrine of degrees of meaning, taken in the present sense, confuses two different senses or meanings of 'the meaning of a statement': (i) the meaning of 'the meaning of a statement' in the sense of what the statement explicitly asserts or states by

---

[33] See footnote 32.

virtue of its components and their syntactic grouping, and (ii) the meaning of the phrase in the sense of its significance (See footnote 33, p. 211) which itself presupposes the meaning of a statement in the first sense. It is in the latter sense, (ii), that the meaning of a statement is the meaning of what it implies. If we ask: "What does this statement mean?" when we already understand perfectly the explicit meaning of the statement, what we are asking about is its significance, what it implies. But note that when we ask for the significance of a given statement, we may be asking for (a) the *statements* it implies, and/or (b) the *states of affairs* it implies, using 'implies' here in a different sense from the formal logician's. For instance, in this latter sense, we may be wondering what the statement implies (or means) about the attitudes, intentions or motives of the person or persons who made the statement. But even in the case of the significance of a statement, this significance, so far as (a) is concerned, is ordinarily thought of as being fixed and determined and not as varying or admitting of degrees. For the statements implied by a given statement are thought of as determined by the nature of the statement itself within a given context of discourse, independently of us, once its meaning is determined by the conventions of language and by the context. Hence we do not and cannot properly speak of *one and the same statement* as being more or less significant in different contexts: if the contexts are different, we will have logically different statements and not two tokens of the same type (*of sentence*). We may say that a given *sentence*, line of verse, and the like, which occurs in a given context, would have been or would be more or less significant, if it were or is used in a different context. For example, "Beauty is truth, truth beauty" can be said to be more significant in Keats' poem "On A Grecian Urn" where it comes as the summation and climax of a whole gamut of ideas and emotions, than in John Smith's crude attempts at poetry-writing.[34] The significance of a *sentence* is determined by and varies with the extent of its implications in different contexts. And

---

[34] This example illustrates another form of significance, namely poetic or æsthetic significance, which is not purely "intellectual" significance or significance *qua* thought.

since for the doctrine of degrees of meaning the meaning of a judgment is determined by and varies with the extent (but also the coherence) of its implications, we may speak of degrees of significance of a sentence in the sense in which this doctrine speaks of "degrees." But apart from the fact that this applies to sentences and not to statements, this is a different meaning of 'the meaning of a judgment' from what we are concerned with here. So far as the latter is concerned no degrees are admissible.

If the doctrine of degrees of meaning is interpreted as affirming (i), then it would follow that 'A' and 'B' do not have the same meaning in the two propositions "A_1 is B_1" and "A_2 is B_2"—they merely have the same form as symbols. For obviously, "A_1 is B_1" cannot *assert* more than what "A_2 is B_2" asserts unless 'A_1' has a different meaning from 'A_2,' or 'B_1' from 'B_2'; since the form of the two statements is the same and cannot be responsible for the difference in meaning; i. e., "A_1 is B_1" and "A_2 is B_2" are logically two different statements (not two different tokens of the same statement), although they are, misleadingly, composed of symbols having the same form. But the difference in what "A_1 is B_1" and "A_2 is B_2" assert may be due either to a difference in meaning between (a) 'A_1' and 'A_2' alone, or between (b) 'B_1' and 'B_2' alone, or between (c) both 'A_1' and 'B_1' on the one hand and 'A_2' and 'B_2' on the other hand. In (a) the metaphysical subjects involved will be numerically different in the two cases, but what is asserted about them will be the same; in (b) it will be the converse; in (c) both the metaphysical subjects and what is asserted about them will be different in the two cases. In (a), (b) and (c) we thus have two logically different statements, each having a definite meaning; and no degrees of meaning are or can be involved.

(7) The incompleteness or partiality of the meaning of a sentence should not be confused with degrees of meaning and therefore with degrees of truth:

(a) it is essential for the doctrine of degrees of truth that it should be possible to speak of the variation in the meaning of a statement referring to the *same* metaphysical subject. If this is possible, then it would be possible to speak of two statements having the same form of expression, as differing in degree of meaning; hence to speak of them as differing in degree of truth in the sense of degree of coherence. For contrariwise, if the metaphysical subject changes with changes in the proposition expressed by a statement, what we would have, logically speaking, would be *two different statements* having the same form of expression, and so with *different* truth-values; assuming that the truth of a statement depends on the inclusiveness or richness of meaning of the proposition it expresses. Increase in meaning will not, in that case, mean an increase in the truth of one and the same statement; hence no increase in *degree* of truth will be involved. Only when we are talking about one and the same thing can variation in degree in it be meaningful.

(b) But suppose it is true that we can have two or more statements having the same form, differing in meaning, and yet referring to exactly the same metaphysical subject. Further, suppose that the difference in meaning is a difference in degree. Still, it does not seem to me to follow that truth can have degrees. A statement "A is B" which is more meaningful than another statement "A is B" referring to the same metaphysical subject A, says *more about A* than the latter; that is, it is more inclusive or less partial or incomplete. Yet this does not make it more true. B may be perfectly true of A in the second statement; and in the first statement what B asserts over and above B in the first statement may be false. For example, "Napoleon lost at Waterloo" in the sense of "Napoleon lost a battle at Waterloo" asserts less about Napoleon than the statement with the same form which means "Napoleon lost a battle at Waterloo and as a result lost his crown." The former statement is perfectly true while the latter is not perfectly true, since Napoleon did not lose his crown merely as a result of losing this battle. This is to say that the degree of a statement's incompleteness may or may not have anything to do with its truth, depending on the particular statement involved. "Water contracts when cooled," asserting literally what it says, is not true as it stands; while "Water contracts when cooled" meaning "Water contracts when cooled provided the pressure is normal and the temperature is above 4° C," is true. And the latter asserts less than the former, though in a different way from the above example about Napoleon's defeat at Waterloo; i. e., in the sense that it describes the behavior of water under restricted conditions. But even in this case the difference between the truth-value of the two statements does not appear to me to be one of degree.

In order to see in what sense we ordinarily speak of "Water contracts when cooled provided the pressure is normal and the temperature is above 4° C" as more true than "Water contracts when cooled," let us consider the following: A statement A may be said to be more true than another statement B if (1) A is (ordinarily said to be) completely true: e. g. "Plato was a Greek philosopher," while B is considered to be only partly true: e. g. "Plato was a Russian *philosopher*"; or if (2) both A and B are only partly true, but A has a greater number of true "constituents" than B; for instance, "Plato was a Greek philosopher who lived in the seventh century B.C.," and "Plato was a Russian philosopher who lived in the seventh century B.C.," respectively. There is also another sense in which we speak of A as more true than B, to be later discussed. On the other hand if (3) A is completely true while B is completely false, we simply say that A is true while B is false; and not that A is more true than B. Similarly, (4) if both A and B are completely false we simply say that A and B are false.

(1) Now what does it mean to speak of a statement as "partly" or as "completely" true? In what sense is "Plato was a Russian *philosopher*" only partly true? The answer is this: Plato was a philosopher; so, insofar as the statement affirms this, it is true: but it is not completely true because it also asserts that Plato was a Russian (philosopher), which is false.[35] Whereas, "Plato was a Greek philosopher" is completely true because Plato was both a philosopher and a Greek. More precisely, Plato was a Russian philosopher" can be logically broken down into a conjunction of

---

35 This is an oversimplification. If in a conversation between A and B, both A and B agree or assume that Plato was a philosopher but are not agreed about his nationality, and A says: "Plato was a *Russian* philosopher," his statement, in that context, will be normally considered to be *completely* false. In short, what the sentence "Plato was a Russian philosopher" is taken to affirm in a given case depends on the context. Above, we are concerned with the said sentence in those contexts in which it is normally said to be only partly true and partly false, and not completely false; i. e., where, in written form, the sentence would be "Plato was a *Russian philosopher*," or (in some contexts) "Plato *was* a Russian philosopher"; and so on.

two statements: "Plato was a philosopher" and "Plato was a Russian." The first of these is true; the latter is false. Similarly "Plato was a Greek philosopher" is logically equivalent to a conjunction of two simple true statements. So the notions of "more true" and "less true" in this context do not involve a notion of degrees of truth. For the sake of convenience, we can speak of "Plato was a philosopher" and "Plato was a Russian" as "components" of "Plato was a Russian philosopher." Similarly with the other statements which are logically equivalent to "Plato was a Greek philosopher." Using this terminology, one of the "components" of the former statement is absolutely false, while the other is *absolutely* true. In the case of the latter statement both "components" are absolutely true.

It must be added, in order to avoid misinterpretation, that we do not hold or imply that a statement has the same *sense* (to use Frege's term) as its "components."

(2) Here, unlike (1), both statements have some absolutely false "components." But one of them (the one which is said to be more true than the other) has a greater number of absolutely true "components": e. g., A has two "components" which are absolutely true and only one which is absolutely false; in the case of B it is the exact reverse. Thus again "more true" and "less true" do not involve the notion of degrees of truth.[36]

The other sense in which we do speak of "more true" and "less true" (and "more false" and "less false") is what Blanshard calls the approximative sense. Consider "$2 + 2 = 5$" and "$2 + 2 = 4.9$." Here we may say that the latter is less false than the former, though we do not normally say that the latter is more true than the former. (Rather, we say that both are false.) Relatively to one another, "$2 + 2 = 4.9$" approximates to the truth, expressed by "$2 + 2 = 4$," more closely than "$2 + 2 = 5$." But taken separately in relation to the truth, both are equally false. In some cases, though not very frequently in this type of case, we do speak of one statement as being more true than another statement; e. g., that "$2.056 + 2.013 = 4.0695$" is more true than "$2.056 + 2.013 = 4.0697$."

---

36 See N.T., vol. II, pp. 305-306.

Neither of these two senses of "more true" and "less true" above is, as Blanshard rightly says, what the doctrine of degrees of truth means by 'more true' and 'less true.' But these two senses seem to me to be the only senses in which we ordinarily speak in this way; and neither involves the notion of degrees of truth. If the doctrine of degrees of truth is to find any support, it is not to ordinary usage that it has to turn. Secondly and importantly, returning to the point from which we originally started, we now see that a statement which is more complete or inclusive than another in what it expresses (in the "proposition" involved) and is also (said to be) more true than the less complete one, may involve no degrees of truth—that a statement's degree of completeness or incompleteness is neither the same as a given degree of truth, nor gives the statement a degree of truth higher than the less complete one.

One way in which the doctrine of degrees of truth is stated and argued for by its adherents is that the truth of any actual statement is relative and not absolute in the sense that it is conditional upon the truth of a system implied (presupposed) by it. This would of course be true in the case of mathematical and logical statements, which form part of deductive systems, if we assume with the advocates of coherence that (pure) mathematical system, are (empirically) true or false. Thus the truth of "$2 + 2 = 4$" would be conditional upon or relative to the truth of our ordinary system of arithmetic; and "$2 + 2 = 6$" would be false because it is inconsistent with this system. In the case of empirical statements, with which alone we are here concerned, the truth of a statement does logically presuppose the truth of some other statements. But since we have attempted to show that the universe is not an all-inclusive internally-related system (in the crucial seventh sense), the statements any empirical statement presupposes are never all the statements, actual and possible, which can be truly asserted of the universe. Apart from this, and concentrating on the fact that if an empirical statement is true other statements must also be true, to say that the truth of any such statement is relative to a set of other statements is not the same as saying that any such statement, because it is relative in this sense, cannot be absolutely, in the sense of perfectly, *true*. A statement may be said to be "relative" and not "absolute" in either of two senses: (1) in the sense that if it is true, other statements must also be true;[37] and (2) in the sense that it is not perfectly or "absolutely" true, as the advocates of the doctrine of degrees of truth understand this. The doctrine of degrees of truth seems to me to confuse (1) and (2). (2) does not logically follow from (1); and it is in sense (2) that it would be significant for the advocates of the doctrine of degrees of truth to hold that actual statements are relatively, and not absolutely, true.

(i) To say that the truth of an empirical statement p logically presupposes the truth of q, r, s. etc., simply means that if p is true, q, r, s, etc. must also be true; that p cannot be alone true, connot be true if q, r, s, etc. are false. But this does not mean at all that p cannot be perfectly true. If the states of affairs which p, q, r, s, etc. assert are internally related, then if the states of affairs asserted by p *exist*, the states of affairs asserted by q, r, s, etc. also exist. But granting this, it would still remain that p's truth depends on the existence of the states of affairs it asserts; and similarly with q, r, s, etc. If now the state of affairs which p asserts does exist, p will be true no matter what else is consequently true—i.e., q, r, s, etc.

(ii) Secondly, it must not be supposed that if one asserts p, one is asserting it "unconditionally" in the sense that he is either asserting or implying that it is true whether any other statements, such as q, r, s, are true or false; independently of their truth. To think so is to confuse the assertion (asserting) of a sentence and

---

37 The meaning of 'relative' and 'absolute' in the sense of 'conditional' and 'unconditional' (or 'conditioned,' to use Bradley's term) respectively, can be seen I think from the following quotation: "The growth of our knowledge consists in a widening and in an increase of systematic mediation. The more the conditions of the judgement are, or can be, included in the judgement, the truer and more real, the less condition*al* and the more condition*ed* does that judgement become. And the judgement that seeks to be at once true and at the same time a more simple and unconditioned assertion of fact, implies the worship and the pursuit of an illusory abstraction.... Such a judgement, the more it attempts to assert itself as absolute, succeeds only the more in emphasizing itself as dependent on and subject to the unknown." (F. H. Bradley, *Logic*,[2] II, 639-40. Quoted from N. T., vol. II, p. 318. Italics in original)

an assertion about this asserted sentence (or statement) itself, and hence to confuse the truth or falsity of the former statement and the truth or falsity of the latter statement. To say that "$2 + 2 = 4$" is true unconditionally or "absolutely" in sense (1) is to make a false (and a perfectly false) statement. But the statement "$2+2=4$" remains, nonetheless, perfectly or "absolutely" *true* (in sense (2). I am again assuming, for the sake of illustration, that pure mathematical statements are synthetic.)

The confusion alluded to is illustrated by the passage by Bradley already quoted:

The growth of our knowledge consists in a widening and in an increase of systematic mediation. The more the conditions of the judgement are, or can be, included in the judgement, the truer and more real, the less condition*al* and the more condition*ed* does that judgement become. *And the judgement that seeks to be at once true and at the same time a mere simple and unconditioned assertion of fact, implies the worship and the pursuit of an illusory abstraction.... Such a judgement, the more it attempts to assert itself as absolute, succeeds only the more in emphasizing itself as dependent on and subject to the unknown.*[38]

Again, Bradley says:

And on this road [of seeking truth in ideas] you not only endeavour to say what you mean, but you are once for all and for ever condemned to mean what you say. Your judgements as to reality are here no less no more than what you have expressed in them, and no appeal to something else which you fail to make explicit is allowed.[39]

This seems to mean that when you say "A is B," and you are told that "A is B" is only true in a degree because it does not specify the conditions under which it is true, you cannot protest that you did not imply to reject these conditions or deny them, or that you did imply that these conditions are present.

My contention is that the demand of the doctrine of degrees of truth that in order for a statement to be more and more true it must include in its meaning (in the "proposition" expressed) more

---

38 Logic², II, 639–40. Quoted from N. T., Vol. II, p. 318. The italics, except in the second sentence, are mine.
39 E. T. R., p. 234.

and more of its conditions, and thus become less and less "unconditional," results from the confusion between or the identification of the two senses of 'relative' and 'absolute,' and the supposition that to assert a statement as such is to assert, or to imply, that its truth does *not* involve the truth or falsity of other statements. If the defenders of the doctrine had seen that such a demand is not required, because to assert a statement is not to assert, or to imply, that it is absolute or non-relative (in sense (1)), they would have seen that a statement does not cease to be perfectly true because it is relative and not absolute in sense (1); and therefore, the doctrine of degrees of truth would not have arisen at all. For only if these things are not seen, and the demand for greater and greater inclusion of the implied conditions in a statement is maintained, that the degree of inclusion of such conditions in a statement could be taken as a measure of *degrees* of truth. In other words, the advocate of the doctrine illegitimately shifts from the first sense of 'relative' and 'absolute' to the crucial second sense, on the strength of the above invalid supposition as a premise.

Another example of this confusion or identification of an assertion about a statement with the statement itself, is afforded by the following passage by A. E. Taylor: "... A proposition is never untrue simply because it is not the whole truth, but only when, not being the whole truth, it is mistakenly taken to be so."[40]

In the case of Bradley, despite what we have said, we must in all fairness mention that he does often distinguish between the degree of truth of a statement and our knowledge of its degree of truth relatively to another statement. Thus a truth which is actually "higher" than another—to use Bradley's terminology—in the sense that it has a higher degree of truth than the latter, may be mistakenly taken by us to be a "lower" or a more "subordinate" truth; and vice versa. Or taking one statement alone, it may be believed to be a higher truth than it really is.[41]

Of course the confusion or invalid identification we are discussing is no accident. It is the result of identifying what a statement asserts with what the maker of the statement has in mind in

---

40 *Elements Of Metaphysics*, London, 1924, Seventh Edition, p. 214.
41 P. L., vol. II, Terminal Essay VIII, p. 684 ff.

asserting it (what he purports or intends to assert); the meaning of the statement with what its maker intends to mean by it; and the truth of the statement with the knowledge of the person making it about its ostensible referent.[42] But we have already argued against all these confusions or identifications and need not go into them again.

Speaking of the "conditions" of a statement we must be careful not to confuse the "conditions" which we have been speaking about in this section, viz., what a statement logically presupposes, and the "conditions" we mentioned earlier in talking about a statement such as "Water contracts when cooled." In both types of cases the conditions of a statement are ones without which the statement cannot be true. But in the case of the former type what this means is that if a given statement A *is true*, certain other statements, B, C, D, etc. must also be true; whereas in the latter type of case a statement A itself is *not true* unless certain *qualifications* are made, i. e., unless it itself is *completed* by adding these qualifications to it. Here the issue is the incompleteness of a statement which makes it false as it stands; in the former type of case the question of incompleteness is not involved. Suppose we take the statement "Water contracts when cooled provided the pressure is normal," in order to clarify the differences involved in the two types of situations. This statement is an empirical generalization and entails (does *not* logically *presuppose*) true statements such as "If X is a sample of water at a temperature of 15° C and under normal pressure, it contracts when cooled," and other, false statements, such as "If T is a sample of water at a temperature of 2° C and under normal pressure, it contracts when cooled." Since some of the statements the generalization entails are false, it itself is false as it stands. In order to make it a true statement, its range of applicability has to be restricted to cases where it will be true, such that it will entail only true statements; and this can be done by adding the qualification "above 4° C contracts when cooled, provided the pressure is normal." *This* new

---

[42] Hence the constant employment, by the advocates of degrees of truth, of the supposed fact of the uncertainty of our empirical knowledge as an argument for the view that no actual statements are or can be absolutely true.

statement, into which the condition which makes it a true statement rather than a false statement has been incorporated, and hence is now "conditioned" so far as the second type of "condition" is concerned, is still "*conditinal*" so far as the former type of "condition" is concerned. It logically presupposes the truth of certain other statements, without which it could not or cannot be true; statements like "Water exists," "Water is capable of being cooled," "The earth's atmosphere can exert normal pressure," and so on. The *empirical* conditions which this statement requires in order to be true are thus seen to be quite different from the *verbal* qualification "above 4° C" which has to be incorporated into the statement "Water contracts when cooled provided the pressure is normal" in order to make it true. The two types of "conditioning" discussed involve two different types of "making a statement true." The capacity of water to be cooled, the atmosphere's capacity to exert normal pressure, etc. "make" the statement "Water above 4° C contracts when cooled provided the pressure is normal" true in a different sense from the qualification "above 4° C," which "makes" true the statement "Water contracts when cooled provided the presure is normal."

Let us return to Bradley's discussion of error in connection with "higher" and "lower" truth. This discussion naturally raises the problem of the criterion of degrees of truth. Let us note, first, that since any actual or possible statement has, according to the doctrine in hand, some degree of truth, the testing of any statement consists not in finding out whether or not it has any truth at all, whether it is or is not perfectly false. Rather, the task of testing, whenever practised, consists in discovering the *degree* of truth of the statement to be tested, and the extent to which the statement coheres with the system of knowledge we happen to have at the time: whether or not it has the same (or as high a) degree of truth as that system. Bradley, as will be remembered, holds that we may err in attempting to find out the degree of truth of a given statement; or, taking it in relation to another statement, whether it has a higher or a lower degree of truth. The basic reason for Bradley, though he also gives some more specific reasons, is that in the case of imperfect knowledge—which is the only knowledge we can ever attain—"coherence" and comprehensiveness diverge more or less.[43] This being so, F. C. S. Schiller is mistaken when he criticizes A. E. Taylor on—

The 'saving doctrine' of the Degrees of Reality, in stating which Prof. Taylor does not seem to have materially improved its Bradleian form.... It still seems to be a pure assumption that what *appears to us* to be the order of ascertained reality, must coincide with the absolute order of merit.[44]

Bradley himself does not hold this. The test which Bradley suggests in choosing between two truths is "... How much of my world is contained and involved on either hand, and how much comparatively, in accepting or rejecting either, do I on the whole gain or lose."[45] But this "world" which is here involved is the world of our finite knowledge, the "body" of knowledge we actually have; and though, taken as true, it can serve to test individual statements or sets of these, the fundamental question is how this body called knowledge is itself to be tested for degree of truth. Obviously the ultimate standard, the ideal system, is not available to us (Cf. our discussion of this point in Chapter IV). We therefore cannot know what specific degree of truth our body of "knowledge" or any other body of propositions, or an individual proposition for that matter, has.[46] In so far forth the suggested test of degrees of truth is defective. For though we can in principle know how coherent is a system, we cannot even in principle know how comprehensive it is without knowing how comprehensive is the all-comprehensive system: something which we cannot know except in a general way and merely abstractly. Nonetheless, the test does give use a relative measure of degrees of truth: it tells us that the apparently more comprehensive and coherent of two sets or bodies

---

43 *Ibid.*, p. 685.
44 "Empiricism And The Absolute, "*Mind*, vol. XIV, N. S., No. 55 (July, 1905), p. 364. Italics in original.
45 P. L., vol. II, Terminal Essay VIII, p. 686. Cf. Bosanquet's dictum: "Either this or Nothing."
46 I. e., how much "modification" the body of propositions or an individual proposition requires to become perfectly true. Cf. Schiller: "... How, we may ask, are we to know *how much* 'modification' or 'transformation' a thing may need to become ultimate reality ?" (Empiricism And The Absolute," p. 364. Italics in original.)

of statements which we have is, in general, more *likely* to have a higher degree of truth. Thus Schiller's criticism that it is not "... in the least self-evident that what seems to need less modification is actually nearer to ultimate Reality and more likely to attain it"[47] seems untenable. The advocates of the theory do not, nor do they need to hold, that what *seems* to need less modification has a higher degree of truth; though they do hold that what *actually* does need less modification has a higher degree of truth.

R. W. Church has a different criticism. Comprehensiveness and coherence (what he calls inclusiveness and harmony, respectively, following Bradley) are taken to be the standard:

> Yet this does (and could) not mean that this standard is anything distinguishable from the very degrees of truth and reality themselves of which that standard is the criterion. The degree to which any finite whole is coherent is in no sense distinct from that appearance itself. For the coherence of that finite whole is that whole itself—that very appearance, which is self-coherent to the degree that it is individual, and is the individual it is in virtue of that self-coherence.[48]

It is true of course that for the doctrine in hand degrees of truth are themselves degrees of coherence and comprehensiveness. For truth is itself coherence. The question of the criterion of degrees of truth therefore reduces to the question of the criterion of degrees of coherence and comprehensiveness. To this the advocate of the doctrine does, as we know, attempt to give an answer. Church's view that there is and can really be no criterion of degrees of truth is therefore not supported by what the advocates of coherence regard as the fact of the identity between truth and coherence. What truth his view has rests, as we have seen in this section, on other considerations; and in earlier sections we have seen that all sorts of difficulties arise when we try to define "degrees of coherence" (or implication) itself, which is allegedly identical with "degrees of truth."

As for intellectual satisfaction, to which the advocates of the doctrine also appeal as a test of degrees of truth, we have already dealt with it, in essence, in Chapter IV.[49]

---

47 *Ibid.*
48 *Bradley's Dialectic*, London, 1942, p. 157.
49 Cf. *Ibid.*, pp. 177 ff.

THE DOCTRINE OF DEGREES OF TRUTH AND FALSITY 225

One more point before we end this already overdrawn discussion of the doctrine of degrees of truth. A. E. Taylor, unlike Bradley, Bosanquet and Blanshard, holds that degrees of truth and reality do not and need not always coincide. He writes—

> There are degrees of truth as well as of reality and the two do not necessarily coincide. The degree of truth a doctrine contains cannot be determined apart from consideration of the purpose it is meant to fulfil. For the special purposes of Metaphysics, the purpose of thinking of the world in a finally consistent way, whatever is not the whole truth is untrue. But what the metaphysician regards as the lesser truth may be the higher truth relatively to other purposes than his own.[50]

Thus "$2 + 2 = 4$," for example, may be considered perfectly true for the mathematician's, though not for the metaphysician's, purposes.[51]

Taylor does not make it clear whether, for him, degrees of truth are determined only by the purpose which the statement or system is taken to serve, or, in addition, by its coherence and comprehensiveness (the latter two resting, of course, on the degree of reality of the statement's or system's metaphysical subject). The latter, more inclusive view, is probably what Taylor has in mind. For if the statement's or system's comprehensiveness and coherence are not to be a determining factor, we will be either led into a purely pragmatic conception of degrees of truth, which the Idealist advocate of coherence would repudiate, or we will have no criterion of degrees of truth on the grounds of the coherence view (assuming for the sake of argument that the criterion given by Bradley and the others does serve its purpose). But even in the more plausible and more inclusive form, Taylor's view does not seem to me to be easier to defend than Bradley's type of view, as Ewing thinks.[52] For it entails that the same statement may have different degrees of truth relatively to different purposes—a flagrant contradiction of our ordinary way of speaking of statements as having a fixed truth-value, even if this truth-value could be some *degree* of truth or

---

50 *Elements Of Metaphysics*, p. 214, footnote 1.
51 Cf. I. C. S., p. 215. See also footnote 1 on same page.
52 *Ibid.*, footnote 1.

falsity. It may seem that Taylor's criterion of degrees of truth, unlike Bradley's type of criterion, makes it possible to measure the degrees of truth of statements and systems. For it would seem that it makes the degrees of truth of an actual statement relative to that of another actual statement, and not relative to an unknown and unknowable ideal system. Unfortunately this is untrue precisely because of the purposes which the statement may be used to serve, taken as part of the criterion of degrees of truth. Consider two statements which have the same degree of truth on the basis of the comprehensiveness and coherence of the system or systems of which they form a part. These statements are used for different purposes. How shall we decide to what extent and in what way these affect the degree of truth they have on the basis of the former grounds? Or take two statements which have different degrees of truth on the coherence-comprehensiveness criterion. Suppose, again, that they are used for different purposes. How shall we decide whether they now come to have the same degree of truth; or whether they will retain the degree of truth they had on the basis of the coherence-comprehensiveness criterion; or finally, if their final degree of truth is different, whether this difference is greater or less than what it is on the coherence-comprehensiveness criterion. That is, how shall we grade different purposes and kinds of context as a measure of degrees of truth?

With this we come to the end of our long journey, though this has been determined by necessity rather than by any completeness of the criticism offered. For the criticism of a philosophical theory, especially a theory of the magnitude and caliber of the coherence theory and the Idealistic system which underlies it, can never be completed. But however partial and fragmentary our criticism has been, it is hoped that enough has been said to show that the coherence theory of truth, in its various aspects, is untenable. We would not be so foolish as to imagine, however, that enough has been said to convince a confirmed advocate of the coherence theory, of the erroneousness of his view. That is too much to expect of any philosophical criticism. To do that all the fundamental metaphysical and epistemological tenets and assumptions on which the coherence view is based have to be meticulously disproved—if that is at all possible. And even that would not be enough: the whole attitude of the advocate of coherence to life and to the world has to be changed. *That*, arguments alone can never do. Our task has been far more modest: to discover for ourselves the truth or falsity of the coherence theory and thereby to have taken the first step toward the more important task of answering the same questions to which the coherence theory adresses itself. It is also our hope that others may benefit, as much as we ourselves have, from our attempt to refute the coherence theory.

One final word. The fact that our conclusions have been negative with regard to the coherence theory should not lead us to think that the criticized theory is worthless. The value of a theory does not lie merely in the amount of truth in it. Moreover, it is always easier to criticize than to offer a plausible substitute for what is criticized. As Rudin says in Turgenev's novel by that name, "you can pick holes in anything." The coherence theory —and the Idealistic system it rests upon—for all its defects, is one of the most coherent and impressive structures ever devised by the mind of man. And that is much more than many philosophical doctrines or systems can boast of.

INDEX

A

Absolute, the, 16 ff., 32 n, 33, 36 f., 50 n, 154, 156 f., 162 f., 170 f., 178 f., 193, 196 ff.
Abstract universal, 66, 66 n, 67 n, 156 ff.
Alexander, S., ix
Appearance, 12, 18, 30, 31 f., 36, 59, 154, 162
Aristotle, 6

B

Blanshard, B., ix, x, 3 ff., 8 n, 14 n, 22 f., 27 n, 29 n, 42 f., 43 n, 51, 56–59, 63 ff., 66 n, 66, 69, 71, 100 n, 102, 105 n, 106, 114, 121 ff., 134 f., 143, 147, 149 ff., 151 n, 154, 158 n, 161 n, 161, 176 n, 175 ff., 176 n, 179 n, 183 ff., 188 ff., 198, 201–209, 216 f., 225
Bosanquet, B., ix, 3, 4 n, 6 n, 12, 14 n, 31 n, 33 n, 43 n, 50 n, 51, 71, 137 n, 137, 141, 147, 153, 200 n, 225
Bradley, F. H., ix, 3 f., 8, 14 n, 16, 16 n, 16 f., 18, 21, 29 n, 29–37, 44, 46, 50 n, 50, 59 f., 60 n, 67 ff., 71, 113 n, 135, 147, 151 n, 150 ff., 155 f., 162–172, 178 f., 197, 204, 218 ff., 222 ff.
Broad, C. D., 31 n, 54, 68 n

C

Caird, E., 29 n
Calkins, M., 29 n, 155
Carnap, R., 144, 144 n
Chambers, L. P., 155 n
Coherence, ix, xi, 13–19, 18 n, 27, 34, 46, 99 ff., 110 ff., 114 n, 122 ff., 134–152, 147 n, 158, 163 f., 170 ff., 184 ff., 192, 192 n, 198, 206, 213, 217, 224 ff.; degrees of, 16 ff., 34 f., 135, 171, 192, 198, 206, 214, 224; test, 100 ff., 106, 114 ff., 120 f., 126, 129, 134, 137, 140 f., 146; theory of truth, ix, x, xi, 3, 20 ff., 27, 27 n, 28 n, 29, 42, 46, 66, 96, 98, 101 ff., 108, 110, 112 f., 116, 134, 141, 143, 145, 147, 149, 156, 160 f., 167, 169 ff., 177 f., 182, 184 ff., 197, 226 f.; theory of reality, 22, 24, 26 ff., 41 f., 46, 96, 98 f., 140, 146, 163
Concrete universal, 18, 66, 156
Correspondence, 13, 27 n, 28 n, 46, 101, 104 n, 115, 138, 143 f., 148 f., 154 f., 158 f., 159 n, 173 f.; test, 126; theory of truth, 27 n, 28 n, 151, 173

D

Descartes, R., 10
Dingle, H., 80 n, 81 n.
Ducasse, C. J., 72
Duhem, P., 125

E

Einstein, A., 101, 129
Ewing, A. C., ix, 20 f., 23 f., 26, 27 n, 31 n, 42, 45, 47 n, 47 f., 50 ff., 59, 63 f., 66 n, 66, 69 ff., 76, 82 n, 87, 90, 96, 99, 102, 102 n, 106, 113 n, 114 ff., 137 n, 140 f., 143, 149, 158 n. 161 n, 161, 166, 225

F

Feigl, H., 130, 144 n
Flew, A., 119 n

G

Goodenough, F., 107 n
Green, T. H., ix, 29 n

H

Hegel, G. W. F., ix
Heisenberg, W., 133 n
Hempel, C., ix
Hoyle, F., 80 n

I

Identity of Indiscernibles, doctrine of, 94 n, 94 ff.

J

James, W., 79 f.
Jeans, J., 81, 81 n
Joachim, H. H., ix, 4 n, 5, 7 n, 8 n, 14 n, 15, 27 n, 47 n, 105 f., 147, 149, 179

K

Kant, I., 6

L

Lewis, C. I., 28 n, 147 f.
Locke, J., 10, 27 n, 155
Lovejoy, A. O., 104

M

Martin, R. M., 117 n.
Marvin, W. T., 43, 43 n, 98 n
McTaggart, J. M. E., ix, 52, 54 n, 56
Meaning, 146 n, 150, 170-177, 184, 196, 202, 205-214, 210 n; degrees of, 16, 171, 186, 196, 201 f., 204 f., 209-213
Modification theory of relations, 30 n
Moore, G. E., 27 n, 66, 66 n, 90 ff., 94 n
Morris, C. R., 12 n

N

Necessity, 13, 17 f., 159, 187, 190 f., 194 f.; degrees of, 13, 186, 188-196
Neurath, O., ix

P

Pap., A., 72 n, 139, 144 n
Perception, 3 ff., 4 n, 12, 45, 48, 50 f., 101, 105 ff., 154
Perry, R. B., 47, 47 n, 85 f., 88 ff.
Pratt, J. B., 31, 31 n

Q

Quine, W. V., 126, 131

R

Reality, x, 37, 11 ff., 16 ff., 21 ff., 27 n, 27 f., 30 n, 31 ff., 41, 44 n, 44 f., 50, 78, 105, 135, 138, 140 f., 151-158, 162-172, 177 f., 188, 193, 197, 200 n, 201, 219, 224; degrees of, 18, 32, 162, 225; organic theory of, 163, 174 f.; system of, 12 f., 16 f., 18 n, 29 f., 34, 195
Reciprocal confirmation, 139, 139 n, 144 n
Reid, L. A., 164
Relations, 9 ff., 17, 19, 21, 23 ff., 29 ff., 37, 39-48, 40 n, 44 n, 51 f., 55-69, 60 n, 61 n, 74, 79, 82, 84 f., 88, 94 ff., 117, 140, 154 f., 159, 162 f., 167 f., 185 ff., 190 n, 190 ff., 206, 209 f.; causal, 45, 52 f., 58, 69-77, 72 n, 76, 82 f., 88, 98 f. 159, 187, 190 f.; external, 29, 30 n, 33 ff., 42 ff., 51, 68 f., 82, 99, 185, 187 f.; internal relations, xi, 20 ff., 27, 29 ff., 30 n, 41 ff., 47, 50 ff., 66-72, 82 ff., 87, 90-99, 141, 178, 185, 188; degree (s) of externality of, 13, 186 f.; degrees of internality of, 13, 17, 33, 35 n, 186 f., 190 f.
Royce, J., 29, 29 n, 46 n
Russell, B., 27 n, 78 n

S

Schiller, F. C. S., 223 n, 223 f.
Schrödinger, E., 133 n
Spaulding, E. G., 29 n, 30, 30 n, 35 n, 35 f., 46 n, 47, 47 n, 82, 84
Stace, W. T., 27 n, 28 n
Stout, G. F., 29 n, 31 f., 31 n, 37 ff., 60 n
Strawson, P. F., 100 n, 118 n, 118 f., 120 n, 146 n, 204 n
System, 11-17, 14 n, 19, 21-29, 35, 42 ff., 71, 77, 82, 85, 98, 101, 104, 108 ff., 115 ff., 120, 125 f., 129 n, 129, 131, 135 ff., 140 ff., 149 ff., 157-166, 164 n, 169, 171-178, 176 n, 182 ff., 187, 189, 192 n. 192 ff., 198, 217, 223, 225 f.; of judgments, 10, 13, 19, 157, 163, 166 f.; of knowledge, 14 n, 13 ff., 19, 45, 101, 137, 149, 160, 173, 181 ff., 222; of propositions, 17, 27, 29, 110, 112, 141 f., 151, 169 ff., 182, 188, 191, 193, 198; of terms, 29 f., 34 ff., 42 f., 162, 178

T

Tarski, A., 144 n
Taylor, A. E., 220, 225 f.
Theory of causality, necessary-connection, 44 f., 71, 75 f., 86, 99; regular-sequence, 70 f.
Thought, x, 3, 4 n, 7 n, 7-16, 42, 45, 106, 135, 153 ff., 162, 165, 170 f., 184, 195 f.; system of, 13, 16 f., 154, 158, 161 f.
Truth, x, 3, 11, 14 n, 14 ff., 27 n, 27, 28 n, 46, 99 ff., 110 f., 114 n, 114, 131, 135 ff., 144 n, 144-153, 163-171, 184 ff., 193, 195, 197 ff., 202, 214 ff., 220, 224; degree (s) of, xi, 16, 19, 31, 135, 160, 163, 164 n, 171 f., 177, 184 ff., 193 ff., 200, 202, 204, 209 f., 213-226, 221 n; nature of, x, 13, 14 n, 18 n, 18 f., 27, 99, 103, 112, 114, 129 n, 143 ff., 144 n, 148 f., 184 f.; test (s) of, ix, x, 14 n, 18 n, 18 f., 99, 100 ff., 110, 112, 114 ff., 121 ff., 126 ff., 134 ff., 140-146, 144 n, 185 f.; system of, 14, 28, 137, 152, 162 f., 166, 170, 173, 179, 182

U

Underlying-reality theory, 29 ff., 35, 41, 46, 50, 61 n, 163, 188

W

Walker, L. J., 67 n, 69 n, 206
Watson, J., 155, 155 n
Weismann, F., 119
Wilson, N. L., 118 n
Wittgenstein, L., 120 n

Corrigenda

Page *ix*. *Line 24*: For 'idealist' read 'Idealist.'
Page *x*. *Line 4*: For 'idealist' read 'Idealist.'
Page *5*. *Line 11*: For 'epistemological dualists' read 'Epistemological Dualists.'
Page *10*. *Line 15*: The ninth word from the left should read 'partially realized.'
Page *25*. *Line 28:* For 'These' read 'these.'
Page *29*. *Line 34*: For 'Card' read 'Caird'
Page *42*. *Line 21:* For 'I' read '(I).'
Page *56*. *Line 34*: For 'Capitole' read 'Capitol.'
Page *60*. *Line 11*: For 'Relations' read 'relations.'
Page *64*. Lines 19-20*:* For '…is a distinction in kind and not of degree' read '… is a distinction not in kind but of degree…'
Page *115*. *Line 11*: For 'truth of falsity' read 'truth' or 'falsity.'
Page *121*. *Footnote 24*: Add '"' at end of 'hypothesis.'
Page *146*. *Footnote 5:* Add '.' at end of last sentence.
Page *155: Line 37*: For 'Waston' read 'Watson.'
Page *189*. *Line 1*: For 'inger' read 'finger.'

www.ingramcontent.com/pod-product-compliance
Lightning Source LLC
Chambersburg PA
CBHW071942240426
43669CB00048B/2556